*f*P

ALSO BY STANLEY COREN

The Intelligence of Dogs

Sleep Thieves

The Left-Hander Syndrome

What Do Dogs Know? (with Janet Walker)

Why We Love the Dogs We Do

How to Speak Dog

The Pawprints of History

How DOGS Think

Understanding the Canine Mind

Stanley Coren

FREE PRESS
New York London Toronto Sydney

fP
FREE PRESS
A Division of Simon & Schuster, Inc.
1230 Avenue of the Americas
New York, NY 10020

Designed by Elliott Beard

Manufactured in the United States of America

ISBN 0-7394-5154-5

This book is dedicated to

Odin and Wizard.

Their companionship, their touch, their love, and

their antics are truly missed.

CONTENTS

PREFACE

DO DOGS THINK? Do they have a mental picture of the world like humans do? Could we say that a dog is conscious and self-aware the way that people are? Do dogs have true emotions? Compared to humans, just how intelligent are dogs? If you ask those questions when you are in a room full of behavioral scientists and philosophers, you are bound to start a heated argument.

Despite the fact that paleontologists have proven that humans and dogs have lived together for at least 140 centuries, there are still many different viewpoints about the workings of a dog's mind, or even if a dog has a mind. For some people the dog is nothing but an unthinking, fur-covered, biological machine, while others consider dogs to be much like little people in fur coats.

Most owners of pet dogs feel that dogs have something like true intelligence and consciousness, although they suspect that dogs often fail to show it for some reason. This notion is captured in a folktale told in Zimbabwe which says that dogs are not only very clever but they even know how to speak. It is just that they choose not to. According to the story, the hero Nkhango made a deal with the dog Rukuba. If Rukuba stole some fire from the god Nyamurairi, people would be dog's friend forever. Dog kept his part of the bargain and gave people fire. Later Nkhango asked dog to help him hunt dangerous animals, stand guard, herd animals, and do other difficult jobs. Finally Nkhango decided that dog should be a messenger. This was too much for dog. After all, since dog had given people fire, he felt he should be allowed to just lay near it in comfort. Rukuba thought, "People will always be sending me here and there on errands because I am smart and can speak. But if I can't speak, then I can't be a messenger." From that day since, dogs have chosen not to speak.

Even educated and logical people sometimes have odd ideas about the mental capacities of dogs. This was demonstrated to me by a lawyer involved in one of the most public and controversial trials in U.S. history. The story of the murder of Nicole Brown Simpson and her friend Ron Goldman, and the subsequent arrest and trial of the sports hero and actor O. J. Simpson, is generally well known. However, there was also a dog involved, an Akita named Kato, which was owned by Nicole. Kato entered the story because one of the neighbors heard the dog's agitated whining. It was then that the neighbor noticed there was blood on Kato's feet and thought that the dog was injured. As he went to return Kato to Nicole, the dog pulled in the direction of the garage. This was how the bodies were discovered. Many people felt that Kato had seen the murder and was trying to get help. One morning, while O. J. Simpson's trial was in progress, I received a phone call from a lawyer associated with the court proceedings. He offered me a lot of money to come to Los Angeles to meet with Kato and to see if I could get the dog to identify the murderer. I tried to explain that, in comparison with humans, dogs have a mental ability similar to that of a two-year-old child. I asked him if he would expect a human two-year-old, with no clear understanding of death and limited language ability, to be able to comment on an event that had occurred nine months earlier. "Look," he pleaded, "couldn't you just come down and interview the dog?" Forgetting that some lawyers lack a sense of humor, I quipped, "You mean something like getting him to bark once for 'yes' and twice for 'no'?" The amazed voice on the phone asked, "Could you do that?"

This book is my attempt to explain to the world (including that lawyer) how dogs think. To understand the canine mind requires that we know a lot about how dogs sense the world and the degree to which they have been genetically programmed to perform their doggy behaviors, as well as what and how dogs can learn and adapt their behavior to changing conditions. In the process of exploring this we will talk about many issues that are of interest to anyone who lives or interacts with dogs. We will learn about the personalities of various breeds of dogs and how early experiences can change their temperaments. We will also explore the changes that occur in the dog's mind as he matures and ages. Along the way we'll even consider some of the stranger questions that people ask about dogs: whether they have an artistic sense, can understand mathematics, have ESP, can sense future earthquakes, or can even detect cancer in humans. This is a book based upon some of the new and exciting scientific research that is beginning to give us a glimpse of the workings of that fur-covered mind. You may find some surprises here, such as some capacities and abilities you didn't know your dog had or some abilities you think he has which he does not. You may also find some ways to understand your dog better, to communicate more clearly with him, and to help shape his behaviors so that he fits into your life more comfortably. You will also find some interesting data and some fascinating stories about how dogs think and behave that you can use if you ever find yourself joining that argument in that room full of behavioral scientists and philosophers.

Finally, I must acknowledge that in many ways this book could not have been completed without the help and support of my clever and loving wife, Joan, who struggled her way through the early drafts.

How Dogs Think

CHAPTER 1

The Mind of a Dog

I myself have known some profoundly thoughtful dogs.
—JAMES THURBER

PALEONTOLOGISTS TELL US that 14,000 years ago a Stone Age man sat next to a fire looking at an animal that we would readily recognize as a dog if we were to see it now. This forefather of all of today's dogs was not just a household pet. He was a sentinel, protector, and hunting partner. His descendants would become, among other things, shepherds, comrades in war, search-and-rescue heroes, law enforcement officers, lifeguards, guides for the blind and deaf, assistants for the disabled, as well as valued family members and companions. One can imagine that this early man, who had just learned to make weapons and tools out of sticks, stones, and bits of bone, might have paused to look into the dark, soulful eyes of his companion and wondered, "What is he thinking about? How much does he know? Does he really have feelings, and if so, what does he think about me?"

It is now 140 centuries since that fire last flickered and died, and we are still asking those same questions about our canine companions. The average dog owner still looks into the eyes of his dog, sees what appear to be sparks of intelligence, emotion, and awareness, and wonders about what is going on in the dog's mind. Historically, many great thinkers have wrestled with this question. Some have intuited that there is a knowing awareness behind those eyes, while others have concluded that dogs merely act according to genetically programmed instincts.

Dogs and Philosophers

The Greek philosopher Plato had a very high opinion of the dog's intellect. He described the "noble dog" as a "lover of learning" and a "beast worthy of wonder." In one of his dialogues he presents a discussion between Socrates and Glaucon in which Socrates, after much analysis, eventually convinces his disciple that his dog "is a true philosopher."

Plato's contemporary Diogenes, another significant Greek philosopher, although more eccentric than most, became known for wandering the world with a lamp claiming to be "looking for an honest man." While he had his doubts about humans, Diogenes thought dogs were extremely moral and intelligent and even adopted the nickname "Cyon," which means "Dog." He would go on to found one of the great ancient schools of philosophy, and he and his followers would become known by his nickname as "Cynics" or "Dog Thinkers." Diogenes' own intelligence and wit were such that Alexander the Great, after meeting him in Corinth, went away saying, "If I were not Alexander, I should wish to be Diogenes."

When Diogenes died, the people of Athens raised a great marble pillar in his memory. On top of the pillar was the image of a dog. Beneath the dog there was a long inscription that started with the following bit of conversation:

"Say, Dog, I pray, what guard you in that tomb?"

"A dog."

"His name?"

"Diogenes."

There are many times when the behavior of my own dogs brings me back to the admiring views of Plato and Diogenes. One cold rainy day, when I was feeling too tired and uncomfortable to take my dogs on their usual morning walk, they had to content themselves with being let out in the yard for a short while. For my flat-coated retriever, Odin, this simply was not an acceptable situation and, late in the afternoon, I was disturbed from my reading by a clatter at my feet. I looked down and noticed that Odin had somehow found his leash and deposited it on the floor. I picked it up, put it on the sofa next to me, and gave him a pat and a reassuring "Later, Odin."

A few minutes passed and there was another clatter at my feet; I found that Odin had now deposited one of my shoes beside me. When I didn't respond, he quickly retrieved the other shoe and put it down next to me. Obviously, to his mind, I was being quite dense or stubborn, since I still delayed going out into the cold and wet weather. It was at that moment that Odin ran to the door and gave a familiar bark. It was a distinctive sound that he only used when my wife, Joan, was approaching the door. I had spent several years teaching at a university in New York City and had developed the habit typical of New Yorkers, which involves always locking doors, even on days when I was inside working at home. This tended to annoy Joan, who grew up in the safer and less paranoid environment of Alberta, Canada. So when Odin gave his "Joan is here" bark, I got up to unlock the door rather than leave her fumbling for her keys in the rain and getting annoyed with my inconvenient habit. The moment I got within a foot or two of the door, Odin dashed back to the sofa and grabbed his leash. Before I had even determined that Joan's car had not arrived in its usual place, he was nudging my hand with the leash he carried in his mouth.

I started to laugh at his subterfuge. I could imagine his mental discourse of the past few minutes running something like "I want a walk, so here's my leash.—OK, I've brought you your shoes, so let's walk.—All right now, while you're already standing at the door, and while I'm now offering you the leash, why don't we just take that walk?" I have obviously added to Odin's behavior a whole lot of reasoning, an internal dialogue, and the idea that there was some kind of conscious planning involved; however, these behaviors certainly would have been consistent with his actions. And by the way, he did get his walk.

Minds More or Less

Although the idea of an intelligent, reasoning, and feeling dog persisted for many centuries, we might say that in the seventeenth century dogs lost their minds. However, according to one of the most influential French philosophers of the time, René Descartes, dogs had no minds to lose. An exceptional mathematician, Descartes also performed some important experiments in physiology, but it seems likely his strong Catholic religious feelings, not his scientific findings, led him to this conclusion. To Descartes, granting dogs any degree of intelligence was equivalent to admitting that dogs had consciousness, which would include awareness and the ability to plan future actions. According to religious doctrines at the time, however, anything that had consciousness also had a soul, and anything that had a soul could earn admission to heaven. That dogs might go to heaven was unacceptable to both Descartes and the Roman Catholic Church at that time.

This left Descartes with the problem of explaining how, in the absence of intelligence, reasoning, or consciousness, dogs could have such complex behaviors. His answer came when he visited the gardens of Saint-Germain-en-Laye, the birthplace and home of Louis XIV. Those gardens featured the seventeenth-century equivalent of animatronics or robotics in the form of elegant statues designed by the Italian engineer Thomas Francini. Each figure was a clever piece of machinery powered by hydraulics and carefully geared to perform a complex sequence of actions. Thus one statue might play a harp, while another danced, and so forth. Descartes reasoned that dogs might be the biological equivalent of these animated machines, but instead of being driven by hydraulics and gears, they are controlled by physical reflexes and unthinking responses to things that stimulate them. The observation that dogs respond to their environment does not invalidate his argument, since those statues also responded to outside events, such as when a person stepped on a particular paving stone, which triggered the switch that in turn activated the statue.

Although Descartes's view of dogs as unreasoning and unconscious bits of biological machinery dominated scholarly thinking for two centuries, it received a major challenge in the middle of the nineteenth century, when Charles Darwin and his theory of evolution emerged upon the scene. Dissenting from the common teaching that each species had been separately created by God, Darwin concluded that humans were not special or unique in their mental abilities. In his book *The Descent of Man,* he stated that the only difference between man and most of his lower mammalian cousins "is one of degree and not of kind." He went on to say that the "senses and intuitions, the various emotions and faculties, such as love, memory, attention, curiosity, imitation, reason, etc. of which man boasts, may be found in an incipient or even sometimes in a well-developed condition, in the lower animals."

Darwin described animals and people as part of a continuum in evolution that gave rise to different levels of awareness, reasoning ability, intelligence, and memory in different species. Since, according to him, these are the components of consciousness, different species would also have different levels of consciousness. Thus a dog might be conscious and self aware, but not to the same degree as a human being.

Recent research has supported Darwin's view by demonstrating similarities between the nervous systems of dogs and humans. For instance, researchers have proven that the nerve cells in a dog's brain work the same way as those in a human brain. The neurons that make up the human brain have the same chemical composition as the neurons in a dog's brain, and the patterns of electrical activity are identical. The structure of a dog's brain contains most of the same organs that are found in the human brain.

Like humans, dogs have special areas of the brain that control specific activities. In fact, if we drew a map of the locations of various functions in a dog's brain, it would be remarkably similar to the map of those same functions in the human brain. For instance, in both dogs and people vision is located at the very back of the brain and hearing is located at the sides of the brain, near the temples. The sense of touch and control of movements are located in a thin strip running over the top of the brain in both dogs and humans.

Even more striking is data from a recent scientific study from the dog-genome project. Ewen Kirkness of the Institute for Genomic Research in Rockville, Maryland, and his research team compared the DNA of a poodle to that of a human. What they found was that there was more than a 75 percent overlap between the genetic codes of humans and canines. All of this physiological similarity is certainly consistent with the belief that there should be a lot of similarity in the behaviors and workings of the minds of humans and dogs.

Minds Lost and Found

In the science of animal minds or animal consciousness, the pendulum tends to swing from one extreme to another. Although Darwin's views never completely disappeared, in the early part of the twentieth century a new psychological perspective called "Behaviorism" held sway. It was an idea more compatible with Descartes than Darwin. This new way of looking at animal behavior was the brainchild of psychologist John B. Watson, at Johns Hopkins University, and would be perpetuated into the present by the research of the well-known psychologist B. F. Skinner at Harvard University.

Behaviorists believe that the only aspects of behavior that can be legitimately studied are those that can be observed and measured by an outside third party. For them, even to talk about "consciousness" or "mind," especially when considering the behavior of animals, is only empty speculation, since we can't really measure awareness, feeling, or thought. Behaviorists believe that we don't even need ideas of consciousness or thought to explain behaviors. No doubt Dr. Watson would have vigorously objected to the "mentalistic" interpretation of Odin's behavior that I gave earlier.

To illustrate the behavioristic view: Suppose that I told Watson that my dog "likes meat." He would likely say that this is a projection of my own feelings. He would note that if I gave the dog a piece of meat, it is legitimate to describe the dog's behavior—the fact that he barks, jumps up, wags his tail, drools, opens his mouth, and eats the meat—but it is not legitimate for me to say that the dog "likes" the meat, or "wants" the meat, or is "aware that the meat will soon be given to him." All such conclusions are merely projections of attitudes or feelings by the human observer onto the dog, and Watson would contend that there is no evidence to support statements that my dog has any thoughts or feelings at all. Like Descartes, the scientist would simply observe that Odin's activity level rises when he is given meat and he performs certain behaviors in response to getting it.

As the field of animal cognition expands, modern psychological theory is becoming a bit more accepting of animal minds again. Biologists and psychologists are starting to talk about "purposive" behaviors and to openly discuss the possibility that dogs might have a true conscious representation of their world. The battle between the "dog as thinker" and "dog as machine" continues, however, and can be heard in the hallways and laboratories of many behavioral science departments around the world. Sometimes these arguments can get quite heated, and often they appear to take on some of the qualities of arguments about religion—the issue becomes one of belief and emotion, rather than of scientific fact.

Canine Mental Abilities

Regardless of whether people grant dogs a mind with consciousness, reasoning, and complex thought, or whether they insist that dogs are simply machines that use neurons rather than silicon chips to process information, there are certain things that can be agreed upon as scientific facts:

- Dogs sense the world and take in information from it.
- Dogs learn and modify their behavior to fit circumstances.
- Dogs have memories and can solve certain problems.
- Early experiences as a puppy can shape the behaviors of the adult.
- Dogs have emotions.
- Individual dogs seem to have distinct personalities and different breeds seem to have different temperaments.
- Social interactions, including play, are very important to dogs.
- Dogs communicate with each other and with humans.

Unfortunately, each of these agreed-upon facts raises a number of new questions. For instance, do dogs perceive the world the same way that we do? If not, how does the world appear to them? What can we sense that dogs can't and what can they sense that we can't? Are dogs' memories different from ours? What kinds of problems can dogs solve, and at what point does their intellect start to fail them? Can dogs understand time, beauty, music, or arithmetic? Do dogs really have ESP, as some people have claimed? When we talk about the temperament of dogs, are we talking about the same thing that we call personality in people? Can dogs learn to do things by simply observing others doing them? All these questions, and myriad others, can be answered even if we can't yet determine whether dogs have true thought and consciousness or whether they are merely fur-covered computers.

Alien Minds

Most people reading this book have much the same hope that I have, namely that we can learn what our dogs are aware of and what and how they are thinking. Realistically, however, we must recognize that this goal may prove to be unattainable and we may never understand the mind of a dog as completely as that of another human being.

The main problem is that we are human and as such we can reason only as a human does. If the experience of the animal is completely different and alien to ours, we may have no human reference that allows us to interpret the "thinking" behind the behavior. Imagine trying to derive how the world appears to a bat, flying through the night, guided only by its natural form of sonar, or how the world appears to a nematode, a tiny worm with no hearing or vision but only a chemical sense and a primitive sense of touch. In each case we might fall back on familiar human experiences, such as supposing that the bat's consciousness during sonar navigation must be like a person's with his eyes closed trying to locate objects in the world by sounds and echoes, but we would be speculating. The bat's sonar might give him a full, rich experience of a world full of objects much like the high-tech sonar used on modern ships, which uses sound reflection and high levels of computer analysis to provide a detailed map of the ocean floor. How that might translate into consciousness is difficult to imagine. What about the experience of the nematode? Can you imagine tasting your way through the environment? Can you build a map of the world in your mind by simply tasting the chemical concentrations that you pass through? We simply may not have the mental capacity to imagine what a nonhuman mind senses and thinks.

Can Mental Process Be Observed?

Even the most careful scientist will have a natural tendency to interpret all behaviors in human terms. Unfortunately, the cause or reason behind a particular human behavior may not be the same reason behind an apparently similar animal behavior. Consider the following simple situation: We tell a child that we have a problem that she has to solve, but we don't give her any details. Next we give her two cards out of a group lying face up on the table. In this case, each of the cards has the number 2 written on it. Now we ask her to find an answer. The child responds by going over to the remaining cards and picking out one that has the number 4 on it. Next we bring a dog into the testing room and present the same two cards to him. Much to our surprise, he responds by also selecting a card with the number 4 on it. Since we can't directly interview the dog, we consult the human child to determine what mental processes were involved. When we ask the child "How did you get the answer 4?" she replies that she took the first number and added to the second number and the sum came out to be 4.

On the basis of our knowledge about how a human solves the problem, can we conclude that the dog that we are testing knows how to add? While that might be tempting, from a scientific viewpoint it is a grave error. To begin with, we view the figures 2 and 4 as numbers, but a dog views them as nothing more than abstract patterns. It is also possible that although we think that the most relevant thing about the cards is the number written on them, there might be other things associated with the cards or the testing situation that the dog responds to. Perhaps the dog's behavior is a lot more subtle than just glancing at the figures written on the cards. For instance, the dog could be looking more intently at us than at the cards. Because we expect (or hope) that the dog has arithmetical skills, and since we are adding these numbers in our heads, we might glance directly at the card that has the 4 on it. The dog, with no knowledge of arithmetic, simply follows the direction of our gaze and then goes to the card that we looked at.

Since the dog views the world quite differently than we humans do, and has different sensory capacities and different priorities, our canine test subject may not actually be working on the mental problems that we have set for him. The dog may well be using mental processes and sources of information that simply don't occur to us. For example, when my children were quite young I had a cairn terrier named Flint. I convinced my children that Flint could read by giving them the following demonstration. First I asked them to draw something. Let's say they drew a cat. Next I had them print three words on three separate pieces of paper; let's say they wrote "cat," "dog," and "horse." I then folded each piece of paper into a sort of a tent, shaped like a Λ, with the word facing toward the dog. Next I showed the dog the piece of paper with the picture of the cat and in serious tones I explained, "Flint, this is a cat. Go find the word that says 'cat.' " In response to this, Flint would dash off with a little yip of delight and would always bring the piece of paper with the correct word written on it back to me. We would repeat this several times, with different pictures and different words. On the basis of this "test," my children became convinced that Flint could read. I even managed to convince some psychologist colleagues of mine that somehow I had taught the dog to associate the shapes of the letters in simple words with either the appropriate image or the sound of my voice saying the word.

The truth of the matter was that I was cheating, using the same kind of misdirection that stage magicians use. Before I would let Flint perform his "reading demonstration," I would stop in the bathroom and scrape the nails of my left hand across a bar of soap. When the children drew the picture, I transferred it to my left hand and put a bit of soap on it. I did the same thing with the paper containing the correct word while holding it in my left hand. My right hand, with no soap on it, was used to carry the papers with the wrong words on it. When I was describing the picture to Flint and saying the word, I held the paper up near his nose, so that he could smell the soap. When he dashed out to "read" the correct word, he was simply seeking another piece of paper that smelled exactly like the one that I placed before him. That solution never occurred either to my children or to my amazed professional colleagues. They viewed the situation as humans, whose dominant sense is vision. The fact that such a minor human sense, such as smell, could really hold the answer did not occur to them.

Thus, returning to our earlier example with the dog and the two cards with the number 2 on them, it could be that that dog had solved the problem in a manner that no human could. Perhaps, like Flint, the dog was solving the problem using scent. Since the child had handled both of the cards carrying the number 2 and also handled the card with the number 4, these cards now carry that child's scent. Thus the dog may be reading the problem that we are setting for him as asking him to "find another thing that smells just like these two." Or perhaps he is using some other mode of thinking that we have no way of fathoming.

This is the caution that we must hold in our minds. The same behavior can result from completely different processes. With human subjects, if we are asked to predict a boy's reaction when a girl that he fancies tells him "No," we must first know what question he was asking! Similarly, when we try to interpret what a dog is thinking or doing, we must know how he interprets the question, what he is trying to accomplish, and which methods and processes he is using. There is no guarantee that his mind will operate like a human mind when faced with a similar situation.

As a first step in describing the mental processes of a dog, we must understand what his world looks like to him and this requires a knowledge of his senses. Some predatory fish hunt their prey by sensing the vibrations or currents stirred up by animals moving in the water near them. Honeybees are guided to their source of nectar because they can see in the ultraviolet range of light (which is beyond human visual ability). Many flowers mark the source of nectar and pollen in patterns that look like dark bull's-eye targets when viewed by an eye that sees ultraviolet light. Many hunting snakes can see in the infrared range (which people cannot). The body heat of warm-blooded animals is a form of infrared energy, so on the darkest night they appear to be bright glowing beacons to the snake. The worlds of these different animals could appear very different from the world that we humans see, since they use senses that either we don't have or we use in a different way.

Since there are significant differences between a dog's senses and a person's, we must first explore what passes through the dog's senses. It is this sensory information that determines the canine view of reality and ultimately shapes the dog's way of thinking about the world.

CHAPTER 2

Getting Information into the Mind

SINCE THE FIRST experimental psychology laboratory was started in Leipzig, Germany, by Wilhelm Wundt in 1873, psychologists have tried to understand the components of human consciousness by performing experiments on the senses of vision, hearing, and touch. Without these senses and those of taste and smell, your brain, which is responsible for your conscious experience, would be an eternal prisoner in the solitary confinement of your skull. Data from the senses are the building blocks upon which thoughts and minds are constructed. The Greek philosopher Protagoras summed up this notion around 450 B.C. when he said, "We are nothing but a bundle of sensations."

If this notion bothers you, then consider the mind as if it were a computer. Mental operations are the way in which the computer processes data. Obviously, the data the computer processes must come from somewhere. In animals, information comes into their "mental computers" from the senses, while the data for the computer might come from the keyboard. Now imagine for a minute that a certain kind of computer has a keyboard with only numbers on it. No matter how powerful that computer is, the only data that it can ever process will involve numbers. A keyboard that contains letters as well as numbers changes the nature of the data that a computer can receive, enabling it to process words and language. But if there is no letter "B" on the keyboard, then the words "brain" and "rain" are not distinguishable. This means that we cannot identify whether the word received by the computer refers to a part of the body or a weather condition. Similarly, if there are limitations on the sensory abilities of an animal, this will affect or bias the conclusions that the animal's mind is capable of reaching. Our senses set limits on the kind of data that our minds can process; thus instead of lacking a "B," an animal may lack the ability to discriminate among colors, which would prevent him from learning things about the world if the most useful information is based upon color differences. If some senses are stronger than others, this may bias us toward seeking out certain sources of information where the sensory data are better and might cause us to ignore sources of information where the data are not very good. Thus we humans have the saying "Seeing is believing" (because vision is our most precise sense), while for dogs it might be "Smelling is believing."

Movies in the Mind?

Most people remember very little that happened before the age of four years. Certainly you were learning many things during the first three or four years of your life, and you did have many experiences that should have resulted in memories. You were probably toilet trained then; you learned how to eat with utensils and how to recognize your parents and other family members; and you probably knew a few children's games and had been to a few interesting places, like the zoo or the seashore. You did form memories of those events, but they were coded or registered in your brain as visual images. Once you developed more advanced language abilities, you changed the way you recorded memories and began to register nearly all of them in the form of a language code. You also began to think by using language rather than images. Those early memories are still there, but because you now think in words, you can't retrieve them—you have lost the key to that part of your past that was registered in images rather than in words.

People who have learned more than one language often find that it is possible to think easily about certain topics only in the language that they were using when they first learned that information. I have a friend who is bilingual in French and English but who was courted by her husband when she met him during her schooling in Paris. Although they now live in an English-speaking culture, they still find that they can talk about their intimate feelings only in French, the language they were speaking when they fell in love! "If I say personal things to Pascal in French, they have feeling and meaning," she told me, "but if I say them in English, they seem fake—maybe even funny. On the other hand, when we talk about things that have happened to us since we began living in Vancouver, we always speak in English. It is as though I can't find the French words for these things."

Dogs do not have language, or at least not the word-based language that humans use. This means that their thoughts will be coded in a form that is quite different from that in humans. In the absence of language, dogs must resort to mental processes that may be similar to the sensory-based thinking that humans use as toddlers. I am not suggesting that dogs are running videos inside their heads, but rather that the substitute for words in their thought processes is a set of images drawn from the experiences that their senses provide them.

Some scientific data suggest that when dogs think about something, their brains act in a manner very similar to the sensory experience of that situation. V. S. Rusinov, a Russian scientist who used dogs to study the electrophysiology of the brain, mounted some sophisticated equipment that measured the brain waves of dogs and transmitted them, via tiny transmitters, to recording devices. Each day, the dogs were brought into the laboratory for various training and perceptual experiments. This was done on a schedule, so for five days each week the dogs began their testing session at the same time. Rusinov soon noticed that as the dogs first came into the testing room, their brains showed electrical patterns that indicated they were fairly relaxed. Once the laboratory session started, however, there were some characteristic changes in the brain wave pattern that seemed to be associated with what the dogs were experiencing. One weekend Rusinov brought a group of visitors into the lab and, although he had no intention of actually testing any dogs that day, he turned on the equipment that normally recorded the brain wave patterns, just to show the visitors how it worked. Much to his surprise, the dog that was normally scheduled for tests at that time on weekdays was producing brain wave patterns that were nearly identical to his regular working patterns. Once the testing time was past, however, the dog's brain waves returned to their normal, nonworking patterns. Rusinov's conclusion was that the dog was sensitive to the passage of time, and when the time came for his testing, he began to think about the testing situation and what normally happened then. Since dogs register memories as sensory images, their thinking activates some of the same regions of the brain that would be used if the dog were actually seeing and hearing what he usually experienced in the lab.

Obviously, if the stuff that a dog's thoughts are made of consists of particular sensory "ideas," and sense images take the place of words in the dog's thinking, then we can understand the dog's thought processes only if we understand the language of his senses. If he fails to sense things as humans do, then he will fail to reach the same conclusions that people do when presented with a particular situation. If he senses things differently from the way humans do, or senses things that humans do not perceive, then his thoughts and understanding of what is going on will be quite different from ours. Thus if we want to learn the language of the dog's mind, we must learn the vocabulary provided by his senses.

The Eyes of a Night Hunter

Human and canine eyes are built around the same general design, but they have significant differences that affect how each species perceives the world. In humans the visual system uses a greater portion of the brain and more neurons to process and transmit information than do any other senses, which means that our interpretation of a situation is usually biased toward what we can see. This is not the case for dogs. Their visual system does not dominate their brains to the same degree, and their interpretation of the environment is less strongly dependent upon sight.

Although in many ways the dog's visual abilities are poorer than people's, the dog does have relatively good vision by animal standards. In some ways the dog's visual processing ability is actually better than that of a human. Certainly, nobody who has ever seen a dog follow the flight path of a thrown Frisbee, and leap into the air to catch it, can doubt that the dog is processing images and has good visual ability. In many dog breeds the ability to do the jobs for which they have been bred and trained depends on their vision. A retriever needs to track birds visually and to mentally mark the places where they fell after a hunter shoots them. Sheepherding dogs can detect small movements of members of a herd, which inform him where he must move in order to keep the flock together. He also needs to be able to see from a distance the hand or arm signals that his master makes to indicate which direction he wants him to go and where to move his flock. Sight hounds, such as the greyhound, have been bred for thousands of years to pursue and catch swiftly running game based solely on vision. Guide dogs for the visually impaired use the visual data they receive through their eyes to substitute for the visual information that their masters cannot detect.

Evolution has fine tuned the senses of every species so that the species can survive. Because humans evolved from tree-dwelling primates, we needed eyes that could see colors (to pick out ripe fruit and nuts from among the leaves of trees), good visual acuity (to see small nuts and berries), and good depth perception (so that we would not misjudge the distance between branches and fall to the ground). The ancestors of dogs were primarily hunters and meat eaters that were adapted to run swiftly on the ground to pursue prey that might be distant but still within chasing range. Canines are also "crepuscular," meaning they are usually active at dusk and dawn and are more comfortable than humans when operating in dim light. The type of eye needed for twilight and nighttime activity requires sensitivity to low levels of brightness, but perception of color is really not very important.

Understanding a dog's visual sense requires some understanding of the anatomy and physiology of the eye, which operates much like a camera. Both the eye and a camera require a hole to let light in (the shutter aperture in the camera and the pupil in the eye), a lens to gather and focus the light, and some kind of sensitive surface to register the image (the film in the camera and the rear surface or retina in the eye). Both the eye and the camera need features to allow them to adjust to various light conditions, and both are continually making compromises between achieving the maximum ability to pick up low levels of light and achieve the maximum ability to see small details.

At every stage in the construction of the dog's eye, however, the choice seems to have been made to sacrifice a certain amount of detail-resolving ability in order to function better at low light levels. For instance, a dog's pupils are much larger than those in most humans. In many dogs you can't really see much of anything except the wide pupil filling the eye, with just a hint of colored iris around the edge. While this lets in more light, such a large pupil also results in a loss of depth of field, which is the range, or near-to-far distance, over which objects are in clear focus. To return to the camera analogy, if a photographer wants to blur out the background behind someone he is photographing, he will use a wide aperture (f-stop) to reduce the depth of field. If he wants everything in focus, including the mountains on the distant horizon, he will use the smallest aperture possible. A dog's pupils can enlarge or contract too, but dogs cannot make their pupils small enough to give them the same depth of field that humans have.

The dog has more light-gathering power in his eyes because of larger lenses. To gather a lot of light, a lens has to be big, which is why astronomical telescopes, such as that at Mount Palomar in California, can have lenses as large as 200 inches (500 cm) across. There are effectively two parts of the eye that serve as lenses in humans and dogs. The first is the cornea, the transparent portion of the eye that bulges out at the front, which is responsible for the actual light gathering. The second, the crystalline lens, is behind the pupil and is responsible for changing the focus of the light. Animals that are active in dim light usually have large corneas. Notice how large your dog's corneas are in comparison to those of humans.

The light that passes through the pupil and the crystalline lens eventually form an image on the retina. Here much of the light is caught and registered by special neural cells called "photoreceptors." As in human beings, there are two types of photoreceptors in the retina: "rods," which are long and slim, and "cones," which are short, fat, and tapered.

The rods are specialized to work under dim light conditions. Not surprisingly, dogs have a much higher proportion of rods in their eyes than humans do, but they also have an additional mechanism to meet the needs of night hunting that is not found in humans.

You might have noticed that at night, when a dog's eyes are caught by car headlights or in a flashlight beam, they seem to glow with an eerie yellow or green hue. This color comes from the "reflecting tapetum" behind the retina, which acts as a sort of mirror. The reflecting tapetum bounces back at the retina any light that has not been caught by the photosensitive cells, thus giving the photoreceptors a second chance at catching the dim light entering the eye. A photoelectric phenomenon in the tapetum causes fluorescence, which adds to the light's brightness and also slightly changes the color of the light that is reflected back. The color shift moves the wavelength of the light closer to that which the rods are most sensitive to and can best detect. Although this light bouncing off the tapetum increases the sensitivity of the eye, there is a cost. The light that hits that reflective surface comes from various directions. Like a pool ball hitting the bumper edge of the table, it does not return along exactly the same path as it entered but bounces off at an angle. Because the incoming direction of the light and the reflected direction are different, lines in the image on the retina are smeared. This is a clear trade-off between sensitivity to low levels of light and the ability to clearly see fine details.

Husky-type dogs, particularly those with blue eyes, may not have a reflecting tapetum and their eyes may not glow when illuminated. This appears to be an accidental occurrence that resulted from selective breeding. The high northern regions that these dogs were bred to work in are covered with snow most of the year. This provides an environment that naturally reflects any light from the night sky and improves visibility of objects. It is possible that the light bouncing back from the tapetum didn't provide any advantage in this environment, and so this special structure just got lost in the breeding. Some researchers have suggested that not having the tapetum in an environment where there is always some reflected ground light might actually be an advantage, since it would provide more ability to see small details without any significant loss of light sensitivity.

Because of the larger aperture, larger light-collecting lens, greater number of rods in the retina, and reflecting tapetum, the dog's eye is considerably more sensitive than the human eye in dim light. It has been estimated that the dog needs only one-quarter of the amount of light that humans do to see things at night. Incidentally, the eyes of cats, who are the ultimate night hunters, are even more sensitive and require only one-seventh the amount of light that humans do to see.

Focusing on the World

In a camera the image is brought into focus by moving the lens forward and back so that the distance between the lens and the film is modified. In human beings the image is focused by muscles that actually change the shape of the lens, making it flatter when objects are far away and round and fat when objects are close. The dog can't change the shape of its lens as much as humans can, but there is some suggestion that, like cats, dogs have a set of muscles that can make the eye slightly longer or shorter to help focus the image. How efficiently the lens changes focus has a direct effect on the visual acuity of dogs.

If the eye can focus the image exactly at the level of the retina, you will get the best visual acuity that the eye's optics allows (this most desirable state is technically called "emmetropia"). If the image comes to a focus too soon (that is, before it reaches the retinal surface) or too late (it really wants to focus on a point beyond the retinal surface), this will result in a blurred image. Each of these two types of failures to focus results in a different kind of visual problem. If the light rays come to a focus too soon, this results in nearsightedness (called "myopia"), which means that close objects can be seen clearly but far objects are blurred. If the light rays come to a focus too late, this results in farsightedness (called "hyperopia"), which means that distant objects are clearly seen but near objects are blurred. It is possible to estimate the focusing ability of an eye using a device called a "retinoscope," which measures the location of the point where light comes to a focus by using a beam of light that is passed through the cornea and crystalline lens. To do this in dogs, you need a cooperative dog and a skillful, patient researcher.

Christopher Murphy and a team of researchers from the School of Veterinary Medicine at the University of Wisconsin reported a study that used a retinoscope to measure the focusing ability of the eyes in 240 dogs. These scientists studied cocker and springer spaniels; golden, labrador and Chesapeake Bay retrievers; German shepherd dogs, poodles, Rottweilers, miniature schnauzers, Chinese shar peis, and several different terriers and mixed breeds. Most dogs had emmetropic eyes, meaning that the focusing ability of the eye is appropriate for the size and shape of their eyes. However, there are some exceptions. More than half of the Rottweilers were nearsighted, as were the miniature schnauzers and German shepherd dogs.

The fact that these effects occurred in specific breeds suggests that they are genetic in nature. Selective breeding seems to play a role, as demonstrated by researchers who tested a set of German shepherd dogs that came from a line of dogs specifically bred to be guide dogs for the blind. Among these German shepherds, instead of having a better than 1 out of 2 chance to be myopic, only 1 out of every 7 was nearsighted. This seems to suggest that we can produce dogs with specific variations in visual ability in the course of breeding them for certain tasks. It is also consistent with some reports that greyhounds, which have been bred to search the distance for game to pursue, are actually a bit farsighted. Although this is a deviation from perfect focusing of the eye, it is a deviation in the direction that makes greyhounds' eyes more suitable for their work, namely to sight distant game and chase it down.

Grainy Sight and Clear Sight

In addition to the focusing ability of the eye, a second factor affects visual acuity in dogs: the type and arrangement of photoreceptors in the eye produce certain effects similar to those seen in photographic film. The film in a camera is covered with an emulsion containing certain photosensitive silver-based salts that react chemically when they are hit by light. Film that is more sensitive in dim light has larger grains of these salts to increase the likelihood that any one grain will capture enough light to produce a chemical reaction. Unfortunately, the resulting image also looks "grainy" (much like a poor-quality digital photo in which the pixels or patches of color are larger), which means some of the smaller details may not be clear. If the light levels are higher, one can use a less sensitive film, in which the grains are tiny and tightly packed, so that even small details can be registered.

The grains in a film emulsion can be compared to the photoreceptors in the retina. Rods (dim light receptors) increase their sensitivity by having a large clump of them all connected to the same "ganglion cell," which pools their information before sending it out of the eye. In effect, the rods act like big grains of photosensitive salt, since any light hitting any one of the rods will trigger that ganglion cell. In contrast, only one or two cones (which operate only in brighter light) are connected to any single ganglion cell that sends its information to the brain. So cones operate much like small grains of photosensitive salt—they perform poorly in dim light, but if the light level is high enough, they have a fine enough mosaic to discriminate small details well.

Since animals cannot change their photoreceptor makeup the way a photographer can change the sensitivity of the film he uses in a camera to fit current light conditions, eyes have evolved to maximize their efficiency for the animal's behavior and survival. In animals whose eyes contain both rods and cones, the photoreceptors are distributed differently in the different regions of the eye. In humans there is a small region, right in the middle of your line of sight, that is called the "fovea." It contains only cones, which are densely packed to provide us with maximum detail vision in bright light. As we move away from the center of the fovea, the number of cones drops off, which explains why our ability to see details in peripheral vision also declines. When you look at something, you are actually aiming your fovea at it, meaning that you are mostly reading this page by pointing your fovea at successive words in a sentence. Words that your fovea is not pointing at appear blurred and become even less distinct the farther away they are from the center of vision. Try this little experiment: Close one eye and let the other eye stare directly at the center of the page. Notice that the page seems fairly clear. Now block your central vision by holding up your finger in front of your eye. Keep the center of your eye pointed at your finger but pay attention to the parts of the page that are not blocked by your finger. The print on the page to the sides of your finger becomes blurry and may be unreadable.

For human beings the rods are found in increasing numbers as you move away from the center of your field of vision. This means that your greatest light sensitivity is outside of the fovea, in the periphery of the eye. That is why people who have to observe dim lights at night often find that the light is more visible if they look off to the side of the target, since the light then falls on a part of the retina that contains a higher density of rods. In effect, then, we have two different "films" in our eyes in different regions—a central area for fine detail vision in brighter light and a surrounding area with greater light sensitivity but poor acuity for small details.

The dog's eye also has separate areas of sensitivity, but the arrangement is different. The fovea of a dog's eye is a bit larger and shaped like an oval lying on its long side. As in humans, it is also a region of densely packed photoreceptive cells, but it is not made up exclusively of cones, as in the human eye. It contains many rods as well, although they are thinner and fewer of them connect to a single ganglion cell. All of this provides better acuity in this part of the eye. From the ends of this oval of densely packed cells, a horizontal streak, which also contains many cells tightly crammed together, extends across the eye. The cells crowded together in the streak give the dog better visual acuity in that region of the eye as well, and would have helped his hunting ancestors search the horizon for prey. This same arrangement is also found in other fast-moving animals that live on the open plains, such as horses and antelope, and is considered an adaptation that evolved to help these animals scan for predators.

The swift-running greyhound, which hunts by sight, has the most pronounced visual streak. Dog breeds that rely more heavily on their noses than their eyes when hunting, such as the beagle, have a less distinct horizontal stripe. Thus our selective breeding for particular behaviors in dogs has caused significant and unexpected changes in the basic physiology and neurology of each breed. Not only do dogs see the world differently than humans, but a greyhound sees the world differently than a beagle.

Do Dogs Need Glasses?

Just how good is a dog's visual acuity? First of all, let's see how we measure visual acuity. If we use a typical eye chart (the kind that you see in the office of an optometrist, with a big E on the top row), the smallest letters that you can read accurately determine your visual acuity. If you are tested at a distance of 20 feet and can read the same line of letters that a person with normal vision can read at 20 feet, then the Snellen measure of your vision is 20/20 (or 6/6 if you are measuring the distance in meters). If your vision is not that good, then you will need the letters printed much larger to read them at that distance. Thus, if the letters that you can just barely read correctly at 20 feet are large enough that a person with normal vision can read them at 40 feet, then your vision is 20/40 (or 6/12).

Since we can't get a dog to read for us, we use another technique to determine his visual acuity. In this test we teach a dog to select a pattern made up of equal-sized black and white vertical stripes instead of a patch that is a uniform gray with no stripes. If he picks the one with the stripes he gets a treat, but if he picks the gray he gets nothing. He is then tested with stripes that become narrower and narrower. Eventually the stripes will be so thin that the dog's visual acuity will not be able to determine that they are there. At this point the stripes blur and smear in the eye, and the card with the stripes will look the same as a card that is a uniform field of gray with no stripes. When the size of the stripes just arrives at this point, we have reached the limits of the dog's visual acuity. The size of the stripes that the dog can see can be converted to the same Snellen acuity measure that we get from an eye chart used to test people.

In actual practice, dogs appear to get a bit frustrated in the testing situation when the lines get very thin and near the limits of acuity. Rather than carefully studying the patterns the way that a person might in order to make out the apparently blurry lines, the dog simply gives up and chooses randomly. It seems that dogs just don't rely on their vision as much as humans, and, after all, even by just guessing, the dog will get a treat at least half of the time. The best performance to date on this test is from a dedicated poodle, tested in Hamburg, Germany. Still his acuity was quite poor and he was only able to discern patterns with stripes that were nearly six times wider than the minimum that humans can perceive. Converting this result to the more usual measures, the dog seems to have a visual acuity of only 20/75. This means that an object that a dog can barely see at 20 feet (6 meters) is actually large enough for a person with normal vision to see at a distance of 75 feet (23 meters). If your visual acuity were worse than 20/40, you would fail the standard vision test given when you applied for a driver's license in the United States and would be required to wear corrective lenses. A dog's vision is considerably worse than this.

Don't let these numbers fool you, however. Although the dog's visual acuity is considerably less than that of a normal human, a lot of information is still getting from his eyes to his brain, even though the focus is "soft" and he won't be able to make out many details. The overall effect is something like viewing the world through a fine mesh gauze or a piece of cellophane that has been smeared with a light coat of petroleum jelly. The overall outlines of objects are visible, but a lot of the internal details will be blurred and might even be lost.

Knowing something about the visual acuity of dogs helps to explain some canine behaviors that otherwise seem incomprehensible. For example, there were occasional times when I would slowly walk out of the house when my dogs were in the yard, only to have them stop and stare at me. As I continued to move toward them at a slow speed, they would take a few nervous steps and might even hunch down in a slightly defensive posture. It seemed quite clear at such moments that they were not quite sure who I was. When I spoke to them, they immediately seemed to relax and galloped toward me, with my flat-coated retriever, Odin, doing his usual goofy greeting dance. Let's change the scenario slightly. I again walk out of the house to find the dogs in the yard, but now I am wearing the broad-brimmed western style hat that I usually wear outdoors. At the moment Odin catches sight of me, his usual response is to dance his way over to say hello, quickly followed by the other dogs in the yard.

Why do they fail to recognize me in the first instance yet immediately identify me in the second? In the first case the dogs had to discriminate who I was based upon smaller, less distinct features, such as the shape of my eyes, nose, and mouth, which are blurry to them at best. However, in the second instance there is a distinctive outline to my shape, provided by my hat, which is a big enough visual feature to be easily seen. No one else in my family has chosen the same style of headwear, so this larger visual feature is quite easily recognized even given the soft focus of their eyes.

If It Moves, I'll See It

Notice that when I spoke of my dogs' difficulties in recognizing me by sight, I was careful to mention that when they saw me I was moving quite slowly. Dogs seem to have eyes that are particularly sensitive to changes in their environment. Detecting that something has moved, and what that something might be, based upon the pattern of movement, is very important for a hunter. Both the scientific and anecdotal evidence seem to support the fact that dogs have excellent motion perception. One study of fourteen police dogs found that the dogs could recognize an object when it was moving even at distances of over half a mile (900 meters), but if that same object was stationary and much closer (just over 600 yards or 585 meters), they could not discriminate it.

A few years ago I witnessed a truly striking demonstration of the advantage that their superior motion sensitivity gives to dogs. I was visiting a man in Florida who was involved in a greyhound rescue project. When I arrived at his small farm, Charlie and his son Ted were talking to Steve and Sue, who were considering adopting a former racing dog. Charlie was explaining that it made good sense to keep a rescued greyhound on a leash most of the time and to use some specific training tricks to ensure good communication with the dog.

"Now they have really sharp eyes. If they catch sight of something, even at a distance of a mile or more, they can tell what it is. So if it looks like it should or could be chased, they'll light out after it in a flash. They're not great at listening to you, and I find that it's better to train them to come to you when you wave or signal."

Charlie gently rested his hand on a fawn-colored greyhound named Jenny. She had black brindled stripes running down her body and looked very much like she had stepped out of an engraving of old-fashioned greyhounds from books printed in the mid-1800s.

"They've got good eyes for finding things. Jenny, here, has learned to find me if someone asks her 'Where's Charlie?' even if I'm surrounded by a flock of people and a mile away."

My scientific curiosity was piqued by this statement and I asked Charlie if he would like to put that claim to a test. With a bottle of bourbon as the stake, Charlie, Ted, Jenny, and I climbed into his van, and with the visiting couple following us in their car, we went out to a nearby stretch of sandy beach. Charlie had chosen this location because it was used by car racers for practice and had flags placed every 100 yards for about a quarter of a mile, with additional marker flags every quarter of a mile up to about a mile and a half from a designated starting line. Charlie, Steve, and Sue drove out to the one-mile (1.5 km) marker, got out of the vehicle, and spaced themselves about 100 feet (30 meters) apart. They then stood perfectly still facing us. Ted then enthusiastically asked, "Where's Charlie?" Jenny clearly knew what her job was and she carefully scanned the horizon, making almost a full circle as she searched for her master. No one was moving, however, and she seemed quite perplexed, even though Ted repeated the question several times. I next signaled for the distant people to start waving their arms. I could barely make out some movement in the distance and could not even tell the woman from the two men. However, now at the question "Where's Charlie?," Jenny glanced at the three distant figures, marked her line of sight to the far right where Charlie was, and dashed straight out to him. A few minutes later the vehicle with the three people and the dog arrived back at the starting line, with Charlie already talking about his prize.

Although Jenny's amazing performance had already established the winner of the bet, I asked everybody's indulgence to repeat the test. This time, however, it would be much closer, at the 100 yard flag (91 meters), with Charlie positioned at the far left this time. With no one moving, Ted again asked Jenny, "Where's Charlie?" At that distance I could clearly identify each of the three people while they stood still waiting for our signal. On the other hand, Jenny seemed totally unaware of their existence, scanning completely around herself looking for her unmoving master. Once we gave the signal to start waving, there was no doubt at all as Jenny fixed her eyes to the left and darted directly to Charlie. The significance of this test is that Jenny could recognize that a moving figure was her master at a distance of a mile (that's 1,760 yards), while she appeared unable to identify him at a distance of only 100 yards when the same figure was motionless!

Dogs not only see motion more easily, but they have the ability to recognize familiar objects on the basis of their motion patterns alone. This was the case with identifying Charlie in the distance. It also explains why dogs may respond to motion pictures or television images of dogs moving but do not act as though they are seeing a canine at all when they are looking at a cartoon dog. Although cartoon dogs clearly move, the dog's motion recognition ability discerns that those movements are not the same as the movements that a real dog would make. Therefore, whatever that figure is that is moving on the screen, to the dog's eye it is not a dog.

At the level of single cells on the retina, a moving target appears to be a flicker. As the image of the target passes over a rod or a cone and then moves on, it causes a momentary increase or decrease in brightness. For this reason, behavioral researchers often use an individual's ability to see a flickering target as a measure of not only the speed at which the visual system can record events, but also of the efficiency of motion perception.

To measure flicker sensitivity, an individual looks at a lighted panel. If the rate of flickering is very fast, there is "flicker fusion" and the panel looks the same as if it were continuously illuminated. A fluorescent light, for instance, seems to be glowing continuously with a uniform light, but it is actually flashing at a rate of 120 times (cycles of light and dark) per second. In the laboratory the ability to resolve flicker is measured by slowing the flicker rate until the person begins to see the light flutter. When humans are tested on this task, the average person can't see any flickering much above a speed of 55 cycles per second, or about half the rate that fluorescent lamps normally flash. (Technically the number of cycles per second is referred to as Hertz, abbreviated Hz.) It is possible to teach dogs to do this same task. When this is done with beagles, they are able to see flicker rates up to 75 Hz on average, which is around 50 percent faster than humans can resolve.

The fact that dogs have better flicker perception than humans is consistent with the data that suggest that they have better motion perception ability than people. It also answers a commonly asked question as to why the majority of dogs don't seem to be interested in the images on a television screen—even when those images are of dogs. The image on a television screen is updated and redrawn 60 times per second. Since this is above a human's flicker resolution ability of 55 Hz, the image appears continuous and the gradually changing images give us the illusion of continuity. Because dogs can resolve flickers at 75 Hz, a TV screen probably appears to be rapidly flickering to dogs. This rapid flicker will make the images appear to be less real, and thus many dogs do not direct much attention to it.

Even so, some dogs ignore the apparent flickering of the television and seem to respond to dogs and other interesting images on the TV screen. Surveys suggest that a dog's favorite programs include anything with animals in it and programs that have images that move rapidly and where there is lots of activity. One dog day-care center owner I interviewed keeps the dogs in her center happy by playing a continuous stream of Marx Brothers, Three Stooges, and old-fashioned Western movies on floor-level TV screens.

Looking Around

Another important difference between the vision of humans and dogs has to do with the field of view—that is, how much of the world each eye sees. Humans' eyes are pretty much oriented toward the front, while dogs' eyes are placed more to the side of their heads, giving them a more panoramic view of the world. In fact, dogs can pick up visual information from events occurring a good distance to the side and even somewhat behind their head.

Humans also have a visual field that extends a bit behind the eye's position in the head, which you can easily demonstrate for yourself.

Simply choose a point that is some distance in front of your head and stare at it. Now raise your hands until they are about a foot to each side of your head and about eye level, with your index fingers pointing upward. Pull your hands back as far as you can so that they are out of view when you stare at the distant point. Now keep staring at the distant target while you wiggle your fingers slightly, and bring your hands slowly forward until the wiggling fingers are just barely visible in your peripheral vision. At this point stop and, keeping your head as still as possible, move your fingers directly in toward your head. You will notice that your hands touch at points on your temple somewhat behind the location of the eye, indicating that you were actually seeing somewhat "behind yourself." If humans' eyes could see only to the front, the visual field would be 180 degrees; however, we actually see about 10 degrees better than that on either side of our heads, giving us a total visual field of about 200 degrees.

An average dog's eyes are set more to the side than ours, which gives it a considerably larger field of view—about 240 degrees. This means that dogs can see more of what goes on around them than humans can. The field of view will differ depending upon the shape of the dog's head. Fairly flat-faced dogs (technically called "brachycephalic" breeds), like pugs and Pekingese, have eyes pointed more to the front and so have only a slightly more panoramic view of the world than people do. Dogs with long noses (technically called "doliochocephalic" breeds) have eyes set much more to the side, so that they can see more of the world around them, with some estimates up to 270 degrees. A dog with that much peripheral vision would be very difficult to sneak up on.

In a discussion with a colleague, who is a professor of physics, about the different "optical abilities" of dogs with different head shapes, I mentioned that I was looking for a quick and easy way to demonstrate the size of a dog's visual field that didn't involve any scientific equipment. He reminded me, "If you can't see the pupil of a dog's eye, then the dog can't see you, since the light from you has to go in a straight line from you through the pupil." This suggested an easy way of testing a dog's field of view that you can try at home.

For this experiment it is best to have two people. One person should simply hold a treat in front of the dog's eyes to keep him looking forward while the other person does the test. Position yourself so that you are at the dog's eye level but off to the side by a foot or so. Now keep your eye on the dog's eye and slowly move back and to the side of the dog until you just reach a point where your dog's pupil is no longer visible to you. That is the outermost limit of the dog's field of view. You should find that you are quite a bit behind and off to the side of the dog's head—demonstrating how panoramic a view the dog has. This extensive field of view accounts for why, even though he is ranging ahead of you, your dog still knows where you are and responds to your movements. You may be lagging behind him, but he can still see you.

The Rainbow Question

Probably one of the most frequently asked questions about dog's vision is whether dogs see colors. The simple answer—namely, that dogs are color blind—has been misinterpreted by most people as meaning that dogs see no color but only shades of gray. This is wrong. Dogs do see colors and can use them to guide their behaviors, but the colors that they see are neither as rich nor as many as those seen by humans.

To understand this, you must think of the light-catching cells in a dog's retina. Dogs have many fewer cones in their eyes than do people. Cones are not only responsible for giving humans their sharpest vision and the ability to see small details, but they are also responsible for the perception of color. So, while dogs may have some color vision, it is likely not as rich or intense as ours, simply because there aren't enough cones.

The trick to seeing color is not just having cones but having several different types of cones, each tuned to different wavelengths of light. Color is a perceptual quality that the brain attaches to various wavelengths, and human beings evolved to have three different kinds of cones: one that responds best to blue (short wavelengths of light), another to green (medium wavelengths), and the third to orange (longer wavelengths). When light comes into the eye, each of these three types of cones responds more or less, depending upon how closely the light matches its particular tuning. The combined activity of these cones gives human beings our full range of color vision, so that a normal person viewing a rainbow sees colors arranged as violet, blue, blue green, green, yellow, orange, and red.

The most common types of human color blindness come about because a person is missing one of the three kinds of cones. With only two cones, the individual can still see colors, but many fewer than someone with normal color vision. This is the situation with dogs. They have only two kinds of cones, one that is almost identical to our blue cone and another that seems to respond best to yellow (which is right in between our green- and orange-tuned cones). This tells us right away that dogs will be a lot less sensitive to reds than people are.

Jay Neitz and his associates at the University of California, Santa Barbara, have been painstakingly testing the color vision of dogs, and their results have given a very detailed picture of a dog's color vision. As of the time of this writing, tests have been conducted on beagles, cocker spaniels, Italian greyhounds, some mixed breeds, and a toy poodle appropriately named "Retina," who was owned by one of the researchers. Similar research has also been done on some wild canids, including foxes and wolves.

To measure color vision, each dog was placed in a testing chamber that contained a display of three light panels in a row. Just below each light panel was a cup attached to an apparatus that would drop a treat into it if the panel above it was pushed. Because of the complexity of the testing, everything was computer controlled. The computer selected combinations of different colored lights to be displayed on the three panels. In each test trial two of the panels were always the same color, while the third was different; the dog's task was to find the different one and to press that panel. If the dog was correct, he was rewarded with a treat in the cup below that panel. A wrong choice brought no treat. The hardest part of the test was training the dogs to understand that they had to find the one item out of three that was a different color. The training period actually took about 4,000 test trials. We already have reason to believe that dogs don't pay as much attention to vision as humans do, but the difficulty in teaching the dog to solve a problem based upon color differences suggests that they pay little attention to colors.

Once it was clear that each dog understood the task, the actual testing began. This involved 200 to 400 tests in each session, with the whole test period extended over a number of weeks. The reason for this large number of tests was to provide a big data set that could be precisely analyzed statistically. The researchers were looking for the color pairs that the dog could tell apart and those that they couldn't. If the dog performed better than 33 percent correct (which is the chance guessing level), the researchers assumed that he could discriminate among the test colors.

These scientists were quite careful in their tests to make sure that the dogs were making their identifications based on color alone. They randomly changed the location of the different colored panel, so that the dog would never know whether it would appear on the left, middle, or right position. In addition, brightness of the colors was also varied randomly, since the dogs could make their judgments based on brightness rather than color.

Neitz and his research team confirmed that dogs actually do see color, but many fewer colors than normal humans do. Instead of seeing the rainbow as violet, blue, blue green, green, yellow, orange, and red, dogs would see it as dark blue, light blue, gray, light yellow, darker yellow (sort of brown), and very dark gray. In other words, dogs see the colors of the world as basically yellow and blue. They see the colors green, yellow, and orange as yellowish, and they see violet and blue as blue. Blue-green is seen as gray. Red is difficult for dogs to see and may register with them as a very dark gray or perhaps even a black.

Recognizing these facts helps to explain something that often puzzles people about their dog's behaviors. Right now, one of the most popular colors for retrieving toys is "safety orange," which is that bright fluorescent orange color used for traffic cones, the vests of road workers, and even the hats of hunters. For a human being this color is so visible that we could easily rename it "screaming orange." Yet when we throw an orange ball or bumper for a dog to retrieve, he will often run right by it and then seems to resort to using his nose to find it finally. Most people can't understand why the dog can charge right past the toy in the first place, without picking it up.

The dog is being neither stupid nor obstinate in his behavior. The reason behind his actions is quite simple. For the dog, the orange of the toy is seen as nearly the same color yellow as the green of the grass on which the toy landed. If the orange color is shifted toward the reddish, it will still appear to be the same color as the grass, but perhaps a bit darker, which still makes finding the orange toy in a field or on a lawn a fairly difficult visual task. The designers of these toys are clearly concerned about whether the dog's owner can find the toy easily, rather than about whether the dog can see it clearly!

This should give us some guidelines for increasing the visibility of an object for a dog. First, think about the color of the background that the dog will be working against. Shades of blue will be best for working on grass. If you can't anticipate the color of the surfaces that the dog will encounter, then use a combination of colors that he can see, such as areas of blue and yellow.

Since this research also suggested that dogs don't pay a lot of attention to colors naturally, but we know that they are very sensitive to variations in brightness, we can use changes in contrast to increase the visibility of objects. One obvious way is to make sure that the target is noticeably brighter or darker than the background against which it will be seen. You could also combine dark and light areas in the same object, but make the areas fairly large and distinct. Too many small areas varying in color or brightness would act something like a camouflage pattern, making the outline of the object less visible and defeating the purpose.

Good coloration for toys used on grass surfaces would include large blue and white sectors. On the other hand, a flying disk that must be caught against the blue sky might best be mostly colored yellow or orange, with perhaps a light blue patch or bull's-eye pattern on the top for those times when the dog misses catching it in the air and has to retrieve it on the grass-covered ground.

The important thing to remember is that dogs are not as visually oriented as humans are. In addition, the visual information that dogs extract from the world is quite different from what people get from viewing the same scene. If something can't be perceived, then it can't get into the brain for processing. If a dog can't see something, it can't solve problems for which it needs that unseen visual information.

Seeing Is Believing?

Dogs also differ quite a bit from people in the way in which they use their sense of sight. Dogs use vision mostly to confirm what they already know. For example, a dog might hear his owner coming up the steps. The dog is already familiar with the sound of his owner's footsteps, so actually seeing him enter the door merely confirms what he already knows from his sense of hearing. The same thing happens when dogs recognize a scent. Their sense of smell tells them that they are following the trail of a rabbit. If the dog gets close enough to a hiding rabbit to actually see it, his sight confirms what it is. Most likely, however, the rabbit will bolt and run at his approach. Once the rabbit is in motion, the dog's eyes become much more useful information-gathering devices. The dog can track the rabbit's movements and plot a path of pursuit that will allow him to intercept the fleeing bunny. Many prey animals have evolved instincts to take advantage of visual limitations of the canid eyes, so they simply freeze in place—one of the simplest and most effective ways to elude detection by a dog. When something is motionless, it becomes virtually invisible to a dog.

Although humans can be called visually dependent animals, dogs use their eyes mostly for the chase; they guide the dog to its fleeing quarry and help him to accurately guide his jaws to grab it. Any other information that the dog gets from vision is just a bonus. The mind of the dog is filled with lots of information about the world, but most of that information is not in the form of visual images.

CHAPTER 3

Playing Life by Ear

I AM SITTING AT MY DESK and working when my dog Dancer jumps up and barks at the door. It is not his "I am alerting the world to danger" bark, but rather, like my dog Odin, his "Joan is coming" bark, which he uses to announce my wife's arrival. I think that Dancer learned this bark from Odin, or if not the specific bark, at least the occasion to bark. Most of my dogs seem to develop some form of signal to indicate when family members or close friends are coming. No two dogs have ever used exactly the same barking sounds, but they are always distinctive enough so that, after a while, I have learned which signals apply to which people. In response to Dancer's signal, I get up to make sure that the door is unlocked and to greet her. I glance out, but no one is there. I have been through this routine enough times to know what is happening. I wander back toward my desk, and a few minutes later Dancer gives his announcement again. This time when I glance out the window, I see her van pulling into its usual parking space.

This is not evidence of ESP, where some psychic sense allows my dog to sense my wife's presence two or three minutes before she actually arrives. It is, rather, evidence of the acute sense of hearing that dogs have relative to that of humans—at least for certain types of sounds. We can rule out ESP quite simply in favor of hearing by noting that Dancer has been giving this bark for several years. However, when Joan's car finally reached a state of disrepair which required that we get her another, Dancer did not give any alerting barks for close to a month after the change in vehicles. It appears that he had to learn that the sounds made by the new van were associated with Joan's arrival. When my son-in-law, John, drops Joan off at home after she has visited my daughter Kari, Dancer does not give his alerting bark. Obviously if precognition were involved, the particular vehicle that my wife was arriving in should make no difference. If the cue were a sound, even though the diesel truck and the sports utility van he drives are both considerably noisier than Joan's van, they are neither familiar nor threatening sounds and hence do not cause Dancer to sound an alert.

Although a dog seems to have better hearing than a human, it is not just an issue of being more sensitive to the same sounds that we hear. I have often read that a dog's hearing is four times more acute than ours, which is not strictly true. This statement comes from an informal experiment conducted by P. W. B. Joslin, whose research involved monitoring the activities of timber wolves in Algonquin Park. He discovered that captive wolves responded to his own attempts at howling from a distance of four miles away, whereas, even on a quiet night, his attempts at howling could not be heard by his human colleagues from more than about a mile away. The fact that a canine can hear sounds coming from four times farther away than a person can is probably what led to this interpretation. The truth of the matter is that for some sounds a dog's hearing is really hundreds of times better than ours, whereas for other sounds dogs and humans have sound sensitivities that are very much the same.

The Limits of Hearing

Sounds are traveling changes in air pressure that hit our ears. The ability to detect a sound depends upon two qualities of the sound signal. Obviously the intensity or volume of the sound is important, but equally important is its frequency. By sound frequency we mean that aspect of the sound that causes it be heard as either a high or low pitch.

If we measured the changes in the air pressure from a continuous tone, we would see that the pressure increases to a peak and then decreases to a minimum pressure many times per second. For simple tones this variation in pressure usually occurs in a regular rhythm, which can be described as a wave pattern. The frequency of the wave is how many times it cycles, from one peak until the next, in one second. The unit of measure is Hertz (Hz), which is equivalent to cycles per second. Differences in frequency produce differences in our perception of the pitch of sound waves. Sound waves with higher frequencies are heard as high pitched, while those with lower frequencies produce a sensation corresponding to low-pitched sounds.

Determining what a dog is hearing was difficult until recently. When testing humans, scientists simply present sounds at different frequencies and intensities and ask if they heard them. To determine the hearing ability of dogs (or other animals), the researcher usually trains the animal to respond to the location of the sound by putting the dog in a test apparatus with a speaker and a panel on both the left and right sides. The experimenter presents a sound to either speaker randomly. The dog has to decide which side the sound came from and, if he presses the panel under the correct speaker, he gets a treat delivered to a cup below it. If he is wrong, he gets no treat. This is obviously similar to the test used for assessing a dog's color vision and is just as tedious, extending over many weeks of training and hundreds of test trials.

More recently a hearing test known as the "brainstem auditory evoked response" (BAER) has been used to measure hearing in dogs. This procedure detects electrical activity in the inner ear (known as the "cochlea") and in the neural pathways that send sound information to the brain. Researchers attach tiny electrodes to the dog's scalp and fit him with earphones or a little sound-emitting device inserted in his ear. It sounds ugly and painful, but it is not, and it is easily done with a relaxed dog, although some fidgety or sensitive dogs do have to be mildly sedated.

During testing, short bursts of sound are sent into the ear, and the brain's response is recorded by a computer. The computer determines if the brain responded to the sound. If the brain did not respond to the sound, researchers assume that the dog did not hear it. The advantage of this test is that dogs don't have to be trained over a long period. In fact, the dog doesn't even have to know what is going on, since we are simply looking at his brain's response to sounds. The disadvantages are that testing at different sound frequencies is complicated, since the process works best if the sounds are very short bursts. If sounds are too short at some of the lower frequencies, there may not be enough sound peaks in the ear to actually activate the hearing process. Second, especially if the dog is under sedation, there is a tendency for the BAER test to underestimate how good the dog's hearing is, at least compared to the more labor-intensive behavioral methods. Still, as a quick and generally reliable method of testing whether or not a dog can hear, the BAER is a good test (especially if you have concerns about whether your dog is becoming hard of hearing).

Regardless of whether we test a dog using the more behavioral methods or the BAER method, the resulting data paint a similar picture of the dog's hearing ability. The largest difference between the auditory ability of dogs and humans is in the high-frequency range. Roughly speaking, a young human being can hear sounds up to 20,000 Hz. If you wanted to have a piano that could produce this highest hearable sound, you would have to add about 28 keys to the right-hand side of the piano (about three and a third octaves). Don't bother trying to create such a piano, however, because most people will not be able to hear the highest notes anyway. As we age, the pounding of sound waves against the mechanisms in our ears causes mechanical damage and we lose the ability to hear higher-pitched sounds first. Exposure to loud sounds (too many rock concerts or too many hours listening to tapes or CDs played at high volume) quickly reduces hearing ability, especially in this high range.

You can conduct a simple test of your own high-frequency hearing by using your television set, although it requires a tube-type TV, not a flat, liquid crystal screen. Turn the set on and lower the volume to nothing. Now lean over the back of your set and listen for a faint, high-pitched whine. The raster (the part that paints the lines on your TV screen) vibrates at about 16,000 Hz. If you can hear it, this means that you can detect frequencies on the order of 16,000 Hz and your ears are in really good shape. Now, try this test on someone who is much older than you are and then on someone who is much younger. You will most likely find that the older individual cannot hear this sound, but the younger one can.

Dogs can hear considerably higher-pitched sounds than people. The highest ranges are between around 47,000 and 65,000 Hz, depending upon the characteristics of the dog. To return to our modified piano, this means that we would have to add 48 extra notes to the right side of the piano to reach the top note that a dog can hear, and the last 20 notes would be completely undetectable by even the most sensitive human ear.

The intensity of sound is measured in decibels (dB), where zero decibels is the average intensity of a sound that can just barely be heard by a young human being. Technically this is called the "absolute sound threshold." Any intensity that is less than zero is written with a minus sign in front of it, and usually represents a sound which is too faint for a human to hear. For sounds with a frequency of 2,000 Hz, and all of the frequencies below this, down to a low pitch of about 65 Hz, dogs and humans have about the same hearing sensitivity. From about 3,000 to around 12,000 Hz dogs can hear sounds that average between –5 and –15 dB, meaning that they are considerably more sensitive to these higher-frequency sounds then people are. Above 12,000 Hz human hearing ability begins to get so bad relative to that of dogs that it doesn't make sense to make any kind of numerical comparison.

The fact that dogs have greater sensitivity to sound than humans do, especially in the higher frequencies, helps to explain why some common sounds, like those made by a vacuum cleaner, motorized lawn mower, and many power tools, can cause great distress in many dogs. Many of these types of equipment have rapidly rotating shafts on motors that power fans, blades, or bits. This arrangement can produce intense high-frequency "shrieks," which for dogs can be painfully loud, while our less sensitive human ears are not bothered since these shrieks are at much higher frequencies than we can normally hear.

Hearing the High Notes

Dogs can hear sounds in the very-high-frequency range because of the evolutionary history of their wild ancestors. Wolves, jackals, and foxes often prey on small animals like mice, voles, and rats, which make high-pitched squeaks, and their scrabbling around in the leaves and grass produces high-frequency rustling and scraping sounds. Although some wild canine species like the wolf can and will hunt larger prey like deer, wild sheep, or antelope, field studies show that the summer diet of many wolves is mainly composed of small rodents like rats and mice, supplemented with an occasional rabbit. The ability to hear the high-frequency sounds that these little creatures make is therefore a matter of survival, and it is likely that only those canines that developed high-frequency hearing abilities actually endured and prospered. Cats, whose entire sustenance may depend upon small rodents, can hear sounds that are 5,000 to 10,000 Hz higher than dogs.

Human ears are also tuned to sounds that are important in our lives. Sounds between 500 and 4,000 Hz are important because they are the frequencies most critical to hearing and decoding speech. The peak sensitivity of the human ear is tuned for a frequency right in the middle of that speech range, namely 2,000 Hz. The maximum sensitivity of a dog is tuned much higher, at about 8,000 Hz, at which our human hearing ability has already begun to drop off. You can hear this difference in sensitivity for yourself if you make a "sh" sound, drawing out its length as if you were trying to signal someone to be quiet. For most people the "sh" sound has a dominant frequency just a bit above 2,000 Hz, which the human ear is tuned for. Now make a "ssss" sound, as though you were trying to imitate the hissing of a snake. For most humans this sound has its dominant frequency just a bit below 8,000 Hz, where the dog's ear is most sensitive. Notice that for the same amount of effort, the "sh" sound sounds louder than the "ssss" sound, mainly because we are less sensitive to such higher frequency sounds. But for the dog, the "ssss" will actually sound a bit louder than the "sh."

The famous Russian physiologist Ivan P. Pavlov was able to demonstrate that in the range where the dog's hearing is best, his ability to detect sounds as well as to recognize their exact pitch is remarkable. In

Pavlov's studies, dogs were trained to respond to tones corresponding to a particular musical note but not to notes that were very slightly different. Dogs were so sensitive to the pitch differences that they were able to discriminate the difference between the musical note C and another note that differs by one-eighth of the distance between that C note and C sharp. Perhaps, then, it is no wonder that my dog Dancer is so good at recognizing the sound of my wife's automobile engine.

Humans have acknowledged and taken advantage of dog's ability to hear high frequencies in several interesting ways. One is the invention of the "silent whistle," which is used by police and protection agencies to signal commands to dogs. The whistle enables police to send a dog to stop or corner a suspect without giving prior warning, especially when spoken commands might be heard by the lawbreaker and might give them time to draw a weapon or escape. These whistles are not actually silent, but just emit sounds that are at a higher frequency than humans can hear (usually around 25,000 Hz). Some hunters use these whistles, mistakenly thinking that only dogs can hear them and the quarry can't. Although some birds cannot hear these sounds, most wild animals that humans hunt for sport usually can. For instance, the sound of a silent whistle would have to be closer to around 40,000 Hz to be heard only by a dog and not by deer, antelope, or raccoon.

A more recent application of the dog's ability to hear high frequencies concern bats. Vampire bats, which are common in some regions of Central and South America, guide their flight by using a sonar that depends upon high-pitched screeches (40,000 to 100,000 Hz). These sounds are at higher frequencies than cattle can hear, which means the bats can safely land on these animals and feed on their blood. Not only does the blood loss weaken the cattle and provide open wounds that can become infected, but the bats also transfer diseases they contracted from infected cattle to healthy animals. Dogs in these same regions rarely are attacked by vampire bats, because the dogs can hear certain components of the bat's shriek and therefore avoid them. Vampire bats do not like to attack moving targets. A new job proposed for dogs is standing guard on cattle herds and listening for bat sonar. When they detect bats, the dogs could then sound a warning to start the cattle moving, which would save many animals from injury and infection.

When Hearing Fails

Just like a human being, a dog's hearing ability diminishes with age. Two general types of hearing loss in dogs, however, are not specifically age-related. Congenital hearing loss, which shows up in the dog's infancy, is usually the result of genetic factors, and induced hearing loss occurs from events during the dog's life, such as serious ear infections that damage the ear and the sound-registering apparatus. Certain chemicals can also damage the ear. Dogs are very sensitive to ear damage from contact with common solvents such as paint thinners and those used in plastic glue or cleaning fluids. These usually get into the dog's system if he inhales vapors or the solvent contacts the skin. Sadly, even certain antibiotics (particularly the aminoglycoside class of drugs) used to help the dog can have negative effects on hearing by concentrating in the fluids of the ear and damaging the apparatus used to detect sounds.

However, the major cause of induced hearing loss in both humans and dogs is exposure to loud sounds. The part of the inner ear called the "cochlea" contains tiny hair cells that flex to register the arrival of sounds; however intense sounds can break these hairs or tear them out by their roots. Once damaged, these hairs do not grow back, so each hair cell that is damaged causes the loss of a fraction of hearing ability. How loud a sound is and how long it lasts determine how damaging a sound can be. In humans some damage to the ear begins after being exposed to a sound of 100 dB for only 15 to 30 minutes. This is the equivalent of the sound of a chainsaw, a motorcycle engine, or a pneumatic drill heard up close, without any hearing protection. Every increase of 5 dB cuts the safe listening time in half, so a sound at 120 dB, which is equivalent to a nearby thunderclap or standing in front of a speaker at a rock concert, can begin to cause damage in a minute or two. By the time the sound reaches 140 dB, the damaging effects can begin immediately.

The ear tries to protect itself from loud continuous noise by using something called the "acoustic reflex." This is a reaction of tiny muscles in the area just behind the eardrum, which control the movement of the bones that transfer sounds into the inner ear. They respond to loud noises by reducing the efficiency of the movements of these bones and thus reducing the intensity of the sound that eventually makes it through to the inner ear for final processing. This reflex is fast, occurring in one-twentieth of a second (50 milliseconds), and protects the system from damage to some degree. It works best if the sound intensity builds up gradually. A very loud sound that reaches its peak very quickly can sneak past the acoustic reflex and cause quite a bit of damage. Such sounds are often called "impulse sounds."

For many years it had been observed that as retrievers age they seem to lose their hearing much more quickly than other groups of dogs. To a lesser degree the same is also true of pointers and spaniels. The conclusion that was first drawn was that this must be a genetic defect in these breeds. However, Andrew Mackin and a team of researchers from the Veterinary School at Mississippi State University came to a different conclusion, suggesting that this loss of hearing may be induced by events in the dog's life. Noise produced by a gun is an impulse noise that reaches its peak so quickly that the acoustic reflex has not even begun to provide its protective effect by the time the sound reaches the inner ear. Furthermore, this noise is very intense. For a 12-gauge shotgun, the sound is in the range of around 140 dB. The much smaller .22 rifle produces a sound intensity of between 125 and 130 dB. Because the duration of the sound is so short, humans don't perceive them as being all that loud; however, impulse noise in the 130 dB range or higher can cause instantaneous damage to the ear. A sensible hunter wears ear protection to prevent damage to his own ears, but obviously the same ear protection is not provided for the dog. Retrievers will be exposed to noise-related damage from the gunfire simply because they are usually close to the hunter and the shotgun's muzzle, where the noise intensity is the greatest. When hunting, pointers and spaniels range well forward of the hunter, which puts them at a somewhat greater distance from the noisy end of the gun, where less damage is apt to occur.

In their study these researchers tested only Labrador retrievers, to minimize any breed differences. They chose dogs that were "middle aged," defined here as four to ten years of age. They wanted dogs that were old enough to have hunted for at least a couple of seasons but were not yet old enough to be showing the loss of hearing associated with old age. The dogs were divided into two groups, those that had been used for hunting and those who had not. While the dogs that had never hunted showed normal hearing sensitivity, those who had been exposed to gunfire for several hunting seasons showed a marked loss of hearing sensitivity. The minimum sound intensity that these hunting dogs could hear was about 60 dB. This means that the sound of a normal conversation would be barely audible, and a conversational voice would have to be raised to a very loud level before we could expect the dog to get enough information to be able to understand and follow commands. Perhaps that is the reason why many hunters insist that their dogs respond better to hand signals than to voice signals—after exposure to the loud, damaging, impulse sounds of guns for a while, the dogs simply can't hear what their owners are saying.

It seems that in rare instances dogs can have their revenge on people for damaging their ears with loud sounds. A large dog's bark can peak at over 100 dB, and, like a gunshot, it is a quickly occurring impulse sound. Isuzu Kawabata, of the Saitama Medical School in Japan, recently reported two cases, one involving a fifty-six-year-old woman and the other a sixty-nine-year-old man, each of whom suffered hearing loss in the lower frequency range that developed quite quickly. It was later learned that in both instances their hearing had been permanently damaged because a large dog had barked directly into their ears.

Congenital hearing loss is mostly due to genetic factors. A recent study by George Strain of Louisiana State University in Baton Rouge involving nearly 17,000 dogs confirmed earlier findings that coat color and other aspects of the dog's pigmentation are associated with congenital deafness. The genetic defect that produces deafness is closely linked with the genes that produce white, roan (a dark color coat that has been liberally sprinkled with white), and piebald (spotty, especially black and white) colors in dogs. The classic example of a piebald dog is the Dalmatian. Twenty-two percent of this breed are deaf in one ear and 8 percent are deaf in both ears, amounting to an amazing 30 percent born with some form of hearing deficit. While all Dalmatians are more or less piebald, in other breeds the white, roan, or piebald genes are found in some individuals but not in others. For example, the bull terrier can be either white or can have prominent color patches. Among white bull terriers, the rate of congenital deafness is 20 percent, while for those with color patches it is only around 1 percent.

The gene that causes whiteness in a dog's coat also tends to make it more likely that the dog will be blue eyed. Since this gene is linked to deafness, we would expect blue-eyed Dalmatians to most likely to be deaf. This prediction is true, and the effect is quite dramatic. Among blue-eyed Dalmatians, 51 percent (or about one out of every two) are deaf in at least one ear.

Where Is It?

In the wild, one of the most important tasks required of the dog's ear is to determine the direction from which a sound is coming. As hunters, the wild ancestors of dogs had to locate game, which can often be heard long before it can be seen. Of course, an approaching sound may also indicate danger, in which case it is important to know which direction to run.

For dogs with pricked ears, the ability to localize and detect sounds is helped by the fact that the outer portion of the ear (the "pinnae") can rotate, so more sound can be captured and its direction better determined. Dogs with floppy ears are at a disadvantage, since their ear flaps hang down and absorb and block some of the incoming sound. Floppy ears also do not rotate very much, so they are less able to locate a sound's source.

Part of the information used by the dog's brain to compute the direction that a sound derives from is the simple fact that one ear is generally closer to the sound source than the other. This causes two small differences in the sounds that are perceived. First of all, the sound reaching the nearer ear will be slightly louder, partly because it is closer and partly because the dog's head blocks the sound from the other ear somewhat. The second difference between the ears is that the sound reaches the nearer ear first and then a fraction of a second later reaches the more distant ear. For this time delay to assist in locating a sound, it should be obvious that a bigger head is better because it provides a larger distance between the two ears.

Generally speaking, predators like dogs do pretty well at locating sounds. We can measure the accuracy of sound localization by drawing an imaginary circle around a dog's head. If two sounds are coming from different locations, we then indicate the directional difference by simply drawing a line from each sound source to the center of the circle and then measuring the number of degrees in the angle formed between them. Results of such a test show that dogs and cats both can tell differences in the directions sounds are coming from when there is as little as 8 degrees of separation. Humans are considerably better than dogs and most other animals that have been tested, being able to tell differences in sound directions that are only 1 degree. The dog's ability to locate sounds means that he can distinguish differences in the arrival time of sounds by as little as 55 microseconds, which is one eighteen-thousandth of a second!

Quite often the first sign of hearing impairment in dogs is an inability to locate sounds accurately. This may show up as confusion when you call your dog and he can't see you. He may look around uncertainly, coming only when he finally catches sight of you. Another sign is that when a loud sound is heard the dog may swing his head first to the wrong side, away from the direction in which the sound occurred. Sometimes this loss of sound localization is the only noticeable symptom that your dog has lost the hearing in one ear, although his other is still functioning.

Can You Hear This?

If you are worried about your own dog's hearing, stand behind him out of sight and either squeeze a squeaky toy, whistle, clap your hands, or bang a metal spoon against a pot. A normal dog will prick its ears, or turn its head or body toward the source of the sound. Be very careful not to stand directly over the dog, since they are sensitive to air currents and may feel your movements or the vibrations in the floor immediately behind them. Also make sure that the dog hasn't seen you before you make the sound. Sometimes it is best to conduct these tests when your dog is sleeping, since that reduces the likelihood that the dog is responding to the sight of your movements.

It is not sensible to try a home test of a dog's hearing when he is a very young puppy. Dogs are not born with all of their exquisite hearing abilities fully matured. Measurements taken in puppies aged eleven to thirty-six days show that their hearing, although functioning at birth, gets better with age over the first month or two. It is their ability to hear the higher frequency sounds that improves the most during the early weeks of growth. So if you are concerned about a puppy's hearing, wait until he is about five weeks of age before testing his hearing on your own.

The ability to hear very sharp loud sounds is the last aspect of hearing that a dog loses. A sharp clap of the hands, or a quick blast on a loud whistle, will often produce an ear flick and a turn of the head that lets you know that your dog heard you, even if he can no longer make any sense of human voice sounds.

Although hearing is important to the dog, you can take advantage of other senses to communicate with your hearing-impaired pet. Remember that if the dog can't hear you, it may miss your approach, especially if it is dozing and becomes quite startled. To wake a sleeping deaf dog, it is often enough to just hold your hand near his nose; he will awake because he detects your scent. Alternatively, you can develop a very heavy step, so that as you clomp your way across a room the vibrations from the floor will reach the dog first and let him know you are coming. Giving the dog a touch as you leave the room lets him know you are leaving.

The most important single thing that you can do for your hearing-impaired dog is to put him on a leash. The leash becomes both a lifeline and a security blanket. A free-roaming deaf animal can't hear traffic, predators, falling objects, or oncoming people, and thus will be at risk. Such animals can also lose their sense of where you are, which can cause them to panic. The leash controls their movements and keeps them out of trouble, and since they can sense your movements, they know where you are, which keeps them calm and secure.

Research is being done on designing a hearing aid for deaf dogs, but there is a more immediate way to assist your hard-of-hearing dog. If possible, simply get him a canine companion. Because dogs are such social creatures, they will pay attention to another dog who lives with them, using whichever senses are still available. Late in his life, my Cavalier King Charles spaniel, Wizard, shared his home with two other dogs, and the average observer would not have noticed that he had gone deaf. When the other dogs ran to the door or began barking at sounds outside the window, Wiz would tag along and check things out. If someone entered the room and the other dogs got up to say hello, Wiz would be right there, joining the greeting ritual as if he had heard the arrival himself. Most important for his happiness, he knew by the behavior of the other dogs that it was time to show up in the kitchen when I called them to supper. His hearing aid was simply the ears of the dogs who shared his life. And it was quite effective.

CHAPTER 4

I Sniff, Therefore I Am

Every species seems to have a preferred or dominant sensory system. For the simplest animals, such as single-celled creatures and simple sea creatures like sponges and coral, it is the "taste" of dissolved chemicals in the fluid in which they live that provides most of the information they need to survive. Somewhat more complex animals like starfish, jellyfish, and sea anemones seem dominated by their sense of touch. Bats, rabbits, shrews, and a number of nocturnal animals seem to respond most strongly to sounds. Humans, apes, monkeys, and birds are visual species and depend upon vision more than any other sense. But for many other mammals, including the dog, the sense of smell seems to reign supreme.

For a dog, his nose not only dominates his face, it also dominates his brain and thus his picture of the world. Human brains are predominantly shaped and structured around vision and processing light-related data, but the dog's brain is built around the information it gets from scents. Humans process many smells at an unconscious level and scents seem to reach our consciousness only if they are quite intense or have particular significance. Dogs respond to many more varieties of scent than humans do, which makes the dog's mind very different from that of his human owner. It also makes the dog's mind an enigma to us. If we could share a dog's consciousness for a moment, it is likely that our familiar world would appear to be quite alien and incomprehensible. How do you interpret a world made up predominantly of smells of different types and intensities rather than visual images? Thus, if we want to understand a dog's thinking and behavior, we must first try to understand his olfactory sense.

Scents and the Brain

The structures that process smells in the human and canine brain are very different. On the underside of both brains are two masses of neural tissue that are the olfactory bulbs, or smell-decoding centers. In humans they look like small swellings attached to the ends of little stems; in dogs the bulbs are so much larger that you can't even see the stems that attach them to the rest of the brain. In humans the total weight of these olfactory bulbs is about 1.5 grams (or half an ounce), while in average-sized dogs they are about 6 grams (or 2 ounces)—four times larger than in humans—even though the dog's brain itself is only one-tenth the size of the human brain. The proportion of the dog's brain that is devoted to analyzing smells, then, is actually forty times greater than that of humans! It has been estimated that dogs can identify smells somewhere between 1,000 to 10,000 times better than humans can.

A Honker Built for Hounds

In addition to the extra brain capacity dedicated to scent recognition, the dog's nose itself is specially designed to detect very faint odors. Let's take a quick tour through this remarkable organ. The hairless part at the end of a dog's nose is called the "leather." It has a distinctive color, usually dark, but it may be brown, pink, or spotted, depending upon the breed. Generally, white dogs or dogs with a significant amount of white on them are more likely to have pale-colored noses. These dogs are more likely to suffer from a condition called "snow nose," which means the nose color will tend to fade to a lighter color in winter. Usually, the normal color returns as summer draws near, although in older dogs the color change may become permanent. Eating out of plastic or rubber food bowls can also lighten or speckle the nose. This condition, called "plastic dish dermatitis," is caused by a reaction between the nose pigment and certain antioxidant chemicals in such dishes.

Look carefully at your dog's nose and you will see patterns of ridges and dimples. That pattern, in combination with the outline of the nostril openings, makes up the noseprint, which is believed to be as individual and unique as a human's fingerprints. For that reason a dog's noseprint has been accepted as providing positive identification of that dog by many kennel clubs around the world. Some companies maintain noseprint registries to help find lost or stolen dogs. If you want to take a noseprint from your dog just for fun (or as a sort of art project), it is quite simple. Dry the dog's nose first. Then pour some food coloring on a paper towel and dab it on his nose. Keep him from licking it off for a couple of seconds, then use a small pad of paper to press gently against the nose, letting the pad's sides curve around to pick up impressions from the sides of the nose as well. You might have to try a couple of times until you get the right amount of food coloring and the right amount of pressure to produce a print where the little patterns on the nose are clear. Don't use ink or paint on your dog's nose. The food coloring is nontoxic and is easily removed, so you won't have to explain to your friends why your dog has a green or blue nose.

Dogs work more actively than humans to gather scents. They don't let them casually drift into the nose but rather gather them from the environment by using certain abilities and structures that humans don't have. To begin with, dogs can move or wiggle their nostrils independently, which helps them determine the direction a scent is coming from. Dogs also have a special sniffing ability that is quite different from their normal breathing. When your dog pushes its nose in the direction of a scent, he is actively interrupting his normal breathing process. As he sniffs, the scent-containing air first passes over a bony shelflike structure in the nasal cavity that is designed to trap the odor-containing air and protect it from being washed out when the dog exhales. This allows the scent molecules to remain in the nose and accumulate. When the dog breathes normally, or pants, the air goes through the nasal passages below the shelf and continues on down to the lungs. Sniffing, however, briefly stores the air in the upper chambers of the nose so its contents can be interpreted.

The difference between sniffing and breathing has some important implications for a dog's ability to follow scents when he is overheated or the weather is very hot. The human body has two types of sweat glands. One type, the "eccrine gland," is designed to help regulate human body temperature by releasing moisture on the surface of the skin in the form of sweat. As the sweat evaporates, it lowers the skin temperature and helps to keep us cool. In humans sweat glands are distributed all over the body, but dogs have them only in the pads of their paws. (This is why when a dog is stressed or overheated, he may leave wet footprints.) A dog has to pant to increase his cooling capacity, because evaporation of moisture from the mouth and tongue provides some relief from the heat. The more he pants, the more evaporation and cooling. Working scent dogs become less reliable in hot weather simply because panting is not sniffing, so while the dog is panting it has, in effect, turned off its scent-processing ability. This is why if you offer a panting dog your hand or a bit of food, he will stop panting so that he can deliberately turn on his smelling ability to check out the available scents. Research has now proven that when dogs are overheated, their ability to track and recognize items by scent is reduced by over 40 percent. Obviously, if the dog is being used for search-and-rescue work in hot weather, this can be a real problem.

There are several solutions to this loss of scenting ability in overheated dogs. The first, of course, is to keep the dog cool. This can be done by spraying him often with water, using the same kind of misting bottles that are used on plants. As the water evaporates from his body surface it cools him, which reduces the need for panting and improves his scenting ability. The second involves simply working the dog in short sessions over a period of a few days under hot conditions. Many dogs will begin to acclimate somewhat to the heat and spontaneously begin to adopt a different strategy. They learn to sniff for a few moments, then stop to pant a bit. This sniff-and-pant routine greatly improves their ability to track a scent, although it slows the procedure noticeably.

Why Do Dogs Have Cold Noses?

Everybody knows that a dog's nose is usually cool and moist. I am often reminded of this after being awakened by a cool nose shoved against my ear by a dog who has decided that it might be nice to wake me so that he might have an early breakfast. This moisture on the leather is produced by many mucous glands in the dog's nose. One purpose of the mucus is to keep the leather cool, but its main purpose is to assist in the collection of odor molecules. All odor molecules are chemicals that can be dissolved in water. The moisture on and in the dog's nose acts like Velcro, and when a scent molecule touches it, it sticks to the surface and starts to dissolve in the mucus. If there is not enough mucus being generated to adequately moisten the outside of the nose, dogs will resort to licking their noses to provide some additional collecting power. Inside the nose are little hairlike structures that keep the mucus flowing back into the nasal cavities. These hairs push the dissolved odor particles inward, concentrating them near the special cells that can identify the smell. It takes a lot of mucus to keep this system working efficiently. This is also the mucus that shows up as drool in certain breeds when it drains down the flews and inner cheek rather than down the throat. An average-sized dog produces about a pint of mucus over the course of a day, which probably explains why dogs drink substantial amounts of water.

Putting science aside for the moment, there is a charming story I was told when I was young that explains why the dog's nose is cool and moist. According to that tale, it all began at the time of the great flood, when Noah had collected all of the animals in his ark to save them from the rising water. Since the two dogs on the ark were both clever and reliable, Noah gave them the job of keeping watch for any trouble. One day the dogs were patrolling the ark and noticed that it had sprung a leak. The hole was only about the size of a quarter, but water was pouring in, and if the hole was not repaired, the ark would sink. While one of the dogs quickly ran for help, the other dog did a truly brave and clever thing. He marched up to the leak and stuck his nose into the hole to stop the flow of the water. By the time Noah and his sons arrived to repair the leak, the poor dog was in great pain and gasping for breath. But the dog's brave deed had saved the ark from sinking. The story goes on to say that God gave the dog his cold, wet nose as a badge of honor and to remind the world of his brave deed. This is the story that I tell my grandchildren, at least until they are old enough to understand and have an interest in mucus and chemicals that dissolve in water.

Ensnaring Essences

The air captured when dogs sniff eventually will reach a set of scroll-shaped, bony plates called "turbinates." These plates are covered with a thick, spongy membrane that contains most of the scent-detecting cells and the nerves that will carry the information to the brain. In humans the whole area containing these odor analyzers is about one square inch (7 square centimeters), or about the size of a small postage stamp. In dogs, this area if unfolded can be as large as 60 square inches (390 square cm), or just smaller than the size of a piece of typing paper. There is quite a bit of variability in the overall size of this surface, depending upon the size and length of the dog's nose. Dogs with longer and wider noses have much more of this surface, while dogs with flat faces and short noses, like pugs or Pekingese, have a considerably smaller surface area in the nose.

The size of this area is an important consideration, since breeds of dogs with larger noses will have more smell receptors and hence greater scenting ability. For example, the dachshund has about 125 million smell receptor cells, while a fox terrier has 147 million and the German shepherd dog about 225 million. Some dogs, in particular the so-called "scent hounds," have noses that are designed to be very wide and deep in order to pack the greatest number of odor-analyzing cells into the available space—even if the dog is not very large. The very scent-oriented beagle, who weighs in at only 30 pounds (14 kilograms) and stands only 13 inches (33 cm) at the shoulder, has the same 225 million scent receptors as the German shepherd dog, which is twice his size at 75 pounds (35 kilos) and 24 inches (60 cm) in height. The grand champion of scenting is, of course, the bloodhound, which checks in with around 300 million scent receptors in his nose. We can compare these canine statistics to the number of odor receptors in humans, which amount to a paltry 5 million or only about 2 percent of the number of smell receptors in the little beagle.

With the added brain capacity devoted to smell, and the fact that dogs have about 50 times more scent receptors than we do, it is not surprising that they are more sensitive to odors than humans are. However, most people do not appreciate just how great that difference is for certain odors. Dogs' noses are specially tuned for animal-related odors, which might be expected, since they are hunters. If we test the human sensitivity to butyric acid, which is a component of sweat, we find that we can detect its odor at a reasonably low concentration of about one five-millionth of a gram evaporated into a cube of air one meter square. Before we get cocky about our scenting ability, however, consider that if we dissolved this same amount of butyric acid in 250,000 gallons (1,000,000 liters) of water, a dog would still be capable of detecting it. If we take one gram of butyric acid and let it evaporate in the volume of a ten-story building, when you open the door you should be just barely able to smell it. If we evaporated that same gram of butyric acid in the air, dispersed it over a 135 square mile area (350 square kilometers) and up to a height of 300 feet (92 meters) in the air, a dog could still smell it. This area is approximately the same size as the area covered by the entire city of Philadelphia! Since that city contains about one and a half million people, all of whom sweat (especially on typically hot muggy summer days), it is interesting to speculate what that metropolis must smell like to a dog!

Smelly Genes

Although all dogs have fine scent recognition abilities, these can, and have been, improved upon through selective breeding. The beagle, basset, and bloodhound are good examples of how sensitivity to odors is partly inherited. These dogs have been bred as specialists—not only in their ability to detect and discriminate scents, but also in their passion to follow, track, and explore odors.

In the 1960s, J. Paul Scott and John Fuller maintained a canine behavior laboratory and field testing station at Bar Harbor, Maine. Looking for genetic contributions to dog behaviors, they tested breeds of purebred dogs. In one test, they used a fenced area approximately one acre in size and released a mouse in it. The mouse, of course, immediately skittered away to hide someplace as far from the release point as it could get. A short time later beagles, with their finely developed noses, were released into the area. It took them approximately one minute to follow the track and find the mouse. When the same test was conducted using fox terriers, they also managed to track and find their tiny quarry, but it took them about fifteen minutes. However, when the test was repeated once more, this time with Scottish terriers, the results were a complete failure. The Scotties did not track the mouse, and one even stepped on it without noticing it. This helps to explain why you don't see Scotties doing search-and-rescue work, or tracking escaped criminals.

The failure of the Scotties is probably due to a combination of factors. First, they have a smaller and shorter nose than either of the two other breeds tested, which gives them a disadvantage in sensitivity to odors. The second possible factor is more behavioral and may reflect the fact that Scotties are simply not as odor oriented and not as motivated to track scent trails.

A breeder of black and tan coonhounds whom I met in South Carolina probably would have explained the Scottie's poor performance in another way, but also one that involved a genetic mechanism. Over a glass of lemonade that had been generously spiked with gin, Tom expounded his theory for me.

"Ya see, if you're picking a hound that you want as a tracker the first thing you got to look at is their ears. Don't matter if it's a coonhound, bloodhound, beagle, or basset, God gave them those big long ears to help them in their work. It goes like this: When they move, them ears flop up and down and that drives the air down to the ground and helps to lift the scent back up to their nose. That makes tracking a whole lot easier. Ain't no prick-eared dog that can match a flop-eared hound in tracking. Just remember, look at the ears—the longer the ears, the better the tracker."

It is a wonderful image—long hound ears flopping up and down and lifting the scent directly to the nose, while the poor Scottish terrier remains clueless because all that his pricked ears are good for is hearing.

As can be verified by anyone who has ever worked behind a prick-eared German shepherd dog doing search-and-rescue work, however, it is just a lovely folk belief that has no scientific merit at all.

Genetics has done something else to distinguish human scenting ability from that of the dog. Like a number of other animals, dogs have a special organ in the nose called "Jacobson's organ," or the "vomeronasal organ." It is a sort of pancake-shaped pouch of special receptive cells located just above the roof of the mouth, with ducts that open to both the mouth and the nose to allow scent molecules to enter it. The large number of nerves and rich blood supply to this organ tell us that it is important to the dog, which is further verified by the fact that there is a special region in the olfactory bulbs in the dog's brain dedicated to processing the information from this special smell receptor.

Up until recently it was believed that human beings, apes, and other old-world primates were completely missing Jacobson's organ. Recent studies have shown that this organ is present but may be a minimally functional vestige of the organ in dogs. The human genome project has found that the gene needed to turn on the sensing ability of Jacobson's organ is not operating correctly and there are very few smell receptors in this organ in people. Furthermore, nerve cells needed to send the information to the brain are absent, and the special section of the olfactory bulb used to process information is also missing in humans.

Aromatic Animals

What kind of scents can a dog perceive that we "nasally challenged" humans cannot? The dog's nose is tuned to a set of smells that have a special biological significance to animals, specifically pheromones, the odiferous chemicals secreted by animals to transmit information to other animals (usually of the same species). The word derives from the Greek words *pherein*, meaning "to carry," and *horman*, meaning "to excite." Researchers originally thought that these smells told male animals when females were ready to mate. Pheromones were thought to excite males to track females and mate. Today we know that these personal chemicals carry a lot more information than sexual readiness.

Researchers studying insects such as ants, bees, and termites found that these biologically generated smells are actually their dominant form of social communication. Pheromones trigger specific complex behaviors in the insect brain, like attracting mates, food-gathering, or fighting. The effects are so powerful that synthetically produced pheromones are used in some insect control programs to bait traps or cause insects to avoid an area.

In primates, including humans, the effect of pheromones is not as powerful as it is in insects, and we are usually unaware of them because pheromones often operate at an unconscious level. The reason seems to be that the olfactory bulbs in the brain send only a small fraction of their sensory information to the cortex, the part of the brain that consciously processes information. Most of the scent information is sent to the "limbic system" of the brain, an evolutionarily old center, found in all vertebrate animals. The various parts of the limbic system concern themselves with three important aspects of behavior: emotions and moods, memory for facts and locations, and the control of the basic animal drives, including sexual desire, territoriality, and social dominance. "Aromatherapy," which uses scents from various essential oils to calm or energize humans, may work through the limbic system, changing moods without requiring any conscious thought from the person or even any conscious recognition of the smell—much the way pheromones seem to operate in animals.

Special kinds of sweat glands, "apocrine glands," secrete the pheromones that carry information about the animal's age, sex, health, and even emotional state. In humans the apocrine glands are found in only certain areas of the body, with the highest concentrations in the armpits and groin area. Dogs and most other mammals have their apocrine sweat glands spread over their entire body, which means that more odor is produced on the animal's body than on the human's. The pheromone-releasing apocrine cells are even found in the hair follicles, so a dog's fur gets coated with these chemicals and concentrated for easier identification by other dogs. Bacteria begin to act on these secretions almost immediately, modifying and intensifying the smell. When the dog's fur rubs against objects, some of the pheromones get transferred to it, leaving a lasting record of the animal's passage. Pheromone smells not only identify the gender, age, health, and mood of the individual but also carry a lot of sexual information as well, such as where the female is in the estrous cycle, if she is pregnant or having a false pregnancy, and even if she has given birth recently.

Reading pheromone scents is, for dogs, the equivalent of reading a written message about the status and feelings of another animal. To carry the analogy a bit further, the canine equivalent of ink is urine. Many pheromone chemicals are found dissolved in dog's urine (and some are also carried in fecal matter), so a dog's urine contains a great deal of information about that dog. Sniffing a fire hydrant or a tree along a route popular with other dogs thus becomes a means of keeping abreast of current events. That tree serves as a large canine tabloid containing the latest news items in the dog world. It may not contain installments of classic canine literature, but it certainly has a gossip column and the personals section of the classified ads. When my dogs are engaged in sniffing at a favorite post or a tree on a city street frequented by other dogs, I sometimes fantasize that I can hear them reading the news out loud. Perhaps this morning's edition goes "Mimi, a young female golden retriever, has just arrived in this neighborhood and is looking for companionship—neutered males need not apply," or "Brutus, a strong young adult Rottweiler, announces that he is challenging the leadership of the neighborhood gang and will take on all comers. Be respectful or beware!"

Dogs prefer to "mark" vertical surfaces with urine because having the scent above the ground allows the air to carry it farther. How high above ground the mark is tells the neighborhood something about the size of the dog that made it. In dogs, size is an important factor in determining dominance. Since dominance seems to be more important to males, they have developed the habit of leg lifting when they urinate so that they can aim their urine higher. Besides, the higher the marking, the more difficult it is for other dogs to mark over it and obscure the message.

Urine marking also conveys information about a dog's emotional state. Changes in emotion are associated with the release of a set of stress-related hormones that work their way into most of the body fluids, including not just the blood but also sweat, urine, and tears, so that an angry animal smells differently from a happy one. Some people claim that animals can "smell fear." I have heard police officers claim that criminals are easy for their patrol dogs to detect because the dogs lock in on the fear of criminals who are worried about being caught. Obviously, fear is an emotion and emotions have no scent, but to the extent that fear causes a change in the chemical composition of bodily fluids, like sweat, and these chemicals can be smelled, certainly fear might be associated with a distinct odor, as may other emotions.

Social Smells

Why would evolution allow emotional signals to work their way into scent-carrying fluids of the body? At first glance, a scent of fear does not seem to provide an evolutionary advantage and it might even be counterproductive. A threatened animal that releases a fear scent could signal its antagonist that the animal is weak; it could even trigger an attack. For social animals like dogs, however, knowing the emotional state of his companions might increase the chances of survival of the whole pack. Thus, what we have been calling "the scent of fear" could be read by an animal's companions as "the scent of danger" and taken as a warning of imminent danger. Also, the absence of the fear scent could signal to a stranger that it is safe for him to approach and perhaps to establish some sort of social contact.

Jacobson's organ in the dog's nose has receptors that can register certain pheromones and may help prepare a dog for a social encounter with another dog. Certainly mutual sniffing is part of the greeting ritual that dogs go through when they meet each other. The exchange of scent information usually begins with the sniffing of each other's faces; however, dogs quickly shift their attention to their acquaintance's rear end, where a lot of information exists in the concentration of apocrine sweat glands. There will also likely be traces of odor from urine, feces, and perhaps from sexual activity. That many different pheromones in one place are certainly worthy of any dog's attention. Dogs process this information quickly and use it to guide further social interactions.

While dogs spend a longer time sniffing at dogs with which they are unfamiliar, even dogs that live in the same household will sniff each other frequently to get a quick update on how their housemate is feeling today and advance warning of any negative or aggressive feelings.

Humans are sometimes embarrassed when a dog comes to sniff them in the crotch. A dog is attracted to the human groin area for the same reason that it is attracted to the genital area of another dog, because the area is a particularly rich source of scents from the pheromone-rich apocrine sweat cells. Unfamiliar humans, like unfamiliar dogs, receive the most attention of this sort, especially if there is a tinge of sexual scent. People who have had sexual intercourse recently seem to attract this kind of attention from dogs. Women in their menses or who have given birth recently (especially if they are still nursing their child) will also often find dogs impolitely sniffing at their genital region.

Ovulation also seems to cause a change in pheromones that attracts dogs. Some researchers noticed that the frequency of crotch sniffing went up dramatically around ovulation and decided to put this fact to use. They trained some Australian shepherd dogs to pick out cows that had just ovulated, allowing farmers and ranchers to successfully breed these cows during their short fertile period. The dog's "sniff test" is considerably easier and more reliable than most other methods of predicting ovulation. Perhaps this could open up a new class of assistance dogs for humans. Millions of women who, for religious or cultural reasons, use only the rhythm method of birth control could be alerted by having specially trained dogs inform them when they are fertile. It would also give a new meaning to the familiar complaint of many husbands that their sex life "has gone to the dogs!"

Many humans have strong negative reactions when a dog starts examining their bodies for scent messages. Perhaps the most public instance of this was the case of Barbara Monsky, a local political activist living in Waterbury, Connecticut, in 1996. Monsky's reaction was so negative when she was sniffed by a dog that she brought a suit against Judge Howard Moraghan and his golden retriever Kodak, charging sexual harassment. The basis for her legal action was that Moraghan often brought his dog to Danbury Superior Court. According to Monsky, it was in the courthouse that the dog sexually harassed her when he "nuzzled, snooped or sniffed" beneath her skirt at least three times. She based her charges on the contention that the judge was complicit in this harassment because he had done nothing about it. Fortunately for dog owners everywhere, when the case was finally brought before U.S. District Judge Gerard Goettel, he dismissed the case. In a later interview he explained that "Impoliteness on the part of a dog does not constitute sexual harassment on the part of the owner."

Odors Observed

The dog's nose initially evolved to help him hunt. As a hunter he requires two things of his nose. First, he has to be able to detect scents. He must also be able to recognize the species of the animal that left the scent and also the scent unique to the particular individual that he is tracking. Discriminating the scent of an individual is important because wild canines often work by chasing their prey until it becomes too exhausted to run any farther or to put up a struggle. Of course this means that they have to stay with that specific animal.

Consider a pack of wolves that has isolated a caribou and begins to chase it. If the animal simply stayed out on the plain and kept away from the other members of its herd, there would only be the task of pursing it until it was weak enough to be attacked. Like many of the animals that wild canines hunt, however, caribou are herd animals. When they are threatened they will seek the safety (and the anonymity) of the herd. Thus, the animal that is singled out by the hunting pack will often attempt to evade pursuit by dashing back into the herd. The wolves may have invested twenty minutes in chasing the caribou. After such a long chase, the caribou should be beginning to tire and to slow, but once it's back in the herd, the wolves must keep track of this individual or their quarry will have time to rest and all of their efforts will have been in vain. Since canines have less than perfect vision, and individual animals in a herd look very similar to one another, they must resort to their sense of smell to identify and continue the pursuit of this already weakened animal.

The concept that canines evolved the ability to pick out the scent of one individual animal, even though his track has been crossed, re-crossed, and trampled over by a whole herd of animals of the same species, boggles our human minds. Our own ability to recognize one scent is easily lost when that scent is covered with another, stronger odor. Thus a human can recognize the scent of a lily, but not after it has been sprayed by a skunk. Dogs differ from us not only in the keenness of their sense of smell but also in their ability to process smells, separate individual scents, and recognize each. In other words, the dog's brain contains a much larger olfactory computer than ours, with much more powerful scent-discriminating programming. Dogs' ability to separate scents can be compared to our ability to separate visual objects.

Imagine a quilt with a bright colorful flower pattern, on top of which we throw a flashlight, a hammer, a pen, and a book. The task of finding, separating, and identifying these objects using only our visual processing system is really quite trivial for humans. We do not see a mishmash of colored blotches that all blend into nothingness but instead easily can separate the quilt from the objects on top of it. We can do this even if we are building levels upon levels of visual stimulation, such as having the book lying open on the quilt and the pen resting on the book. We easily single out these objects and identify them.This is the way the dog's olfactory system treats scents. Scientific research shows that dogs separate smells into distinct, recognizable odors. They don't blend them or respond only to the dominant scent. This is sometimes called "odor layering." As an example, suppose you walk into a kitchen where someone is making chili. What you smell is chili from the pot on the stove. What your dog will smell is the meat, beans, tomato, onions, and each of the spices. The dog has separated this "olfactory scene" into layers of scents in much the same way that we easily separated the visual scene involving items on a quilt into layers.

Sorting Scents

If dogs did not have the ability to separate one scent from another, to ignore irrelevant odors, and to focus on the important ones, then they would be considerably less useful in many of the jobs that we require of them. Explosive-detection dogs have shown their remarkable discrimination skills on many occasions. For example, some terrorist groups have tried to smuggle explosives past dogs by covering the scent with perfume or scented oils. In one case the explosives were hidden in sacks of coffee. One person was apprehended when a dog detected explosives that he had tried to hide in his suitcase by wrapping them in smelly soiled socks and inserting this noxious package in a plastic bag. Another tried to hide explosives in a pail containing soiled baby diapers. Recently an explosives-detecting dog found a case of dynamite that had been hidden by burying it two feet underground.

Drug and narcotic smugglers don't fare much better at attempting to disguise the odor of their contraband by masking them with strong smells. An Arkansas state policeman, Creston Hutton, working with a yellow Labrador retriever named Meg, was inspecting a vehicle when Meg alerted him that drugs were present. Officers searched in all of the usual places but found nothing. Meg insisted that contraband was there and indicated a particular location along the side of the vehicle where nothing was visible to the officers. Nonetheless, Hutton was confident about Meg's accuracy and insisted that the search continue. The place that Meg was attracted to was near the opening to the gas tank, so police probed inside it. Sure enough, there, immersed in gasoline, was a plastic container filled with 35 pounds (16 kg) of marijuana!

Attempts to hide narcotics by disguising their scent simply doesn't work. If it did, then the Labrador retriever Snag would not have been able to discover 118 drug stashes worth over $810 million dollars. Despite the drug lords' best efforts at concealing the scent of drugs, the team of "Rocky" and "Barco," who patrolled the Texas and Mexico border (in a section nicknamed "Cocaine Alley"), still had good enough scent discrimination to help in 969 drug seizures (all in the same year, 1988). With attempts at concealing the drugs proving to be a failure, these drug smugglers resorted to another way of evading detection—they put up a reward of $30,000 for anyone who could kill these dogs. Fortunately, this plan was also a failure and the two dogs lived to enjoy a happy retirement.

There are some scents that dogs don't like very well. Among these are citrus smells, such as lemon, lime, and orange, and spicy smells like red pepper. They particularly dislike the smell of citronella, which is why it's often used in sprays to keep dogs away from certain areas. It's also used on antibarking collars. The collar has a little microphone that picks up the dog's barking and delivers a little spray of citronella, which is supposed to stop the barking. It does for a while, until a dog acclimates to the odor, after which it has no effect on the animal. This means that drug smugglers might be no more effective in trying to hide their contraband in truckloads of limes than by immersing them in tanks of gasoline.

Dogs can be so good at detecting narcotics that they can virtually put themselves out of work. At Erlestoke prison in Wiltshire, England, a border collie named Rebel had virtually wiped out drug-taking by the prisoners by finding nearly all of the narcotics before they could be used. Because of his effectiveness, fewer attempts were being made to smuggle drugs in, so Rebel had lots of time on his hands without much work to do. Therefore, he was given additional training so that he could also signal when he detected alcohol. Prisoners have found ingenious ways of making home-brewed alcohol and of hiding it. Alcohol can be as disruptive in a prison population as drugs and is often the cause of violent incidents. Rebel's handler, Neil Pollard, described Rebel's first search for alcohol.

"We suspected hooch was being brewed but couldn't find it by normal search methods. So we sent Rebel all round the prison, and when he got to the showers he stopped. He had picked up the scent even though it wasn't noticeable to the human nose.

"I started having a look round, then got a ladder and found a recess in the roof. Inside we found twenty-two liters of hooch—much to the disappointment of the prisoners."

Pungent People

Dogs are very good at identifying individual humans by scent. A person's scent is produced in perspiration, which is then altered by bacteria that act both upon the sweat and the skin. Five kinds of bacteria are most typically involved, each present to a greater or lesser degree in every person. Human sweat also has eight major chemical components that can exist in varying concentrations, depending on a person's physiological state and mood. Skin composition will also subtly differ, depending upon race, age, exposure to sun, oil secretion by specific glands, and diet. The combination of all these variables suggests that there may be millions of different human scents, and that each can be unique to a single person, at least for a period of time. An individual's scent will be affected also by perfume, deodorant, cigarette smoke, and other odors that linger on skin and clothing. Eating certain foods, such as garlic or onions, can alter the chemical compositions and change a person's "scent signature." Changing certain aspects of the combined chemical signal that makes up a person's individual smell, say with a new perfume or deodorant, can confuse a dog and cause him to make errors in scent recognition, but only until he learns to focus on those aspects of the scent that have remained the same rather than those aspects of the scent that have changed.

To get an idea of how well dogs can identify people by scent, let's compare it with people's ability to identify other human beings using our dominant sense, vision. The most systematic research on our identification ability comes from forensic psychologists who have studied the accuracy of identifying people in lineups. Witnesses to a crime are asked if they can identify one of a group of people who are the same race and sex and approximately the same size. Since humans are so sight oriented, these identifications are principally done just by looking at the people in the lineup. Research indicates that people are really not all that good at this sort of identification. For instance, psychologists Ralph Haber and Lyn Haber statistically analyzed thirty-seven different studies of how well people can identify other people in lineups. Overall, it turns out that under the best conditions, with lineups containing six suspects, people are correct in their identifications only 55 percent of the time, or a bit better than half the time.

The canine equivalent to a visual lineup is a so-called "scent lineup," where some item that was associated with a crime is given to a dog to smell. Next, instead of parading a group of people into the room, the dog is presented with a set of six to twelve steel cylinders or cloth diapers. One of these items has been handled by the person suspected of the crime, while the others have been handled by different individuals.

The dog's task is to see if one of these has the same scent as the item from the crime scene, and to pick it out. A number of countries will accept this evidence in court as being the equivalent of "witness identification." Several studies, using different techniques to assess dogs' accuracy in this task, found that they are correct about 80 percent of the time—many times better than human witness identifications by sight. In the end, a person will be correct in only one out of two identifications, while a dog will be correct four out of five times.

Dogs that make errors in the scent identification of people may well do so because they are too sensitive to smell differences. Researchers have demonstrated that dogs not only can match the scent of an individual person, but can also respond to which part of the body the scent came from. Thus dogs can tell the difference between cloth pads that have been scented by holding them in a person's hand, rubbed on an elbow, or rubbed under an armpit. According to the dog's nose, each person has many different scents. An identification failure in a scent lineup might thus be due to a test object having been scented by a different part of the criminal's body than the crime scene object. The better a dog gets to know a person, or the more scent samples he gets from different regions of the body and taken at different times, the more likely the dog will begin to learn the specific basic scent that discriminates one person from another.

Looking at the scent identification errors that dogs make tells us about the kinds of things that a dog is paying attention to. Dogs are most likely to confuse members of the same family who all live together in the same home. Dogs also sometimes confuse the scents of identical twins. They are less likely to confuse the smell of twins if they are eating different diets, but it appears that the ability to tell twins apart is much easier if the dog first gets to sniff each of them. Under these conditions, it appears that the dog's exquisite olfactory mind kicks into high gear and begins to search for subtle differences between the two scents. Now, having directly compared them, the dog can tell them apart by smell and even track a trail left by one of them, ignoring places where the other twin has crossed the path or tried to confuse the dog by walking the same path and then veering off.

Sniffing the Past

Sights and sounds are gone in an instance, but odors linger. A scent trail is a snapshot of the past: an animal passed by here a while ago and the dog's nose can determine its identity, the direction it was going, and perhaps how long ago it was here. This allows him to find that animal if it is a potential quarry or to avoid that animal if it is a potential threat. This same ability also allows humans to use dogs as trackers or in search-and-rescue tasks.

In early days people thought that tiny droplets of blood made their way through the skin and provided the trail that tracking dogs followed. This is how bloodhounds got their name. Researchers now think that scent consist of tiny bits of skin cells, referred to as "rafts" or "scurf," that carry a person's odor because they are covered with sweat and acted on by bacteria. Because the human body sheds about 50 million cells each minute, these rafts fall from the body like a shower of microscopic snowflakes. With their noses tuned for biological odors and pheromones, dogs easily detect these rafts and can follow them to the person who shed them.

Detecting the traces of the person who passed is just the first part of the dog's task. He also must determine which way the person went. One direction leads him to his target, while the other leads him in the wrong direction. Researchers at the University of Oslo tested dogs' abilities to determine the direction of a track. They had someone walk a path through a field or over a paved area, and then twenty minutes later they brought a tracking dog to the middle of the path. The dogs' performance was striking. They would take about three or four seconds to sniff around five footsteps' worth of the path, and then confidently strike off in the correct direction that the person had gone. They were clearly following the scent trail, rather than anything about the shape of the foot imprints, since even if the person had walked the path going backward (so the footprints point in the wrong direction), the dogs still followed their actual direction of movement.

Earlier footsteps are a few seconds older and just a fraction weaker in the intensity of the scent that they give off. This gives the dog the clue that he needs to follow in the correct direction, toward the stronger scent. However, the dog needs distinct patches of scent to do this correctly. When the researchers laid the trail by riding a bicycle, rather than walking, the dogs did much more poorly. Because the change was so gradual from one part of the track to the next, picking up the direction became nearly impossible. When the researchers put leather patches on the rear wheel of the bike so that now there were gaps between these scent marks which would be more like those of footsteps, the dogs again had enough information to determine the correct direction by the difference in the intensity of the scent patches.

I once decided to test how dogs determine the direction of a trail using my best tracking dog, my flat-coated retriever Odin. I set up the situation so that if I were correct, he would track in the *wrong* direction. I enlisted the aid of a friend, rubbing the soles of his shoes with pepperoni sausage. He then walked a distance of about 100 yards (around 90 meters). I next brought Odin up to around the middle of the path and gave him a piece of cloth that I had rubbed with the same pepperoni sausage, to tell him which scent I was interested in following. The trick involved in this tracking task is that as my friend walked the pepperoni would gradually wear off of his shoes and the scent would actually become weaker in the direction that he was moving. If Odin was tracking in the direction that the scent was strongest, this means that he should move in the direction that the track started from, rather than in the direction that was actually walked. This is exactly what happened. Each time that we tried this, Odin took only a few moments to make up his mind and then struck off confidently following the path to its beginning rather than to the end, where my friend was waiting. This clearly indicates that the direction of a track is given by the strength of the scents left in the trail.

As a trail grows older, the scents fade, which makes determining its direction much more difficult. Warm days with sunshine will weaken a scent quickly. The ultraviolet rays destroy some of the odor-bearing chemicals, eliminating much of the scent. This is why hanging a sweat-soaked T-shirt out in the sunshine makes it seem much fresher after a few hours. This does not mean that an old scent trail is too weak to be followed, but rather that the direction of the trail becomes more difficult to determine. Under these conditions, tracking dogs will often look toward their handlers to get some clue as to the direction to go. If the handler doesn't know, or makes a bad guess, the dog may not find the person. However, if the direction that the path started in is known, dogs can perform in a remarkable manner even under adverse conditions with an old trail.

Canine Constables

One of the major uses of dogs by law enforcement agencies is to track and find criminals and escaped prisoners. For instance, James Earl Ray (who some years later would be convicted of the assassination of civil rights leader Martin Luther King, Jr.) managed to escape from maximum security Missouri State Penitentiary near Jefferson City where he was serving a sentence for another crime. It was several hours before his jailbreak was noticed and the usual procedures for recovering prisoners were put in action; however, he was not found. More than forty-eight hours later, a bloodhound named Buttercup was brought in to join the search. The one clue that the police had was the direction in which Ray had started. There were clear footprints in the moist ground from a pair of rubber boots Ray had stolen because he thought that they would keep any dogs from picking up the scent. This kind of deception really doesn't work, since the rafts of skin that carry the scent are shed by every part of the body, and there is always quite enough for the dog to follow. The weather had been drizzly, however, and the ground was damp, but Buttercup did not need the added information from a fresh trail. She struck off and never once deviated from the scent trail. A few hours later she stood excitedly howling at Ray's hiding place, some seven miles (eleven kilometers) from the prison!

Buttercup's performance seems astonishing, but there are reports of dogs tracking even older trails over longer distances. The longest I have been able to verify comes from a search-and-rescue bloodhound named Randy, whose handler, Stephen Johnson, was called upon to track a pair of children who had been lost in a large wilderness park. The children had last been seen playing at one end of the campground, near a path, so the search began there. Randy sniffed some of the children's clothing and then confidently started down the path at a brisk pace. It was nearly five hours later, and close to 35 miles (56 kilometers) from the campsite, that Randy found the two frightened and hungry children. They were still moving as quickly as their little legs would allow them in a direction away from where they started in a misguided and misdirected attempt to get home when the big brown dog came to their rescue.

Adventure and crime stories have often misled the public by describing how criminals escape from tracking bloodhounds by jumping into a stream and running down it to wash away their scent and obscure the trail. The idea that this strategy would work is only a half-truth. The problem is that water retains scent. If the stream is large and deep enough, and if the flow is fast enough, the man's scent may dissipate. But if the stream is not very deep, and the flow not very fast, or if there are breezes wafting across the water, the scent will actually spread out along the banks of the stream and cling to moist surfaces there. For a fresh trail this still provides more than enough information for the tracking dogs. Five or six hours of direct sunlight will, however, probably destroy the odor. High winds can also dissipate and scatter the scent just as flowing water can. So the ideal conditions for a prison break that would evade the tracking dogs would either be during a heavy downpour of rain, with high winds, or alternatively a very hot, sunshine-filled day, with high winds and a head start of five or six hours.

A good tracking dog does not depend solely upon the scent of his quarry to follow its trail. Footsteps disturb the soil and bring up fresh odors. Walking on grass or other vegetation crushes or breaks bits of it, again stirring up new odors. When the track is fresh, these will mix with the scent of the quarry. Fortunately for the tracking dog, many of these scents persist longer than sweat and pheromones, even in direct sunlight, so that even if the quarry's scent is fading, the dog can use these smells to keep on the trail, as long as not many other people are walking over the same ground.

Tracking, Trailing, and Sniffing the Air

Dogs use their noses to follow a trail by either tracking, trailing, or air-scenting. Different breeds of dogs prefer different methods, each of which is best suited to a designated task and certain conditions.

Tracking and trailing are often referred to as if they were the same, but they are not. Tracking is the most precise means of following an individual, since the dog follows the track of the quarry with his nose down, moving from one footstep to the next. Tracking dogs work best if the trail is relatively fresh, and they are most likely to use the smell of disturbed ground and broken vegetation to help them. Because they follow the exact path, they are also likely to find objects that had been dropped or hidden by the person being followed.

Trailing is the most common way that dogs follow scent paths, by scenting the flakes of scurf shed by the body rather than the footsteps themselves. Because scent rafts drift as they fall, depending upon the wind speed and direction, the dogs may follow directly along the person's path but also may be many yards away, walking parallel to it.

In both tracking and trailing, the dogs can easily find people at night, when human vision is of little value. Tracking and trailing dogs are almost always kept on a long leash while following a scent trail so that they don't outrun their handler in their enthusiasm to follow the track.

An alternative to tracking and trailing is air-scenting, in which dogs run with their heads up trying to catch the person's scent and ranging around the area until they do. Once the dog catches the scent, he follows it directly to the person, moving in a straight line upwind rather than following the actual path. Wind and weather affect how well an air-scenting dog can find someone. On a hot sunny day, with no wind, the person's scent will not travel far, and the dog has to make a number of closely spaced passes through the area to detect it. Under the best conditions—at dusk or dawn, with the ground cool, a bit of humidity, and a steady breeze—the person's scent will carry a long distance and the dog is more likely to catch it on one of his passes over the area.

Bloodhounds are the superstars of trailing. They have a fine memory for scents and, while most breeds have to be reminded every few hours by being exposed to the scent-carrying article that belonged to the person that they are tracking, bloodhounds can track all day without a single reminder. However, like most hounds, they are not as good as other breeds at air-scenting, since they push their noses down to catch rising scents rather than lifting them up to catch scents wafting in the breeze. The preferred air-scenting breeds for most search-and-rescue teams are German shepherd dogs and Labrador retrievers.

Air-scenting dogs are used in disaster areas, such as collapsed buildings, where the task is to detect a victim's location rather than follow any path. These dogs are trained with odors that smell like a mixture of different people so that they use their noses to find any person in the vicinity. Hopefully, as the dogs pass systematically over the disaster area, they will hit a scent that will lead them to a living individual who can be rescued. Most respond best when they find someone who is alive, and some get quite upset when they find a dead body. If the missing person is assumed to be dead, a so-called "cadaver dog" is called in.

Cadaver dogs are trained to detect scents associated with decomposing flesh. They have also been used in criminal investigations in which murderers confessed to killing someone but couldn't remember exactly where they put the body. Cadaver dogs can also detect trace smells rising through water and thus can find victims of drowning or bodies hidden under water.

In 2001, Kimberly Szumski, a thirty-six-year-old woman, was missing from her Philadelphia home for three months. Suspicion of foul play had fallen on her estranged husband, who was involved in the construction business. Operating on a hunch and some fragmentary witness reports, searchers brought in a pair of cadaver dogs to search a building that the husband had worked on. The dogs soon found a particular place in the building and gave the signal that something was present. Nothing appeared at all amiss to the humans on the scene, but the police had strong faith in these dogs and had the wall torn down. They found Kimberly's body wrapped in plastic, sealed in duct tape, buried under cinderblocks, and cemented into a wall reinforced with steel bars. Nonetheless, the dogs detected the trace odor and discovered her location.

Some cadaver dogs are "human remains specialists." A classic example of this is Eagle, a Doberman pinscher who proved his ability in central Michigan in 1999. A physician, Azizul Islam, and his wife, Tracy, had been having difficulties, and on December 20 Azizul told his children that their mother had gone back to England to stay with relatives. Two days later parts of a dismembered body were found in a restaurant dumpster, and a week later more of the body was found in a trash bag left in a field. The police suspected that the body belonged to Tracy Islam, went to her home, and obtained her toothbrush, from which they extracted a DNA sample. Next they asked the doctor if they could bring in Eagle for a search of the premises. He agreed. When they arrived, the police noticed strong bleach odors just about everywhere, and Eagle's handler was worried that this might make it impossible for Eagle to do his work. They started their search in the basement and almost immediately the dog gave an alerting signal to a paint roller; a bit later he indicated something on the floor that Islam had been painting. Later analysis would show that there was blood in the paint and some traces on the floor. The DNA matched that of Tracy, and Islam was later convicted of first degree murder.

Professional Noses

The wonder of the dog's power of smell is perhaps best shown by the variety of different tasks to which humans have asked dogs to apply their noses. In many cases dogs are called upon because electronic means of detecting scents simply can't match canine sensitivity and discrimination. In some cases where the scientific measuring devices are available and sensitive enough, they are so large and cumbersome that they can only be used in fixed facilities, such as laboratories or testing stations.

In a typical year in the United States, about 75,000 buildings are set afire deliberately by people who are seeking to collect insurance funds, or trying to harm, kill, or terrorize someone, or attempting to destroy property or criminal evidence. Arson kills around 500 people in the United States each year. In the year 2000 alone, arson resulted in 1.34 billion dollars in property damage. The majority of arsonists use a flammable hydrocarbon, like gasoline, paint thinner, or solvents, to set fires.

Sometimes the evidence from the pattern of burning may be sufficient to suggest arson, but it is difficult to confirm that an accelerant was used with field equipment, so arson-detecting dogs are widely employed in investigations. These animals are trained to detect the presence of the various flammable liquids that could be used to intentionally set fires. Research has established that a dog can detect the presence of accelerants up to eighteen days after the fire has been extinguished. Using electronic equipment, however, requires the fire investigator to get to the site immediately for reliable readings, but some burned buildings remain unsafe and smoldering, with the chance that fire could break out again for a substantial period of time. With the arson dog, investigators can wait until the site is safe enough to enter. The preferred dogs for this kind of work are black Labrador retrievers. (Yellow labs work just as well, but after nosing through the soot they come back black and thus just require too many baths.) Many insurance companies now have their own arson-detecting dogs, and the Federal Bureau of Alcohol, Tobacco, Firearms, and Explosives has about fifty such dogs.

Another case of dogs detecting hydrocarbons occurred in 1974, when a newly buried natural gas pipeline was scheduled to open in the Province of Ontario in Canada. Initial testing found that a quantity of gas was being lost in transit, which meant that the pipeline was leaking. Using every bit of technology at their disposal, the engineers and scientists were still unable to find the leaks. The chance of a disaster resulting from a leak was high, and yet the line was due to be opened in only nine days. It was then that someone came up with the idea of contacting Glen Johnson, who trains dogs to do various types of scent work. Working under time pressure, Johnson took three dogs that already had been trained to do other types of scent discrimination and in only two and a half days he reeducated them to dig for articles scented with butyl mercaptan, the chemical used to "odorize" natural gas so that humans can smell it in high concentrations. When taken to inspect the first 20 miles (32 km) of the pipeline, which was where the pipeline workers thought there might be three small leaks, the dogs actually found twenty the first day. The engineers insisted that this was impossible and that the dogs were in error. However, when the sections that the dogs indicated were dug up, the presence of leaks was confirmed in every instance. This means that the dogs detected odors at a distance of 40 feet (12 meters) below the ground. Before they finished their final inspection, the dogs had found more than 150 potentially dangerous leaks.

Evolution did not design a dog's nose as a replacement for high-tech chemical sensing equipment, of course. A major use of a dog's scenting ability has always involved hunting, first for himself and then later in the service of humans. Few places in the modern world today depend completely upon hunting for survival, but there are still some. For many northern people, a major source of sustenance was, and still is, seal hunting. Seals use breathing holes in the ice to get their air and gain access to the surface. When they use the hole, some of their scent rubs off on the outside and the cold moist surface holds the scent like a magnet. Finding these holes is a difficult task for a human, since they are often covered by blown snow and floating ices flakes and thus are virtually invisible, so seal hunters rely heavily on their dogs. A husky breed that the natives called Kimmiq is kept hungry before a seal hunt. When these air-scenting dogs are then taken out on the ice field, they pass up and down the ice until they find the seal scent and then follow it straight to the nearest ice hole. There the dog circles or lies down until the hunters arrive.

With several hunters and dogs working together, the seal hunt is a group effort. Once the dog has alerted, the hunter informs his comrades of the discovery. The dog's task is to find all of the breathing holes in the area because the hunters have to plug all but one or two with a clump of wet snow that quickly freezes, effectively closing it off. They then guard the open holes, and when a seal comes up to breathe, they harpoon it. A small feast is usually held on the ice before taking the seal home and the hungry dogs are included in this, since it is important to keep them strongly motivated to find more seal holes in the future. At the end of the hunt, the dogs drag a sled and transport the meat back to camp.

Dogs are sensitive to the scent of insects, even though they did not evolve to hunt them. For this reason, dogs are now used to detect termite infestations. Termites cause over a billion dollars of damage to homes each year in the United States. Yet studies indicate that termite infestations at the early stages go undetected by human insect control inspectors nearly two-thirds of the time because the inspectors rely on visual signs of damage. Unfortunately, by the time damage is visible there is usually already significant structural damage. William Whitstine's Florida home was inspected for termites and given a clean bill of health, but three months later a massive infestation of termites and a great deal of damage were discovered. Whitstine trains dogs for drug, explosive, and arson detection, and he reasoned that dogs could be trained to detect the chemical odors termites give off. Research has proven him right and, in one University of California study, termite detection dogs identified forty-nine of fifty specially prepared blocks of wood into which researchers had bored holes and inserted termites. The 95 percent accuracy of the dogs is remarkable, given that the chemical-sensing device that they were tested against was correct less than 50 percent of the time.

Other pest-detecting dogs have been trained to detect egg masses laid by gypsy moths. Accidentally introduced into North America in the mid-1800s, these moths are devastating forests, damaging hundreds of different species of trees.

Dogs are also being used to help insects. Honeybees are threatened by a condition called "foulbrood disease," which infects entire hives and spreads quickly. As pollinators, bees are extremely important to agriculture. Inspecting hives for foulbrood disease is slow and laborious work for a beekeeper, but a trained dog can inspect 200 hives in a day with almost perfect accuracy. Infected hives can then be cleansed before the disease gets a chance to spread.

Dogs have also been trained to find toxic molds. These grow in areas of a building that have been exposed to water due to floods or leaks, since moist conditions in drywall, wood, or carpeting are the ideal conditions for their growth. In North America, people spend 75 to 90 percent of their time indoors, which means that the risk of exposure to such molds is quite high. The spores of many molds can be quite toxic and have been associated with health problems, including asthma, sinusitis, skin rashes, and severe respiratory problems (including some forms of pneumonia). These molds are often difficult to discover because they are under carpets or furniture, in walls, behind moldings, or in attics and crawl spaces, but after dogs have detected them, the contamination can easily be removed and neutralized.

Doctor Dog

Some dogs seem to have the capacity to sniff out the presence of cancer in humans. This startling discovery was first reported in the prestigious medical journal *Lancet*, in April 1989, by Doctors Hywel Williams and Andres Pembroke. A female patient sought advice about a mole on her thigh. Her concern was aroused by her dog, a cross between a border collie and a Doberman, who often spent several minutes sniffing at a particular mole, even through her pants (the dog paid no attention to any other moles on her body). She decided to see the doctors after the dog tried to bite off the mole while she was wearing shorts. Analysis showed that the mole was actually a malignant melanoma. Williams and Pembroke noted, "The dog may have saved her owner's life by forcing her to seek medical advice while the mole was still at a thin (noninvasive) stage." They guessed that the dog's sense of smell was the true lifesaver here and that malignant tumors, "with their aberrant protein synthesis, emit unique odors, which though undetectable to man, are easily detected by dogs."

If this were just an isolated incident, we could dismiss it as a chance occurrence, but there are now seven published case reports in which dogs have detected and brought to their owner's attention moles or skin lesions that have later proven to be cancerous. After seeing one of these reports, Dr. Armand Cognetta, a dermatologist with the Tallahassee Memorial Regional Medical Center in Florida, decided to see if a dog could be specifically trained to detect cancer. The actual training was done by a retired police dog handler, Duane Pickel. The test case was a seven-year-old schnauzer named George, who had already had a successful career as a bomb-sniffing dog. George learned to locate and retrieve tissue samples of melanoma that had been removed surgically from patients and stored in glass vials. In 1996, Cognetta informed the U.S. National Cancer Institute that George was more than 99 percent accurate in finding tiny cancer samples that had been wrapped in gauze and placed in one of ten holes in a plastic tube, or when finding melanoma samples taped under bandages on a person's body. Cognetta had George examine seven volunteer patients with cancer and some patients that had been declared cancer free. He successfully identified four of the seven patients and located the sites of their cancers. One cancer-free patient was misidentified by George, who obsessively kept sniffing at one particular mole and giving his alerting signal. Just as a precaution, this mole was removed and examined. It turned out that the doctor had been wrong, but George was correct and the mole was malignant!

With such initial promise, the dog's nose is now being put to a variety of new medically related tests. Researchers in California claimed that they were able to train a standard poodle named Shing Ling to detect lung cancer. This was done by collecting breath samples from cancer-free patients and patients with untreated lung cancer. Preliminary reports indicate that the dog achieved 85 percent accuracy in this task. Other ongoing research at Cambridge University is attempting to discover if dogs can be trained to detect prostate cancer, which kills more men than any other cancer. This will be done by allowing the dog to sniff the urine of normal and cancerous men. Many men find the screening procedures used to detect the disease so embarrassing that they do not get regular checkups. If dogs could be trained to detect the early stages of prostate cancer from a simple urine sample, they would doubtless save many lives. Some dogs are even being trained to detect tuberculosis from sniffing human saliva samples. This disease often erupts in poorer countries and in refugee camps set up to house survivors of military actions or natural disasters. In such places, medical staff and sophisticated equipment may be in short supply and the rapid olfactory-screening ability of trained sniffer dogs might save thousands of lives.

A dog's sense of smell is not only exquisitely sensitive, but it also communicates with a brain that can make fine discriminations among scents and learn new ones when they become important. The use of dogs for medical diagnoses raises an interesting question: If your doctor's big yellow Labrador retriever discovers a cancer on your leg, should you be charged for a lab test?

CHAPTER 5

A Matter of Taste

GIVEN THE DOG-FOOD ADS that talk about "cheesy flavors that dogs love," "rich beef flavor that dogs can't resist," "a taste of bacon that dogs will do anything for," and so forth, you might conclude that one of the most important senses that a dog has is his sense of taste. While it is certainly true that dogs love food and love to eat, taste is a lot less important to dogs than it is to people.

In evolutionary terms, taste is a very old sense. The gustatory (taste) sense evolved from direct interactions of the first living things with the giant bowl of chemical soup in which they were immersed. The substances that were suspended or dissolved in water were important to the survival of these primitive living things. Some substances provided food, some gave warning, and some could cause damage or even kill. As animals evolved, the taste system became more specialized and sophisticated. Sensations of pleasure and disgust provided by taste serve a survival function. A reasonable rule of thumb, at least for natural substances, is that bad tastes are a signal that the animal has encountered something that is harmful, indigestible, or poisonous, while good tastes signal useful, digestible substances.

Because it is important for survival, taste is one of the earliest senses to begin functioning in dogs. Young puppies seem to have only their sense of taste, touch, and smell working at birth, but the taste sense still requires a few weeks to completely mature and sharpen.

How Taste Works

As with humans, the dog's sense of taste depends upon special receptors, or taste buds, which are found in small bumps on the top surface of the tongue called "papillae." Some taste buds are also on the soft part of the roof of the mouth (the palate) and the back part of the mouth where the throat begins (the epiglottis and the pharynx).

To taste anything, some of the chemicals in that substance have to be dissolved and the fluid used to do this is saliva. Dogs have four pairs of salivary glands located under the tongue, at the back of the mouth, behind the ear and under the eye. They also have different types of saliva, some watery and others more like mucus, apparently for different types of food. When the dog eats meat, the saliva that is produced is mostly of the mucus variety, while eating vegetable matter produces more of the watery saliva.

An animal's taste sensitivity depends upon the number and type of taste buds that it has, much the same way its sensitivity for smell depends upon the number of olfactory receptors. Humans win the sensitivity contest for taste, with around 9,000 taste buds compared to a dog's 1,700. Dogs have considerably more taste buds than cats, which average only about 470.

The life span of any taste bud is only a few days, and like the skin cells that they evolved from, they must be replaced. As an animal's physical abilities begin to slow with age, the ability to regenerate or produce new cells of any kind becomes less efficient. This is true for taste buds in dogs and people. With fewer taste buds available, the keenness of taste is reduced in older animals. Some diseases, especially those typical of old age (such as diabetes or hypothyroidism), and even some of the drugs that are used to treat diseases can also affect the production of taste buds and can change taste sensitivity.

How Many Tastes?

Specific taste buds appear to be tuned to specific chemical groups. Traditionally, when talking about human tastes, we have identified four basic taste sensations: sweet, salty, sour, and bitter. Early research showed that a dog's taste receptors respond to the same kind of chemicals that trigger human taste sensations. The one clear difference, however, is that dogs are not as sensitive to, nor do they have as strong a craving for, salt. Humans and many other mammals have a strong taste response to salt. We seek it out and like it on our food. Pretzels, potato chips, popcorn, and other snack foods are liberally dosed with salt. Salt is needed to balance our diet and there is not much of it to be found in vegetables and grains. Dogs, however, are primarily carnivores and, in the wild, most of their food is meat. Because of the high sodium content in meat, the wild ancestors of dogs already had a sufficient amount of salt in their diet and did not develop the highly tuned salt receptors and salt craving of humans.

Evolution has shaped other aspects of the dog's taste system and preferences. We can see how this has happened by considering another common domestic pet, the cat. Cats have a reputation for being finicky eaters and being more sensitive to tastes than dogs. This clearly makes no sense, since cats have only one-quarter the number of taste buds of dogs. However, the cat's taste buds are tuned specifically to flesh: Cats are true carnivores. Anything other than meat from animals, birds, and fish is difficult for a cat to digest. For this reason, their taste buds evolved to react to certain chemicals found in flesh (nucleotides) and the cat will tend to reject virtually anything that does not cause a response from these "meat detectors." Dogs are not exclusively carnivorous but are usually classified as omnivores, meaning that they eat, not only meat, but plant material as well. Nonetheless, in the wild, more than 80 percent of a canine's diet is meat. Thus, in addition to sensors for sweet, salt, sour, and bitter, dogs also have some specific taste receptors that are tuned for meats, fats, and meat-related chemicals. Dogs will tend to seek out and clearly prefer the taste of things that contain meat or flavors extracted from meat.

Some chemicals that seem to trigger the meat taste sensors in dogs include the glutamates, which are associated with building the proteins that make up flesh. The most common chemical of this sort is monosodium glutamate (MSG), which is used as flavor enhancer. It is a favorite additive in Chinese cooking. Because of these research findings, some scientists have wondered whether humans, who are also omnivorous and like the taste of meat, might also have such meat taste receptors. Indeed, Japanese researchers found such a taste sensor in people, and they named it the "umami" taste receptor. It responds to the same chemicals that the dog's meat-tuned taste buds do, and people report that when these taste buds were activated, it produced a flavor sensation described as kind of "meaty" or "savory."

The sweet taste buds in dogs respond to a chemical called "furaneol," which is found in many fruits, including tomatoes. Cats are virtually "taste blind" for this substance, but dogs like this flavor. Preference for sweet probably evolved because in a natural environment dogs frequently supplement their diet of small animals with whatever fruits happen to be available. My dog Odin, for example, loved pears. He could not pass by the pear tree on our farm without stopping to pick up a wind-fallen piece of fruit, which he would wolf down with great gusto. Unfortunately, if the pear was very ripe his face would get covered with pear pulp, meaning that he couldn't return to the house until he had been hosed off or wiped down. A dog's sensitivity to furaneol and many other sugars is accompanied by a preference for foods containing these substances. Many dogs show a quite pronounced "sweet tooth," while cats have no interest in sweets at all.

The sweet tooth that dogs have can be fatal. One of the most frequent sources of poisoning in dogs involves automobile antifreeze containing ethylene glycol, which strongly activates the dog's sweet taste buds. As little as two ounces of this sweet-tasting substance can kill a medium-sized dog. Several surveys in the United States have suggested that between 10,000 and 30,000 dogs die each year of ethylene glycol poisoning. The problem peaks twice each year, as people add antifreeze in the fall or remove it in the spring. However, antifreeze may be available at any time of the year due to leaks from the car's radiator or coolant system, which are usually noticed as puddles of greenish colored liquid in the driveway or on the street. Dogs that are housed part of the time in the garage are at particular risk of poisoning. While most dogs are attracted by the sweet taste and drink it directly, some become indirectly poisoned as they wash their soiled paws and fur.

Detecting antifreeze poisoning is not always easy. Early signs generally include wobbling, staggering, and "drunk" behaviors, depression, vomiting, and diarrhea. The fatality rate, however, is high and requires immediate action if you suspect that your dog has ingested ethylene glycol. First induce vomiting. Use a 3 percent hydrogen peroxide solution mixed half and half with water; the dosage should be about two teaspoons for every 10 pounds (4.5 kilograms) that your pet weighs. Use an eyedropper or cooking baster to squirt the mixture to the back of your pet's tongue. This should cause vomiting within five minutes; however, if it does not, the treatment may be repeated two or three times, allowing ten minutes between doses. If hydrogen peroxide is not available, mix three tablespoons of salt into a half a cup of warm water and administer it in the same dose. Get the dog to the veterinarian immediately, since there is an effective treatment if it is started within the first nine to twelve hours. After that length of time, the liver begins metabolizing the ethylene glycol into substances that cause kidney failure and ultimately death.

There is a simple preventative for ethylene glycol poisoning and that is to use a less harmful, propylene glycol–based antifreeze in the car. Propylene glycol, although not entirely nontoxic, is considerably less toxic than ethylene glycol. It is also not as sweet tasting, which makes it less attractive to the dog. There appear to be no performance differences between ethylene glycol and propylene glycol antifreezes; hence, this seems like a safe alternative to keep your dog's love of sweets from doing him harm.

Taste buds for the basic flavors are not distributed equally across the tongue. The arrangement in dogs is somewhat similar to that in humans, with minor variations. All areas of the tongue can respond to all of the taste stimuli if they are strong enough, but the following areas are noticeably more sensitive. The front portion of the human tongue is most sensitive to sweet tastes, and in dogs the sweet taste buds are more to the sides. Dogs' sour and salty taste buds are also on the sides but farther back, with their salt-responding area much smaller than human's. The rear portion of the tongue is most sensitive to bitter tastes. Sensitivity to meaty tastes is scattered over the top of the tongue but mostly found in the front two thirds.

Dogs also have taste buds that are tuned for water, which is something they share with cats and other carnivores but not humans. This taste sense is found at the tip of the dog's tongue, the part that he curls to lap water. This area responds to water at all times, but when the dog has eaten salty or sugary foods, the sensitivity to the taste of water increases. This ability to taste water may have evolved as a way for the body to keep internal fluids in balance after the animal has eaten things that will either result in more urine being passed or will require more water to adequately process. One thing that will do this is meat, with its high sodium content, which makes this a particularly useful sense for carnivores. It certainly appears that when these special water taste buds are active, dogs seem to get an extra pleasure out of drinking water and will drink copious amounts of it.

Terrific and Terrible Tastes

Dogs, like people, do have distinct taste preferences, but they are not always easy to measure. When you are testing the taste preferences of people, you only have to ask them which foods they prefer. When you are testing dogs, however, the situation is more complex. You might think that all that you have to do is to give a dog two types of food at the same time and see which one the dog eats first, or eats more of, but dogs have a strong tendency to snatch and gulp the nearest bit of food that they can reach. Some dogs simply continue to eat out of whichever bowl they happen to have their nose in. Many will continue eating until all of the food is gone, regardless of how much food you put in it. The majority of dogs will try to gobble both samples of food if possible.

You can control these tendencies by setting up conditions so that the dog learns that he can have only one of the two food samples and the other becomes unavailable after they've made a choice. Under these conditions, some definite patterns of food preferences become clear. Dogs have a mild aversion to sour-tasting substances, such as citrus fruits, but they have a very strong dislike for bitter-tasting substances. This is so strong that it overpowers their sweet tooth. For example, saccharine tastes sweet to most people, but if it is used in strong concentrations it leaves a slightly bitter aftertaste. For dogs, that trace of bitterness is enough to make them avoid any substance with saccharine in it.

Because dogs dislike bitter tastes, various sprays and gels have been designed to keep them from chewing on furniture or other objects. These compounds often contain bitter substances, such as alum, or capsaicin from hot peppers, which not only has a pungent taste but also causes a burning sensation in the mouth. Coating items with bitter-tasting material will eventually keep most dogs from chewing on them, but the key word is *eventually* because the taste buds that sense bitterness are located on the rearmost third of the tongue. A quick lick or fast gulp will not register the bitter taste. Only prolonged chewing will let the bitterness work its way back to where it can be tasted. Then the dog must also learn to associate the bitter taste with the particular object for the avoidance to be learned.

An example of the problem associated with trying to use bad taste to stop unwanted behaviors involved a cocker spaniel named Blondie, who had developed a food-snatching habit. Blondie would brazenly jump on a chair and snatch toast or cookies that the children were about to eat and then race away with her prize. The usual "cure" suggested by many dog behaviorists is to "set a trap" for the dog by taking a few pieces of toast, coating them with a bitter substance, and leaving them on the table—apparently free for the taking. The idea is that the dog will learn that food that is taken from the table is bitter and unpleasant and will not do so in the future.

For Blondie, the bittering substance that was used was alum, which was painted on a few pieces of toast that the children of the house apparently left behind at the table. The result was less than heartening. Within moments after the children had turned away, Blondie was up on the table and had snatched the piece of bitter toast. It was wolfed down in seconds, and although Blondie looked momentarily surprised, the toast must have passed over the bitter-sensing portion of the tongue well after the front of her tongue had sensed the sweetness of the bread. Even after several "baited" pieces of toast, Blondie still did not stop snatching food. Sometimes she still made it to the table and grabbed food intended for the children that was not made bitter. Simply licking at the food with the front of her tongue did not give her any sign that it was bitter or not, and she was food-motivated enough to take the chance.

With the failure of the alum treatment, a more powerful stimulus was required. A noxious-tasting solution of Tabasco sauce and lemon juice was prepared and applied to the toast, liberally enough so that it was a bit moist. Remember, things must be dissolved in liquid to be tasted, so this would be unlikely to pass by the portion of the tongue that can taste bitter things and go unnoticed. We also rubbed a bit of lemon peel on the plate containing the nasty-tasting bit of bread. Now when Blondie snatched the newly baited bit of toast, she did catch some of the bitter taste before she swallowed and also smelled the citrus. This game was repeated a number of times with a plate that had been rubbed with lemon peel and contained a bitter "treat." After a couple of days, it was becoming clear to Blondie that she should avoid any plate with a lemon smell, since it was associated with a bitter aftertaste. Next, to solve the food-snatching problem permanently, a faint lemon scent from a lemon-scented cleaning spray was spread around the edge of the table. This meant that at the same time that the table was being cleaned with such a spray, a large sign was in effect being posted for Blondie, that said "Anything around this smell tastes bitter sooner or later." Treats given to her while she was on the floor, with no lemon scent around, were of course safe and good-tasting snacks. Although dogs dislike bitter tastes and will stop eating things that taste bitter, they often need cues from other senses (such as smell or sight) to learn to avoid them all together.

When it comes to taste preferences, dogs prefer meats over vegetables. They prefer beef and pork over lamb, chicken, and horsemeat, although these preferences are weaker if the scent of the food is not available. They prefer moist food over dry food, probably because the taste is more readily available if the taste chemicals are already dissolved in some fluid.

Dogs also prefer warm foods over cold foods, partly because the tastes are somewhat stronger when the food is at body temperature or a bit warmer but also because odors are stronger from warm food. In dogs, just as in humans, the sense of smell and the sense of taste interact. Try this little experiment: Cut pieces of crisp apple, hard pear, and raw potato to about the same size. Close your eyes and hold your nostrils closed. Now have someone give you bits of the three items to taste and you will find it virtually impossible to tell the three foods apart, since much of your appreciation of the food is based upon smell rather than taste. This also explains why, when you have a cold and a stuffed nose, most foods are relatively tasteless and the finest wine tastes like a cheap "plonk."

Based upon all of this information, we can derive a simple way to make commercial dry dog kibble more desirable and flavorful. Simply pour a small amount of warm water over it before giving it to the dog. The warmth and moisture augment both the taste and smell of the food. This also works when dealing with older dogs, who, because they have fewer taste buds, find their food relatively unappealing.

There are other ways that food can be made more palatable to dogs. Adding fat to food seems to make it more desirable; however, rancid fat (which produces a sour taste) will cause the food to be avoided. However, manipulating the type of food is not the only important factor in determining food preference. The Waltham Centre for Pet Nutrition in Leeds, England, found that all foods seemed to be more acceptable to dogs if they were fed directly from their owner's hand. As it is with people, for dogs love and a smile make all foods taste better.

Comfort Foods

Some food preferences in dogs seem to be learned, and this learning can occur quite early. Familiarity with food tastes actually occurs before the puppy is born. The mother's diet influences the composition of the amniotic fluid in the womb, and the taste buds (as well as the olfactory receptors of the nose) are stimulated by the chemicals that the developing puppy is floating in. This is really the very first stage of the development of taste preferences. Some taste-related chemicals also make their way into the mother's milk that the puppy nurses on, helping to establish particular taste sensations as being associated with safety and security—the doggy equivalent of "comfort foods."

Generally speaking, dogs prefer new tastes over familiar ones, a phenomenon known as "neophilia" from the Greek word roots *neo* meaning "new" and *philos* meaning "fondness for." From an evolutionary point of this makes sense, since it encourages the animal to try different things that might prove to be nourishing, which makes survival more likely because the animal comes to accept more items as food sources. There is a restriction on neophilia, in that the new food has to have some aspects of similarity to familiar foods. Thus its taste, texture, and smell should remind the dog of other things that it has eaten in order for him to try the new food.

The opposite of neophilia is "neophobia," from the Greek *phobos* meaning "fear of," and when it comes to food, this is much rarer in dogs. It appears most commonly in stressful situations. A sudden change in environment accompanied by an abrupt change of diet is the most common trigger, but an illness or physical injury, again in association with a change in the food regimen, is another possible scenario. Here dogs will revert to the most familiar foods and often will not accept anything else.

When a dog feels psychologically threatened, it develops a craving for tastes that were associated with earlier periods of safety, in the same way that a person under stress might crave macaroni and cheese or ice cream and feel comforted by eating these foods if they were associated with childhood experiences when they felt happy and protected. From an evolutionary standpoint, this is adaptive behavior, since it could help a dog to avoid eating things that might be toxic when he finds himself in a strange environment.

A Malamute puppy named Kody (short for Kodiak) showed strong food preferences. He was purchased from a breeder located just outside of Juneau, Alaska. At just under seven weeks of age, he was removed from his litter, put on a cargo plane, and flown to Seattle. When he arrived it was obvious to Ed, his new owner, that Kody had been taken from his litter when he was too young. The combination of a noisy plane ride (in rough winter flying conditions), the absence of his familiar littermates, and the presence of a new environment had all added up to a traumatized, frightened, insecure puppy. Ed tried feeding him kibble designed for puppies, but Kody would not eat it, or canned dog food, or even cooked beef. The pup lapped unenthusiastically at milk, consuming only a little of it, and worrying Ed quite a bit. The very next day he took Kody to a veterinarian, who said that there was nothing physically wrong with the dog. "He'll eat when he's hungry enough," Ed was told.

Ed was still worried about his new pup and contacted the breeder to find out what Kody's mother had been fed. It turned out that her diet was mostly fish (often still frozen) that had been caught by the husband of the woman who bred her. On the basis of her advice, Ed served some fresh salmon that had been chopped into small bits and the puppy seemed to relax a great deal as he gobbled this familiar food down greedily. Gradually, Kody was weaned off his fish diet as Ed introduced kibble mixed in with the fish. Today, like most dogs of his breed, Kody happily eats just about anything that can be called food or even vaguely resembles food.

Familiarity effects explain why dogs living in different cultures seem to have different taste preferences. It is the food preferences of the dog's owner, as well our notions of what we think dogs want to eat, that ultimately determines what goes into a dog's bowl. Thus in North America and the UK there is a belief that dogs prefer meat and cats prefer fish, which is why Ed never thought of giving Kody fish when he was looking for an acceptable food. Dogs in North America generally do not like very spicy foods; however, in Mexico and Central America, where the human cuisine often is quite spicy, dogs are much more accepting of pungent foods. I once saw a Mexican dog happily take a chilli pepper that it was offered and gulp it down. Conversely, a friend of mine who was a vegetarian had reared her dog on a meatless diet consisting of rice, beans, and cooked vegetables, plus some milk, cheese, and eggs for extra protein. When the owner became ill, the dog was cared for by another family member, who was surprised to see the animal refuse both beef and chicken, regardless of whether it was cooked or raw.

In a familiar environment, dogs will often ignore the taste of things that they eat, especially if other dogs are around that might compete for the food. Most dogs do not eat delicately, savoring each morsel, but rather gulp their food down without stopping to enjoy the taste or even to evaluate it. This is how their wild ancestors ate—quickly, so that they had the food safely in their bellies before some bigger animal or another canine in the pack came along and tried to steal it. This way of eating, however, can sometimes lead to difficulties.

Consider a boxer owned by the Miller family of Chicago. When they named him Chomper, they had no idea how perfect that name would be. Most of the time Chomper devoured his food and snacks in what seemed like only a couple of big bites. One day Chomper became ill with what seemed to be an awful stomachache. When the veterinarian operated, he found that Chomper's stomach contained a man's sweat sock, a lady's bracelet, and an 8-inch (20-cm)-long butter knife. Obviously, Chomper was not choosing these doggy snacks because of how good they tasted.

CHAPTER 6

In Touch with the World

WE SHARE WITH DOGS the sense that the boundary between what is truly "me" and what is the "outside world" is most clearly defined by touch. Touch may seem simple at first consideration, but it really involves four different forms of perception: pressure or contact with the body, sensation of heat or cold, perception of pain, and "proprioception," which monitors where limbs are at any point or how quickly parts of the body are moving. Dogs have developed a high degree of expertise in using their sense of touch to communicate with other dogs and humans, too. Besides giving him information about the world, as the other senses do, touch is intimately associated with the arousal of emotions and the formation of emotional bonds.

Discovering the World

Perhaps the association between touch and emotion in dogs arose simply because it is one of their first sources of information that puppies use to learn about the world. The newborn pup is functionally blind and nearly deaf, and although his scent receptors function, they are immature, so he relies mainly on what he can sense by touch. When a two-day-old pup is separated from his mother, he tends to whimper and to swing his head from side to side like a pendulum, seeking his mother's touch. Evolution has provided an additional source of sensory information to help the puppy at this critical time. These are special heat sensors in his nose. Yngve Zotterman of the Swedish Research Council discovered these unusual receptors, which are sensitive to heat radiated from warm objects in the form of infrared energy and are located around the nostril slits and openings to the nasal passages of puppies. When the puppy swings his head, he is trying to locate the heat source that is his mother. Once he senses it, he follows the "heat trail" back to her. When he touches her body, he stops whimpering and curls up against her and, once relaxed, drifts off to sleep. Mature dogs do not seem to have these special heat-detecting receptors, so we must conclude that they disappear or become nonfunctional as their other senses mature.

The puppy also uses touch as his first means of communicating his needs, nudging at his mother's nipples with his nose and in subsequent days with his paws. This nudging stimulates the flow of milk, which feeds him and also provides emotional comfort. This process also stimulates the development of his mind. The feedback from his sense of touch tells his brain that there is a world out there. Because his actions cause things to happen, he learns that he can interact with that world and even change or control it to some degree with his own behaviors

Each of the four forms of touch sensations is associated with its own special sensory apparatus. The pressure sense, for example, has two different classes of receptors. The surface contact receptors are located near the surface of the skin, frequently near the base of each hair follicle in hairy or fur-covered skin. Light touches and anything that twists or stretches the skin will trigger responses that send information to the brain. Evolution used the principle of the lever to increase our sensitivity to touch long before Archimedes discovered it as a mechanical principle. Since each hair serves as the long end of a lever, its tip is easily moved, while the force of the movement is amplified at the base of the hair.

The second class of touch receptors is located deeper in the skin and responds to compression. Human beings also have both surface touch and compression sensors, and the special sensory receptors used for each are virtually identical for dogs. If you pay attention to the weight of your body resting on your buttocks as you sit on a chair reading, that feeling of weight is due to the deeper pressure receptors. This is different from the feeling of the texture of the paper as you touch this book, since that comes from the surface touch receptors located nearer to the skin surface.

Different places on the dog's body have different degrees of touch sensitivity. For example, around the nose and muzzle is a rich supply of sensory nerves, making the nose and lips extremely sensitive to touch. Dogs' feet also convey a lot of touch information. The pads of the feet have specialized nerves that respond to vibration and allow the dog to determine how stable the surface is when he is running. Some researchers believe that this is a form of proprioception that monitors the dog's running speed. Some very sensitive nerve endings are also located near the surface of the skin in the deepest portions of the spaces between the pads of the feet. The presence of extra nerve endings in this region probably explains why most dogs hate being touched around their feet. This is well understood by other dogs since, although dogs touch each other a lot as part of their communication and play, they always avoid mouthing, or even sniffing at, each other's feet.

The World of Whiskers

Dogs do have one set of touch receptors that differs from anything that humans have; these are a set of specialized hairs, called vibrissae, on their faces. Popularly called "whiskers," they are not at all like the nonfunctional whiskers that men sometimes grow on their faces. In cats the common term is "feelers," and this may be a better name, since vibrissae are really sophisticated devices that help the dog feel its way through the world. They are quite different from most other hairs on the dog's body, since they are considerably more rigid and embedded more deeply into the skin. At the base of each vibrissa is a higher concentration of touch receptor cells than are associated with other hairs. Because each whisker is longer and less flexible than normal hairs, it makes a better lever and amplifies small, light touches to a greater extent.

Vibrissae are universally present in carnivores and are also found in a variety of other animals, including cats, rats, bears, and seals, which suggests that they must serve a useful function. Neuropsychologists tend to agree that the amount of the sensory cortex of the brain that is devoted to processing information from a particular body area is a good indication of how important that area is in the perceptual world of the animal. Of those areas of the brain that register touch information in the dog, nearly 40 percent of them are dedicated to the face, with a disproportionately large amount of that dedicated to the regions of the upper jaw that include the vibrissae. You can actually map each individual vibrissa to a specific location in the dog's brain, suggesting that great importance is assigned to information from these sources.

Many dog fanciers are unaware of the importance of vibrissae to the dog. Many dog groomers seem to consider vibrissae as a purely cosmetic feature, as if they were the same as human facial hair. Dogs of many different breeds routinely have their vibrissae cut off in preparation for the show ring. It is argued that this gives the dog's head a "cleaner" look. Amputating vibrissae is both uncomfortable and stressful for dogs, and it reduces their ability to perceive their close surroundings fully.

Most studies of the function of vibrissae have involved rats and cats, but the few dog studies confirm that the wiring and functions of the vibrissae are similar in all animals that have them. The vibrissae serve as an early warning device that something is near the face, protect the dog from colliding with walls and objects, and keep approaching objects from damaging the dog's face and eyes. You can demonstrate this for yourself by tapping gently on the vibrissae of a dog. With each tap, the eye on the same side of the face will blink protectively, and the dog will tend to turn its head away from the side tapped.

The vibrissae also seem to be involved in the location of objects and perhaps in the recognition of the objects themselves. Most animals use vibrissae much the way that a blind person uses a cane. First, the little muscles that control the vibrissae direct them somewhat forward when the dog is approaching an object. Next they actively "whisk," or vibrate slightly while the dog swings his head to drag these hairs across surfaces. Whisking gives information about the shape and roughness of surfaces near his head. Laboratory studies show that rats can even learn to discriminate between rough and smooth textures based upon the information from their whiskers alone. Since the dog's eyes can't focus very well on close objects, and this makes it difficult for him to see things near his mouth, the information from the forward-and downward-pointed vibrissae appears to help him locate, identify, and pick up small objects with his mouth.

Dogs whose vibrissae have been removed seem more uncertain in dim light. Under these conditions they actually move more slowly, because they are not getting the information that they depend upon to tell them where things are that they might collide with. With intact vibrissae, the dog actually does not have to make physical contact with a surface to know it is there. These special hairs are so sensitive that they also register slight changes in air currents. As a dog approaches an object like a wall, some of the air that he stirs up by moving bounces back from surfaces, bending the vibrissae slightly, which is enough to inform him that something is near well before he touches it.

I encountered an example of how important vibrissae can be for a dog when I met Willie. Willie is short for Wilhelmina, and she was a blue merle Shetland sheepdog owned by a computer programmer named Bruce. When Willie was around four years of age it became apparent that she had developed a condition that clouded both of her eyes. Although she still could make out light and dark, her vision was probably equivalent to trying to make your way around the world using only the visual information that you can get looking through several layers of tracing paper. Bruce contacted me to ask how to help Willie and I provided him with a list of things that would keep his dog safe and happy at home, even with her severely impaired vision. My recommendations included leaving items of furniture in their same places so that she could form a consistent "map" of her environment and using scents or textured materials such as throw rugs to mark areas. Willie adapted well and would zoom around the house like a sighted dog most of the time, with only an occasional stumble or collision that reminded the family that she was blind.

Bruce's daughter, Susan, was just finishing her second year of college when Willie's condition was diagnosed. She truly loved the dog and was emotionally affected by Willie's virtual blindness. Susan had been thinking about going to medical school but had not fully decided; however, now she announced to the family that she would not only get a medical degree, but she would become an ophthalmologist so that she could help people with the same kinds of visual problems as Willie.

As Susan's college graduation date neared, she insisted that since Willie had been the crucial factor in her choice of a medical career, she wanted a formal picture of herself in her graduation cap and gown seated with Willie. Bruce thought that this was such a sweet, special request that on the day before the photograph was to be taken, he took Willie to be professionally bathed and groomed so that she would look her best.

You can probably anticipate what happened. Following the dictates of show dog fashion, the dog groomer brushed and trimmed her, which included cutting off Willie's vibrissae. She did look beautiful, but when Bruce took Willie home that night he suddenly feared that something had gone terribly wrong with her. As she ran up the steps to go into the house she collided with the door jamb. As she tried to make her way through the house she banged into a chair and table leg. Now looking a bit distressed and confused, she began to slow down and move quite tentatively. A bit later, when she went to drink some water, her head actually missed the bowl completely and she bumped her nose on the floor.

Bruce was frantic and called me to ask if a dog could have a sudden mental deterioration that could leave it disoriented. After I learned what had happened, I was able to reassure him that Willie's problem was not mental—she could still process information—but that an important source of information had been amputated when the groomer cut Willie's whiskers. Fortunately, the groomer had left some short stubs of the vibrissae, and these special hairs grow fairly quickly, to compensate for the fact that their ends often break off from all of the brushing and banging against objects to which they are subjected. After a month or so, enough of Willie's vibrissae had grown back so that she was again navigating through her familiar world with confidence.

On the basis of the evidence available about the importance of vibrissae to the dog, there is an obvious recommendation that should be made to kennel clubs holding conformation shows. That is not to penalize dogs entered into such events if their vibrissae are intact. Unfortunately, cosmetic considerations often appear to be more important than considerations of a dog's comfort and safety to officials in such organizations, so I do not expect good judgment to prevail. Unless you are in active competition, however, I would strongly recommend that you leave your dog's vibrissae intact.

Hot and Cold

Dogs and humans use the same mechanisms for surface contact and also for deep pressure touch, but we are quite different in how we sense temperature. Human skin has two types of temperature-sensing cells, one for registering heat and the other for sensing cold. With the exception of those heat sensors around the nostrils in puppies, dogs have only cold-sensing temperature receptors. This doesn't mean that dogs cannot feel warmth, but rather that the mechanism is quite different from that in humans. Researchers suggest that a dog will seek a warm spot to lie down in an attempt to turn down or turn off the unpleasant response to cold. They note that pressing warm or even moderately hot items against a dog's skin produces very little response. If the heat is intense enough, however, the skin will be damaged and the dog will respond to the signals from the pain receptors in the skin.

Handling heat seems to be a flaw in the evolutionary design of dogs. Obviously it is not good that a dog does not recognize hot items against his skin before they burn him. Dogs are also often placed in jeopardy because their bodies can't adapt efficiently to hot environmental conditions. You might guess that one reason they can't deal well with heat is that they are covered with fur, which could make their bodies quite hot in the summer. This is only partially the case, since fur is actually an insulator that serves as barrier between the outside environment and the dog's interior. Thus, in the winter the fur preserves body heat and keeps out the cold. In the summer it is a barrier to the outside heat. In a hot environment, however, heat can build up in the body, and the fur then becomes an impediment to cooling down, since excess heat can't easily dissipate through it. Because dogs can cool themselves only by panting or sweating through the pads of their feet, rising temperatures can result in heatstroke, which can be life threatening. Each year hundreds of dogs lose their lives from heatstroke simply from being left in cars in the summer. Death can occur in as little as twenty minutes in a hot car.

The Puzzle of Pain

Odin died with my hand caressing his head and my eyes wet with sorrow. Throughout his disease he never whimpered and he never cried. My beautiful black dog had developed a form of cancer that causes a quick but painful death in humans, yet Odin did not sob and moan. Is this because he felt no pain? Some people might argue that a situation like this proves that dogs have little or no conscious experience of pain in the sense that people do. They can even call upon a long philosophical history to justify their claim. They are wrong.

Pain is almost always a response to damage to some part of the body. As an important evolutionary development, pain helps keep animals alive in several ways. Survival often depends upon the ability to get away from or to terminate harmful environmental situations before they do damage. Pain signals that something dangerous is happening and it is time to do something to make it stop. In addition, since pain is noxious and emotionally unpleasant, animals generally learn behaviors that will allow them to avoid pain (and bodily damage) from that source in the future.

Another survival function of pain is that it sends signals that help animals cope appropriately with an injury when it does happen. Generally speaking, pain induces individuals to be still and not move, so that healing may occur. It is nature's way of "putting on the brakes" and encouraging the rest needed for healing. Humans and dogs both tend to "lie low" or "sit things out" while pain persists.

There are many reports of cases where people have received serious injuries but have not felt pain until sometime later. This does not contradict the basic functions that pain serves. Sometimes, when an injury first occurs, actions such as escaping or fighting for one's life may be required, and pain would only interfere with these. A wild canine, such as a wolf, may often be injured when hunting large animals, defending cubs, fighting for territory, or attempting to establish social dominance. Under such conditions, delaying the perception of pain until such a time when it is safe to engage in behaviors that promote healing may save the individual's life.

Without a sense of pain we would have a hard time living long enough to reproduce. This is often the unfortunate fate of people who are born without the ability to feel pain. For example, psychologists Ronald Melzack and Patrick Wall from McGill University in Montreal reported the case of a woman who died at the young age of twenty-nine due to massive infections that were the direct result of numerous injuries, including cuts and scrapes that damaged her skin, unhealed bone and joint injuries, and internal damage from various collisions or falls. In normal people, any one of these injuries would have sent a pain signal that would have caused them to seek treatment and to rest and recuperate. However, this woman had not detected most of the injuries, nor had she noticed the onset of infection, because she lacked adequate pain sensitivity. Although pain is unpleasant, it saves lives. Certainly an animal that must hunt for a living, and whose body is in constant danger of injury, such as a canine, would benefit from such a mechanism.

Do Dogs Feel Pain?

Neurologically dogs and humans have very similar pain response systems. In both species the first signal for pain usually comes from free nerve endings in the skin; and the pathways that take pain signals into the brain are virtually identical. Thus, dogs have all of the neural apparatus needed to feel pain. In addition, many of the apparent symptoms of pain in dogs are controlled by the same kinds of medication that are used to manage pain in humans.

If dogs have the equipment that is used to register pain, and behaviorally seem to benefit from the warnings provided by pain signals in the same way that people do, why should there be much doubt as to whether they feel pain? The answer to this question actually has little to do with whether dogs actually hurt when they are injured and much more to do with human speculations about whether dogs have minds similar to those of humans, which give them consciousness and self-awareness.

There are two possible ways of comparing ourselves to dogs and other animals. The first is to suggest that dogs and humans share the same general mental and sensory structures, and that the only differences between us are a matter of degree: thus we have better vision, reasoning, and memory than dogs, and they have better scenting and hearing abilities than we do. Just because humans have better reasoning does not mean that dogs do not have *any* reasoning ability, just as the fact that dogs have better scenting ability does not mean that people don't smell anything at all.

The alternative, which was advocated by the French philosopher René Descartes, is that humans differ from dogs and animals because they have abilities that differ in kind, not degree. This argument would suggest that we reason better than dogs because we have different types of reasoning abilities that are not available to dogs and, furthermore, that humans have a consciousness and self-awareness that dogs and other animals do not have. Thus Descartes would have described your dog as just some kind of machine filled with the biological equivalent of gears and pulleys. This machine doesn't think, but it can be programmed to do certain things. He also denied that animals could have feelings or emotions, including a sense of pain. According to him, the cry of pain that one hears when one strikes an animal is not pain but rather the equivalent of the clanging of springs or chimes much like the sounds you might get when you drop a mantle clock or some windup toy. This idea was picked up and extended by Nicolas Malebranche, a French philosopher who claimed that animals "eat without pleasure, cry without pain, act without knowing it; they desire nothing, fear nothing, know nothing." This kind of reasoning allowed Malebranche to dismiss the objections of a visitor who saw him kick a pregnant dog hard enough to cause a shriek of pain by saying, "Don't you know that it does not feel?"

The sad outcome of this kind of reasoning is that it can be used to justify cruelty of any sort to animals. In past centuries, dogs were nailed to boards by their four paws so that surgery could be performed on them to see the circulatory system working in a live being. People who felt sorry for the pain inflicted on the poor creatures were laughed at as fools. They were told that dogs were merely "animate machines" and thus feel no more pain than a clock would if you were taking it apart to study how it works. According to this viewpoint, there is no moral issue associated with inflicting pain on a nonhuman animal because it does not feel real pain.

I would like to say that we could dismiss these kinds of arguments as simply reflecting attitudes of an unenlightened and best forgotten past. However, Descartes' theory that nonhuman animals can feel no pain and have no conscious awareness is still being advocated by some prestigious figures in the twenty-first century. For example, Peter Carruthers, who is Professor of Philosophy and the Chairman of the Department of Philosophy at the University of Maryland, continues to deny that animals can consciously feel pain. For this reason he claims that we have no need to exercise any ethical restraint on inflicting the kind of injuries upon animals that we know would cause pain in a human being. In a paper published in the *Journal of Philosophy* he summed up his viewpoint saying, "since their experiences, including their pains, are nonconscious ones, their pains are of no immediate moral concern. Indeed, since all of the mental states of brutes are nonconscious, their injuries are lacking even in indirect moral concern."

Even veterinary scientists disagree about how much they should concern themselves about the experience and treatment of pain in dogs. The research literature, however, is quite clear in showing that adequate pain management after surgery is usually associated with a more rapid recovery. Pain control seems to be especially important after surgery, in the immediate postoperative stages, such as when the dog is awakening from anesthesia. Those dogs whose pain is medically controlled start eating and drinking earlier, get up to relieve themselves more quickly, and ultimately can be sent home sooner.

Chronic pain, experienced over a long duration of time, can actually be a danger to a dog's physical as well as his mental health. The reason is that pain is a stressor, and in response to stress the body—a human's and a dog's—begins to release a set of stress-related hormones that affect virtually every system in the body. They alter the rate of metabolism, generate neurological responses, and cause the heart, thymus glands, adrenal glands, and immune system to go into a high state of activity. If this situation continues long enough, these organs can become dysfunctional. In addition, the tension that the state of pain-related stress induces can decrease the animal's appetite, cause muscle fatigue and tissue breakdown, and also rob the dog of needed, healing sleep.

Yet many veterinarians seem to be unaware of these research findings. A recent survey found that only half of the surveyed veterinarians routinely prescribe painkillers after surgery. Some still insist that the dog's sensitivity to pain is minimal, except for certain "wimpy breeds." Attitudes seem to be changing, however. Younger practitioners are most likely to administer analgesics, with the highest rate of such prescriptions coming from recent graduates of veterinary school. From a psychological point of view it is interesting to note another factor that also increased the probability that the veterinarian would give painkillers to a dog, which was if the veterinarian himself had experienced severe pain in his life because of injury or disease. Apparently such a shared experience increases our sympathy for suffering in dogs.

Pain control, however, is a two-edged sword. Dog owners have to exercise a certain degree of discretion when using painkillers with their pets after surgery. If enough pain control drugs are given to the dog so that he feels that he can resume his normal activities too soon, wounds may reopen and the dog's long-term health may be placed at risk.

Stoic Dogs

Dogs do not overtly show symptoms of pain to the same degree that humans do. This fact has clearly contributed to the doubt that some people have about their ability to experience it. Yet there are many reasons having to do with the dog's evolutionary history that are consistent with the idea that dogs can consciously feel pain but may adopt behaviors that hide it from plain view. Expressing pain is adaptive in humans, since it usually encourages others to provide social support and medical help. Dogs, however, are predators whose hunting strategy involves focusing their attention on the most vulnerable individuals in a group. Signs of pain and injury in one canine can automatically trigger the predatory instincts in other canines. This is an adaptive response for the hunter, since he is less likely to be hurt when attacking an animal that is already injured, and that animal is less likely to be able to escape.

If a dog reads behaviors consistent with pain and injury as an invitation for an attack, then it is reasonable to expect that at some level dogs are aware that others in their pack would also read such behavior in themselves in the same way. Therefore, if a dog is hurting, expressing that pain openly might elicit an attack from packmates because of their predatory predispositions. The attack on a hurting dog might also be triggered by more social concerns, since a dog whose status in the pack is lower than the injured animal's might view his rival's incapacitated state as the perfect opportunity to challenge him to improve his own status.

All of this would suggest that dogs in the distant evolutionary past adapted so that they appeared to act in a stoic manner. They will suppress many of the more obvious signals of pain and injury to protect themselves and their social standing in the pack. They hide their pain to appear to be more in control of the situation, and this makes it difficult for humans to recognize when their dog is hurting. However, you can detect certain signs of pain in the animal—the better you know your dog, the more likely you will be able to appreciate when your dog is in pain.

Obviously, if your dog is whimpering, crying, or yelping, then the pain has reached a degree of intensity that has broken through his protective barriers and his normal reserve. This is a dog that is hurting so badly that he doesn't care who knows it. Usually, however, the signs are less obvious and include excessive panting and rapid breathing even when the dog is at rest and not heat stressed. The dog may shiver or tremble. Sometimes he may appear to be extremely restless and change positions frequently while lying down or sitting. At the other extreme, he may appear extremely reluctant to change body positions. The dog may pull away when being touched, may appear to be guarding one part of his body, and may even show uncharacteristic aggression, growling or threatening when touched or even approached. Licking or chewing at painful areas is also common. Dogs in pain will often lose their appetite. Other physical signs of pain can include a rapid heart rate, dilated pupils, and a rise in body temperature.

Why Did You Hurt My Tail?

If you are in the mood to start a heated argument in a group of dog fanciers or veterinarians, just raise the issue of tail docking in dogs. The arguments against this practice are usually based upon suggestions of cruelty, pain, and mutilation. Dog breeders whose animals' tails are docked believe that not enough pain is involved to be an ethical issue. In one survey of 100 dog breeders in Australia, 87 percent felt that the idea of the pain caused to the puppies by tail docking was overblown by the press and public. In fact, 25 percent of them believed that at the age at which puppies have their tails docked they so young that they are actually incapable of feeling pain. Another 57 percent were convinced that the pain was at most mild and quite brief. Nonetheless, this issue has been catapulted into the political realm, and public pressure has caused several countries to entirely ban tail docking.

Many opponents of tail docking claim that this practice is done solely for cosmetic purposes and any level of inflicted pain is not warranted. Historically, tail docking did not begin simply as a matter of fashion, with breeders striving for a particular look in the show ring. Many breeds of spaniels that have their tails routinely docked would have quite elegant, well-plumed tails that make them more handsome to my eye if they were not docked. The practice of tail docking began for very practical reasons that related to dogs' working lives.

Take the case of independent guard dogs. Suppose, for example, I am a criminal trying to get past a Doberman pinscher. If this Doberman has a long tail, it is a detriment to its guarding ability because I can simply seize the dog by the tail and thus control its actions while avoiding its teeth. If I could immobilize the dog long enough in this way, my accomplice could severely harm the dog without any threat of injury to either of us. For this reason the tails of many guard dogs are often closely docked. If there is no tail, there is no easy way for bad guys to grab and control the dog.

Partial or full tail docking occurs in more than fifty breeds of dogs. In many, it was originally intended to prevent tail damage, which is particularly common in hunting breeds that have to pursue game through heavy vegetation and thick brambles or over rocky terrain. The natural action of their tails, as they whip back and forth, can easily lead to torn, broken, and bleeding tails, which are painful, often difficult to treat, and may require amputation of the tail—potentially a high-risk operation in an adult dog. Obviously, docking the tail eliminates the risk of this injury. Dogs with thicker, well-muscled tails, like Labrador retrievers, do not have their tails docked and seem less likely to suffer injuries. In some breeds, such as vizslas, the lower part of the tail is quite strong while the section of the tail nearer the tip is often turned upward (making it more likely to snag on obstacles) and carries little fat and muscle as protection from brush and rocks. For this reason, only the upper third of the tail is usually docked in this breed.

Recent research suggests that tail injuries are simply not an issue for pet dogs, at least for city-dwelling dogs. For example, one study was done at a university teaching hospital in a typical urban setting, in which over 12,000 dogs with docked and undocked tails were examined. Tail injuries in these pets were extremely rare. There were only 47 cases, which is less than four-tenths of 1 percent of the dogs in this survey. These researchers concluded that tail docking had little protective value.

Regardless of the reasons for tail docking, the question in which we are interested here is whether it causes pain. A study of fifty dogs conducted at the University of Queensland in Australia found that *every single puppy tested shrieked loudly* at the moment of amputation. In the minutes that followed, most of the puppies did settle down and show less distress. It is this quick-settling behavior that breeders point to when they suggest that the puppies must not feel much pain. They note that within about fifteen minutes of being returned to their mothers, most of the puppies go to a nipple to feed or nuzzle next to her to sleep. However, eating immediately after a painful experience may be a survival mechanism that is left over from the dog's evolutionary history. Feeding provides sustenance and energy reserves to cope with other, future traumatic events. In addition, there is some evidence that the act of sucking releases endorphins, which are natural pain-killing hormones that work exactly like morphine analgesics by blocking the pain signals transmitted to the brain. Thus the sucking behavior of puppies whose tails have just been docked may well be evidence that they are still in pain and trying to engage in activities that will make the hurting go away.

Remember, however, that expressions of pain in dogs are often less than the actual amount of pain that they are feeling, simply because they are living with other predators that might take advantage of what could be evidence of weakness. The puppies will have that same predisposition, perhaps even to a greater degree, simply because their small size and weakness already make them vulnerable. Thus yelping and whimpering would only draw unwanted attention to them. At this young age these dogs are already practicing stoicism, and an overt denial of pain, regardless of the actual degree of hurting that they are actually experiencing.

Love and Touches

One of the most interesting aspects of touch is the role that it plays in the psychological well-being of dogs. Touch is critical for establishing emotional and social bonds among dogs and even between dogs and people. Touch is also an important aspect of canine communication.

The first laboratory demonstration of the psychological importance of touch came from the University of Wisconsin, where Harry Harlow was working with baby macaque monkeys that had been deprived of the usual caressing provided by their mothers. In the beginning these monkeys acted very much like emotionally disturbed people do. They would crouch motionless for hours, sometimes simply clasping themselves, sometimes rocking their bodies in a monotonous, repetitive way, sometimes banging their heads against the wall, or chewing or scratching at parts of their body until open wounds appeared. These monkeys would eventually grow up to suffer from serious behavioral and emotional disturbances and an inability to relate to other monkeys.

To show that it was the actual absence of a gentle touch that was important, Harlow provided these monkeys with "surrogate mothers." These were constructions with the head of a monkey and sometimes a bottle from which the infant monkeys could nurse. One of these "mothers" was a wire model, which gave little contact comfort, while the other was padded and covered with terrycloth to provide some gentle touch sensation. Even if the wire mother fed them with the bottle and the cloth covered did not, the infants preferred to stay with the softer mother. Clinging to her and feeling the soft touch from her seemed to give the infant monkeys a sense of security and safety. They would even run to their "cloth mother" for safety and security when threatened by any strange event.

Since those classic studies on monkeys, similar research has been conducted using dogs with virtually identical results. Puppies that are separated from their mothers show a great deal of distress. They do not seem to be comforted by providing them with food, or hard play toys, but soft objects, whether a cloth, padded mother substitute or simply some squares of soft cloth did reduce their signs of anxiety.

The calming effect of touch can be provided by a human as well as another dog. If dogs are in some form of emotional distress, such as a strange situation, social isolation, or because they have been exposed to unpleasant events, gentle petting by a person can have a soothing effect. The beneficial aspects of touch can actually be measured physiologically: The heart rate slows and breathing becomes more regular.

The effects of touch can actually "teach" a dog to cope with anxiety-producing situations. If a dog is comforted by petting immediately before and after events associated with discomfort, and if this process is repeated a number of times, physiological measurements show that the dog eventually displays less anxiety in the distressing situation and recovers more quickly. It is almost as though the comforting touches begin to teach the dog something like "This will only bother you for a short time and then everything will be all right again."

All touches are not equal in their ability to calm dogs, however. Michael Hennessy headed a team of psychologists from Wright State University and Ohio State University at Newark in a study of the effect of touch on shelter dogs. Dogs that were petted and stroked were more relaxed and generated fewer stress hormones during the taking of blood samples than dogs that did not receive petting. The best form of petting seems to begin with encouraging the dog to maintain body contact with the person doing the petting. It is best to have the dog lean against the person or to sit or lie down. The technique is more like a massage than simple petting, with special attention to the dog's shoulder, back, and neck muscles. Another effective way of petting involves long, firm strokes of the hand, moving from the dog's head back to the hind quarters. The idea is to not just to move the skin but also to massage the underlying muscle. This means that the pressure on the dog should vary from medium to firm. In addition to stroking the dog, the person should talk to him in a gentle and soothing manner throughout the session.

Probably the best-known advocate of specific touching techniques for dogs is Linda Tellington-Jones, who developed a massage procedure for reducing tension and changing behavior in dogs that she calls the Tellington Touch (or T-Touch). She first used these techniques on horses but found they worked well on dogs, cats, and other animals, too. Her method is loosely based on a set of body-awareness exercises for human therapy developed by Moshe Feldenkrais. In general, T-Touch uses circular rotating movements of the hand and fingers to press and move the muscles and skin in calming manner. Tellington-Jones also found that beginning at the head and moving back and down the body works best.

One form of touch that humans find pleasurable but most dogs hate is hugging. For a dog the experience of hugging is perceived as confining and restricting his movements. Among dogs, freedom of movement is important for survival, whether it involves the freedom to run away from some form of threat or the ability to move freely to defend themselves. When you hug a dog you effectively immobilize him, which raises his anxiety level. Most dogs will struggle to free themselves from the restraints of your arms, and some may become anxious enough to snap or threaten in order to break loose.

Puppies that are touched a lot early in their lives, even before they are weaned from their mother, display lasting positive effects, including increased vitality, higher activity levels, and greater disease resistance. Psychologically, these dogs exhibit more confidence, are more socially responsive, and are less likely to show negative emotional reactions. There is even evidence that puppies that are extensively handled and touched by humans early in their lives become better problem solvers and learn what their trainers are trying to teach them more easily. We'll return to this aspect of early touching in a later chapter, when we deal with how to turn a puppy into the "perfect dog" by controlling his early experience.

All of this shows that the touch sense is doing more than simply informing the dog's mind that there are things out there that are hot or cold, sharp or blunt, or pleasant or hurtful. Information from the sense of touch is actually shaping the dog's mind and modifying his present and future behavior.

CHAPTER 7

A Canine Sixth Sense?

THE MAN'S NAME was William Becker and he had come up to speak to me after I had given a talk in Toronto.

"You talked all about dogs' abilities and senses," he said, "but you left out one of the most important ones."

"What was that?" I asked.

"Their extrasensory perception," he replied.

I have heard this kind of statement before in various guises. A number of respectable authors have written books for a general audience suggesting that dogs are able to use information from sources other than their five senses. Many people who make such claims have had extensive experience with dogs and include respected dog trainers, veterinarians, and canine behavioral consultants.

Certain claims of canine extrasensory perception (ESP) tend automatically to bring out the natural skepticism of most scientists. My own doubts are strongest about suggestions that dogs have precognition (psychic knowledge of something in advance of its occurrence), clairvoyance (psychic ability to see things beyond the range of the power of vision and to know things that are occurring, or have just occurred, at a great distance), or mental telepathy (literally, "distance feeling" or mind-reading in the sense of discerning another's thoughts).

If, however, extrasensory perception means the ability to perceive things in ways that humans do not yet understand and cannot perceive through the senses, I can be a bit more accepting. After all, it was only in the late 1950s that the fact that bats can detect and identify insects by echolocation (a sort of biological sonar) became accepted by the scientific community. At about the same time, scientists also learned that electroreceptive fish can read changes in the electrical fields around them. Some of these fish actually generate their own electrical fields and read the changes in them, while others, like certain catfish and eels, simply read the changes in the electrical fields caused by living things near them. As in the case of bats, this ability helps fish to detect things that they prey upon and eat. Prior to the scientific research that showed that such abilities existed, the hunting skills of these animals would have been considered to be "extrasensory."

A "proof" of the extrasensory perception of dogs is usually based on a particular incident in a family's history. Like many others, William Becker tells of a dog who seemed to know in advance that some disaster was looming and made frantic attempts to protect his master. William's story dealt with his father, Josef Becker, who was living in Germany, in a town called Saar Louis. One day he went off for a stroll with his German shepherd dog, Strulli, and decided to stop in a local inn to have a drink. Strulli, who was usually a well-mannered, quiet dog, became quite agitated as his master sat down and began to do everything in his power to get Josef's attention. He ran back and forth between Josef's chair and the door to the inn. He circled his master and grabbed at his clothes, trying to drag him from his seat. When that didn't move him, Strulli leaned back and gave a loud howl. To get some peace and quiet to finish his drink, Josef took Strulli outside and closed the door as he returned to his chair. Strulli, however, would not desist. Somehow he found another way into the inn and once again began tugging and howling at Josef. The man accepted that this was a losing battle and, rather than disturb the other patrons any further, quickly quaffed his beer, made a comment that the dog was probably following his wife's instructions to keep him from wasting too much time in taverns, and strolled out of the door with the dog.

Josef and Strulli walked outside and crossed the road. They had gone only a short distance when they heard a rumbling and cracking sound. As Josef spun around, he saw the inn disintegrating into a pile of timbers, masonry, and bricks. The building took only a minute or so to collapse, and few of the patrons had a chance to escape. Several people died and there were more who were injured. The collapse appeared to be the result of an excavation dug for a new construction next to the inn. During the digging the builders had inadvertently damaged the old inn's foundation. Nobody suspected any danger except, according to William, the dog Strulli.

"It was his premonition that saved Josef's life," he told me, suggesting that this was an example of precognition. Such phenomena are extremely difficult to prove scientifically, however. The requirements of science are that before we accept an explanation based upon undetectable forces or psychic abilities, we must first rule out any less exotic but plausible alternatives.

Listen to the Future

We know, for example, that dogs have very sensitive hearing and this can account for some apparent instances of precognition. Thus, a more recent incident that sounds very similar to the tale of Josef and Strulli involved Valerie Smith of Plymouth and her collie, Tommy. Valerie, who is partially deaf, was walking down a public path with Tommy. She reported, "He stopped and just stared at the trees. As I stepped forward he turned and barked at me, which he never normally does. When I went to walk on again he really turned, baring his teeth. He stood still again as if to say 'Stay there.' " Within seconds, a large tree crashed down on to the path, so close to Valerie that it scratched her right arm. "I was just so shocked to see the tree, which was about five meters long. It was covered in ivy and you could see the bottom half was rotten, but Tommy knew it was coming down." Although one could attribute Tommy's behavior to some form of precognition, in this case it seems more likely that dog's sense of danger came from the popping and cracking sounds the tree made as it began to fall.

Can the same explanation be used for Strulli's actions? We do know that dogs have sensitive hearing, at least for some frequencies of sounds. The dog's sensitivity to specific frequencies depends, in great degree, on the size of the dog or, more specifically, on the size of the dog's head. For a large dog with a large head the ear is correspondingly larger. That means that the canal that lets sound into the ear is wider, and every structure in the ear is correspondingly bigger. A small ear is tuned for higher-pitched sounds while a large ear is tuned for lower-pitched sounds, much the way that a small, narrow organ pipe will produce a high-pitched sound while a long, wide organ pipe will produce lower sounds. This means that smaller dogs have an advantage in hearing high-pitched sounds but may have greater difficulty in hearing lower-pitched sounds. On the other hand, some researchers believe that dogs with big, square, mastiff-type heads, which includes the Saint Bernard, Newfoundland, and Great Pyrenees, can actually hear subsonic tones. These are very low-frequency sounds, which are far too low for humans to hear. This may explain how the Saint Bernard is able to hear the faint low-frequency sounds made by people trapped under snow by avalanches, while dogs with smaller heads might not sense them at all. The dogs detect these avalanche victims, not because of some psychic power of location, but simply because they hear the low-frequency sounds that make their way through the snow.

A Seismic Sense

There is a heated debate going on among scientists as to another ability that dogs have that may be due to their hearing. Some dogs seem to be able to predict events such as earthquakes or avalanches before they occur. There are many reports of Saint Bernard dogs in the Alps who warned travelers, or members of search-and-rescue teams, of an impending avalanche in time for them to escape or take some safer mountain path. Researchers have confirmed that hours (or sometimes days) before a major earthquake, dogs begin pacing and acting distressed and restless. They become anxious and seem to sense trouble that their human companions cannot. In some cases they seem to bark at nothing and in other cases they run away from home.

I encountered this phenomenon myself on the evening of February 27, 2001, although I didn't understand the implications at the time. Barbara Baker, a senior instructor with the Vancouver Dog Obedience Training Club, was working with the advanced class, and this evening was not going well.

"What's going on here?" she finally asked in an exasperated voice. She was distressed by the behavior of her class of eight highly trained dogs. Each of these dogs had earned at least one Canadian Kennel Club obedience degree and was a reasonably reliable obedience competition dog. Yet these dogs had just failed to respond properly to a simple "stay" command. Instead, they whimpered, shifted around, or ran across the room looking for their masters. All the dogs seemed worried and upset for no apparent reason.

Barbara's question would be answered thirteen hours later when a 6.8-magnitude earthquake shook the Pacific Northwest. Focused near Seattle, only about 150 miles south of that classroom, it was felt through much of Washington State and the Province of British Columbia. In retrospect, it seems that the dogs were warning their human companions of the impending seismic event.

The idea that animals can sense earthquakes before they occur was first recorded in Greece in 373 B.C. The report was that dogs howled and many rats, weasels, snakes, and centipedes moved to safety several days before a destructive earthquake. More recently, James Berkland, a geologist from Santa Clara County, California, scanned the lost-and-found sections of local newspapers to determine the number of dogs and cats that were reported missing in and around the city of San Jose. According to his research, a major increase in lost pets predicts that an earthquake of magnitude greater than 3.5 on the Richter scale will occur within a seventy-mile radius of downtown San Jose within a couple of days. He claims that these predictions have been 80 percent accurate over a twelve-year period.

The predictive ability of dogs (and some other animals) has been recognized as being so good that, in China and Japan, along with high-tech scientific instruments, animals are considered an integral part of the national earthquake warning system. Their usefulness was proven first in 1975, when officials in the Chinese city of Haicheng were alarmed by the suddenly odd and anxious behaviors of dogs and other domestic animals. Those on earthquake watch recognized that the dogs' behaviors had occurred previously and usually just before major earth tremors. On the basis of these observations, officials ordered 90,000 residents to evacuate the city. Only a few hours later, a massive earthquake struck. It measured 7.3 on the Richter scale, which is stronger than the 1989 earthquake that collapsed part of San Francisco's Bay Bridge, caused three billion dollars in damage, and darkened parts of the city for three days. After the Haicheng earthquake, nearly 90 percent of the city's buildings were destroyed. It is estimated that, without the early canine warning, thousands of additional lives would have been lost in this disaster.

Because of events like these, there have been some wild speculations that dogs have special senses that enable them to detect changes in electrostatic charges in the atmosphere or subtle vibrations of the earth to which humans are insensitive. Other, more cautious suggestions are that the dogs were sensitive to low-frequency, subsonic sounds that are made as large masses of earth begin to move below the surface.

I used the opportunity provided by the Vancouver earthquake to do a bit of research. A few hours after the event I sent out an e-mail questionnaire to a list of local dog owners and also to some local dog training clubs and animal shelters. In the questionnaire I asked them to recall the behaviors of their dogs during the twenty-four hours before the earthquake and to indicate if there had been any noticeable changes during that interval. In all, I got reports back for 193 dogs within that week. The number of dogs that showed distress during that interval was 41 percent—a remarkably high number. On average, most people noticed strange behaviors in their dogs around three hours before the actual earthquake, although a few reported that their dogs were acting differently up to a full day before the quake.

The idea that hearing was involved in the prequake, stress-related behaviors of the dogs was tested by looking at the seventeen dogs in the group that had known or suspected hearing losses. Of this set of animals, only one hearing-deficient dog showed any odd behaviors during that interval and she lived with another dog in the household with normal hearing who was acting distressed. This makes it likely that the dog with a hearing deficit picked up on her companion's anxiety.

If the signals of an earthquake were coming from lower sound frequencies or subsonics, a higher percentage of the big dogs should have detected the sounds. I divided the dogs roughly into three groups: big dogs (over 22 inches at the shoulder), medium dogs (between 14 and 22 inches at the shoulder), and smaller dogs (less than 14 inches). The results do not support low-frequency hearing, since only 20 percent of the large dogs showed agitated behavior compared to 51 percent of the medium dogs and 64 percent of the smaller dogs. This suggests that the higher-frequency sounds are most important. Dogs hear higher frequencies best, as do the other animals most likely to signal earthquakes—small rodents and snakes.

Thus we might extrapolate and suggest that it was probably the high-frequency sounds of wood fibers breaking and masonry cracking that upset Strulli and Tommy and caused them to warn their masters of danger.

Dogs Foretelling Doom

People who believe in psychic phenomena might accept the dog's acute hearing as the explanation in these cases, but they are most likely to counter the argument by bringing up other stories that they feel supports some form of precognition, clairvoyance, or telepathy. The most common claims about precognitive dogs are that they seem to know that someone in the house is about to die. The usual sign of this is agitation on the part of the dog and, quite frequently, mournful howling. Since domestic dogs do not howl all that often, this behavior is noticeable.

Verna Simmons told me a story about her grandmother's dog, a Labrador retriever named Eddie. Verna had flown to California to help care for her grandmother, who appeared to be terminally ill but who wanted to remain in her home in a Los Angeles suburb rather than stay in a hospital. Eddie had been the old woman's constant companion ever since her husband had died. She had taken him everywhere with her, and because he was so quiet and well-behaved, he was always accepted by her friends and family. Before she had become too ill, Eddie had spent countless hours at her feet while she did needlework, read, or watched television. The old woman would also occasionally talk to the dog the way that you would talk to a person. By the time Verna arrived, Eddie appeared to be quite anxious and upset. He hovered around Verna's grandmother's bed and had to be shooed away or even locked outside to keep him from getting in the way while Verna and her aunt took care of the failing woman. Verna had been there only a few days when the events that so impressed her occurred.

"Grandma had had a really bad day and had been quite uncomfortable. We called in the nurse who had been seeing her, and she gave her some morphine and told us that we should watch her closely. She thought that we should probably think about getting a machine that would provide some oxygen, since Grandma's breathing was getting a bit weak. Aunt Connie picked up an emergency oxygen tank from the pharmacy just in case there was a problem that night. I put Eddie out in the yard and agreed to watch Grandma for the night and Connie would take over in the morning. I must have dozed off, but around two A.M. I was awakened by the most mournful howling I ever heard. It was really loud and at first I thought that there must be a wolf or a coyote around, but each of the howls started with one or two deep barks. Then I recognized that it must be Eddie. I have never heard him howl before, and Connie said she had never heard him do that before either. He sounded sadder than I ever imagined a dog could sound. I felt a feeling of anxiety and jumped up to see if his howling had awakened Grandma. She didn't seem to be breathing, so I shouted for Connie. We called 911, and the ambulance was there in minutes, but she was dead. Eddie knew the moment that she died. He was out in the back yard, and Grandma was in the front bedroom, so there wasn't any way he could have heard any sounds, like Grandma gasping for breath or that sort of thing. I don't know how he knew, but I've heard that dogs have a special sense for this sort of thing. I understood then that that he was howling because he sensed—he knew—that his best friend and his soul mate had died."

While the story of Eddie is poignant, it can be explained without any need to invoke clairvoyance or precognition. Howling is a sound that is usually made by a dog that has been relatively isolated, such as being locked away all day in a yard with no access to human or other companionship. When combined with a leading bark, it carries two messages.

The leading bark is an attempt to bring his pack members or family to him, just in case there is a problem, while the howl indicates the fear that no one will respond. In effect this sound means, "I'm worried and alone. Why doesn't somebody come and help me?"

Eddie had been put outside and isolated from his customary human companionship and could have been howling from loneliness. It is common to remove a dog from the house when someone is seriously ill. We also know that a seriously ill person may die and that a lonely, isolated dog is more likely to howl—add these components together and you have the basis for the apparent association between a dog's howling and the death of someone in the house. Verna notes that the dog never howled before, but he had also never been locked out and isolated from his family before. From such chance associations legends and beliefs in psychic phenomena may grow.

Numerous stories tell of dogs who appear to know about events that are occurring at such a distance that some kind of direct perception is impossible. One story that was told to me by a female acquaintance involves an incident that occurred during the Korean War.

"I got a phone call at work from my mother, who told me that she was having a hard time with her arthritis that day and wondered if I could pick up some things for her at the market and drop them off on my way home. Since I knew that Mum was worried about my brother, who was with some front-line unit in Korea, I told her that I would not only bring her the stuff that she needed, but I would make dinner for her that night.

"When I got to Mum's house I expected that I would be met at the door by Max, my brother's boxer, but Mum told me that he seemed pretty depressed that day and if he was still like that in the morning she would probably take him to the vet to get him checked out. My brother had gotten Max as a pup, and they were inseparable when he lived at home. Anyway, I made us some dinner and then we sat down in front of the TV. Mum always watched this one news show with John Cameron Swayze, which used to start at 7:30 P.M. It was just as the show was beginning that Max leapt up and started pacing wildly, whimpering, shaking, and crying. He looked so frantic that I thought that he was having some kind of a seizure. I tried to calm him down, but he ran away from me and hid under an end table. Max had always been such a calm and unexcitable dog that this was really strange behavior. I called my mother the next day to check on him, and she said that he was better but was still depressed.

"The next afternoon Mum received the news that my brother had been killed in a mortar attack. He had died at about 9:30 A.M. Korean time, which would have been just about the time that the news report was going on the air. It coincided exactly with the time that Max began acting weirdly, and Mum and I knew that Max must have somehow known that my brother had just died. There was simply no other explanation that made any sense to us."

Predicting Arrivals

Probably the most common example of a dog apparently knowing about an event occurring at a distance is the familiar observation that dogs seem to know exactly when their owners are coming home. I have already mentioned that my dog Dancer has a specific bark to indicate that my wife is approaching. He frequently anticipates her arrival by several minutes, although I have never actually timed her appearance or kept systematic records. I have always attributed this behavior to his ability to hear her somewhat noisy car from a distance of a few blocks away. Rupert Sheldrake, however, who holds a Ph.D. in biochemistry from Cambridge, might disagree with my explanation. He has collected numerous reports from people whose dogs seem to know when their owners are returning long before any sounds from a nearing vehicle could provide clues to their arrival. Furthermore, he claims that this is not due to some innate canine ability to tell time, because the dogs seem to anticipate their owners coming home even when the time is not regular or predictable and when they are returning by bus, train, or plane rather than the family's automobile.

One striking case that Sheldrake describes is that of Carole Bartlett of Chiselhurst, Kent, who often leaves Sam (a mixture of Labrador retriever and greyhound) with her husband when she goes to the theater or to visit friends in London. To return home requires a twenty-five-minute train journey and then a five-minute walk from the station. Carole's husband does not know which train she will return on because she might arrive at any time between 6 and 11 P.M. Sheldrake quotes Carole saying, "My husband says Sam comes downstairs off my bed, where he spends the day when I go out, *half an hour before my return* and waits at the front door." The reason why this report appears so remarkable is that the dog seems to begin waiting for Carole around the time that she is just starting her journey home—while she is still many miles and thirty minutes away from her front door. Since the train runs on a regular schedule, and the dog can't pick up any clues based upon sounds or scents as to which train his mistress might be traveling on, Sheldrake argues that, "The most convincing evidence for telepathy between people and animals comes from the study of dogs that know when their owners are coming home. This anticipatory behavior is common. Many dog owners take it for granted without reflecting on its wider implications." In his book *Dogs That Know When Their Owners Are Coming Home,* Sheldrake claims to have collected more than five hundred cases of dogs that anticipate their owner's arrival and encourages people to test their own pets to help confirm the telepathic and clairvoyant communication between dog owners and their pets.

The most closely studied case of ESP in a dog concerned a mixed-breed terrier named Jaytee, who lived in Ramsbottom, England, with his owner, Pamela Smart. Jaytee seemed to anticipate Pam's return by running to the window or outside to sit on the porch just about the time that his mistress was beginning her return home. This anticipation occurred even when Pam's schedule was irregular and her travel times were unknown to other members of her family. In an attempt to verify Jaytee's telepathic abilities, the Austrian State Television network sent two film crews. One crew followed Pam as she walked around the downtown area while the other stayed at home and continuously filmed Jaytee. After a couple of hours, the crew with Pam decided to start home. At that moment Jaytee went out on the porch and remained there until Pam returned. The results of this experiment received a lot of media attention, and television commentators described the dog as "psychic" and always correct in his anticipations.

Sheldrake decided to invite a team of researchers, headed by psychologist Richard Wiseman of the University of Hertfordshire, to test Jaytee's telepathy. The results of this research were subsequently published in the *British Journal of Psychology.* Wiseman reported that his first task was to eliminate any possible nontelepathic clues that might trigger the dog's behavior. This meant that Pam could not leave and return at a familiar expected time, or use a car whose sound was familiar and might be picked up at a distance. They also had to eliminate any possible clues that the dog might pick up from the behaviors of other people in the house who knew when Pam was returning. To do this, Wiseman and his team designed an experiment in which no one, including Pam, would know in advance exactly what time she would start her journey home. For this reason, they took Pam to a remote location and used a special calculator to generate a random time for their return. Pam was told only that they were going to start back a few seconds before they actually started back. Meanwhile, another member of the research team had remained at Pam's home and made a complete video record of Jaytee's behavior. This was done on four separate occasions.

The next thing that Wiseman did was to have an independent researcher judge the videotapes. This individual was not given any information about Pam's return time and simply scored any times when it might be reasonable to feel that Jaytee was signalling that his owner had started home. What the researchers found was that Jaytee was an extremely vigilant dog, and he typically responded by running to the window or out on the porch more than a dozen times during any of Pam's absences. Sometimes an event, such as person walking by or a car pulling up to the sidewalk, was the obvious reason that he ran to investigate. A few times there was no obvious reason for Jaytee's going to the window. Unfortunately, the majority of these "unexplained" trips to the window did not coincide all that closely with the times that Pam started home. In a subsequent interview, Wiseman summarized his results saying, "At a randomly selected time the owner returned home and yes indeed the dog was at the window at that point. When we rolled back the film and looked at the rest of it we found the dog was constantly going to the window. In fact, it was at the window so much it would be more surprising if it wasn't at the window when the owner was returning home!"

So why were Pam and her family so sure that Jaytee was accurately signaling her return? It is likely that this has to do with some well-known thinking biases that human beings have. These often involve a kind of selective memory based on what psychologists call a "confirmation bias," a type of selective thinking in which people tend to notice and look for events that confirm their beliefs and, conversely, do not look for, ignore, or perhaps undervalue the relevance of facts that contradict their beliefs. The classic example is that if a person believes that during a full moon there is an increase in crimes, accidents, or arguments, then they will take special notice when these events occur during a full moon. The flip side of this coin is that they are less likely to remember or take notice of these same kinds of events if they occur during other times of the month. Obviously, a tendency to do this over a long enough time would unjustifiably produce a strong belief in the relationship between the full moon and the rate of crimes, accidents, and disputes.

The confirmation bias and some selective remembering probably explain the belief in Jaytee's telepathic abilities. He was at the window many times, but his family tended to remember only the times his watching exactly coincided with Pam's returning home. All of those other times that Jaytee had been at the window were simply dismissed, forgotten, explained away by attributing them to outside noises or events, or perhaps not noticed in the first place because there was no startling coincidence with his mistress's arrival.

Seeing Through Distant Eyes

Our love for our dogs makes us long for evidence for some kind of special abilities or links to us. Virtually every dog owner has some "spooky" story about one or another of his dogs and its anticipation of some special event. What we conveniently forget is all of the times when our dogs acted strangely and nothing out of the ordinary happened, or our dogs acted quite normally when major events or crises were affecting us or our close family members.

Dogs do have some sensory abilities that are extraordinary to us but normal to them, some of which I have already mentioned and some that we will encounter later. They also have the ability to read our moods and intentions. It is tempting to attribute these abilities to higher-level psychic phenomena and to feel that some form of telepathy is responsible, but scientific testing has yet to confirm such abilities.

For example, Richard Wiseman (the same psychologist that tested Jaytee) tried to confirm telepathic links between a person and a dog in another case involving Laura "the dog communicator." Laura advertises on the Internet that if you've lost your animal you can telephone her and she will psychically tune into the animal's mind and tell you what it's looking at, which in turn may identify the location so that you can go and retrieve your pet. Wiseman's first test of Laura involved taking a dog to a particular location in Britain and then letting it run free. When he asked her where she felt the dog was and what it was seeing, he reports that she could sense it but her descriptions of the place were not very accurate. Rather than give up, Wiseman tried to confirm her psychic ability and the telepathy of dogs using a simpler, more objective set of measures. In these tests he released the dog but took a photograph of the place where it was. The photo was shown to Laura with nine others, and she was told that the dog was in one of the ten locations. She was to look at the photos and select the one that matched the telepathic images from the dog. On two successive tests Laura chose the wrong locations.

Based on his actual research findings, Wiseman has become quite dubious about ESP in dogs and telepathic links between people and dogs. In an ABC interview with Ann Warburton about his research with Laura, his scepticism became quite evident. He explained to the interviewer, "Laura's website is one of my favorites because sometimes she can't get to the case immediately and so offers some commonsense advice which is basically to go out into the neighborhood where you've lost the dog and to call its name out rather loudly. And it does make you wonder the intelligence of the people going to the website if they need to be told that. And second, the whole website is about forming this intuitive and mystical link with your animal, but when push comes to shove you're out there calling its name!"

CHAPTER 8

The Preprogrammed Dog

I AM STANDING in a room full of puppies ranging in age from three to five months and watching several social "dramas" unfold. One pup named Hugo, which looks like it will grow up to be a mostly German shepherd dog, approaches a yellow-colored cocker spaniel pup named Amber. Hugo uses a stiff-legged walk, his head is low, his ears are up, and he is staring directly at Amber. The blond dog responds by immediately lowering her body and then rolling on her back. Across the room is a Siberian husky named Tiska, who is moving toward a soft-coated Wheaten terrier named Ike. Tiska suddenly lowers the front end of her body so that her front legs are flat on the ground to the elbows while her rear end and tail are held high. Ike responds by adopting the same posture for a moment, and then the two pups dash off in a merry game of chase.

Anyone who knows something about dogs can read these two scenarios quite easily. Hugo and Amber are working out an issue of dominance and submission, each declaring their presumed status and their intentions, while Tiska and Ike are merely inviting each other to play. These behaviors are the same in dogs born and reared in Nashville, Beijing, Rome, Moscow, or Johannesburg. They represent the kind of preprogramming of behaviors that is encoded in the genes of every dog. They do not depend upon any kind of learning but rather display themselves under certain conditions, or when certain events occur in the dog's life.

Things Already in the Mind

Information gets into a dog's mind through his sensory systems. But the dog's mind does not start out as a totally blank slate. Every behavior is not the result of environmental influences and learning. A human child begins life with a mind that is a relatively empty book and must learn how to act and communicate with the world, but the book that is the dog's mind contains several chapters' worth of useful behaviors available from birth. In many respects we depend upon this genetic storehouse of behaviors to make our dogs useful companions and coworkers. We expect that herding dogs will have a predisposition to herd, guarding breeds will be protective, hounds will track, pointers point, retrievers retrieve, and so forth. A dog is not born with a full repertoire of perfectly shaped behaviors, but it will have recognizable examples of aspects of the expected adult behaviors. The herding dog will need to have his prewired stalking and chasing tendencies modified so that they can be put under some degree of human control, while the guard dog must be taught to inhibit some of his inherent aggressive tendencies.

These genetically predetermined behaviors are usually called instincts, and one of the major controversies in behavioral science involves how large a role they have shaping the mind. This is often referred to as the *nature versus nurture question,* where "nature" refers to genetics and instincts and "nurture" refers to learning and experience. Biologists and zoologists usually tend to feel that a great deal of behavior has been genetically prearranged, while psychologists tend to feel that there is a good deal of flexibility and that an individual's personal history and his interactions with the environment are more important in shaping the final behaviors. In many respects trying to determine whether the contributions of genes are more significant than those of learning through personal experience for any behavior may be impossible to answer. It is much like asking the question, "Is the height or width the most important factor in determining the area of a rectangle?" Obviously this is a nonsensical question, because without both height and width you would not have a rectangle, and there is no way to ascribe greater importance to either.

What biology has preordained is a set of behaviors and abilities with which the animal begins life and that may also limit how and what an animal can learn. Experience and learning will determine the specific skills that are learned and the final shape of behaviors. Biology or genetic programming makes it easier for us to create a dog that can do particular things, through selective breeding, although it may also make it more difficult for us to eliminate particular behaviors. For example, terriers are specifically bred to bark. The job of a terrier is often to go down into an underground den to eliminate a fox or a badger. A functional terrier must bark when the least bit excited or aroused. Its furious barking alerts the hunters to the location of the burrow. The sound of the barking underground tells the hunters where to dig to uncover the quarry and, often, to rescue the terrier, who may get trapped beneath the earth. Conversely, because this genetic tendency is so strong, training a terrier *not* to bark in certain circumstances may be difficult. It will certainly be much more difficult than training a retriever to stay quiet, since retrievers were bred to sit silently so as not to frighten away the birds that are the hunter's quarry.

From Hunter to Herder

Some of the behaviors that are related to survival seem most likely to be genetically determined: caring for young puppies, sexual behaviors, some hunting behaviors, and some social and communication behaviors. When humans deliberately intervene to change the genetic predispositions of a breed of dogs, we usually try to select aspects of these "prewired" behaviors for our own purposes. Probably the most spectacular success in breeding for useful behavior been in the creation of herding dogs. Without herding dogs the progress of human civilization would have been much slower because we would not have had the organized animal husbandry that provides us with meat, wool, leather, and many other needed products. When it comes to controlling a flock of sheep, a single shepherd and one dog do better than ten men without the assistance of a dog.

The herding ability of dogs is based on the same genes that control pack-hunting behaviors in wolves and other wild canids. Hunting large animals requires coordinated activity to control the movement of a group of potential prey animals so that eventually a single animal may be isolated for the kill. The hunting behaviors in wolves that serve as the foundation for herding behaviors in sheepdogs are genetically programmed. The first genetic instruction has the pack position itself around a herd of prey animals with each individual at approximately the same distance. Each wolf will try to remain equidistant from its hunting partners on its right and left. The action of these instructions results in an elegant, complex pattern of encirclement, with the pack forming an almost perfect circle that closes steadily during the hunt and keeps the herd together.

A single sheepdog tries to do the work of many wolves. Actually, the herding dog performs the entire programmed pattern as if it were taking the part of every member of the pack. First the dog decides on the proper or "key distance" that it should be from the flock and then dashes around to occupy the remaining stations that normally would be filled by other packmates. As the dog goes from one position to the next, he circles the flock in a wide casting motion. This curving path has pauses at each "outpost" where another wolf should be. It drives the sheep on the outer fringes to the center of the circle and thus keeps the flock together.

The next genetically programmed predisposition deals with setting an ambush. It is often the case that when a wolf pack hunts, one wolf may separate from the rest of the pack and hide from their quarry, crouching down to hide and wait. The rest of the pack then tries to drive the herd toward that location. This is why sheepdogs tend to run and then drop to the ground staring at the flock of sheep. It is, in effect, playing the part of the wolf that waits in ambush. The sheep appear to be quite aware of the dog's presence when the dog gives them the "eye" or stares; it seems to mesmerize any sheep that may have started to wander away from the rest of the flock. The staring dog tends to hold them in position, but the moment the flock as a whole starts to move again, the dog immediately resumes its encircling actions.

Driving the herd in a particular direction is also a genetically encoded program. Wolves have been known to maneuver herds of prey animals into areas where their movements can be restricted by the terrain to make it easier to split off and isolate an individual for the kill. The wolves drive the herd by making short, direct dashes toward the animals. This causes them to run in a direction that takes them directly away from the charging hunter. Sometimes the wolves nip at the heels or flanks of the driven animal to alter its path; they may even use a shoulder to bump the animal in a particular direction. When Ronald Reagan was president of the United States he had a Bouvier des Flandres, a large cattle-herding breed from Belgium, named Lucky. Following her instincts, Lucky was continually trying to herd the president and visitors by nipping at their heels and buttocks. She even punctured the president's pants and drew blood on one occasion when, unluckily for her, photographers were present who later published pictures of the president being herded by his dog. To avoid future embarrassments, Lucky was sent back to the Reagan ranch in Santa Barbara, California, and replaced by a Cavalier King Charles spaniel named Rex that had no herding instincts and was too small to reach up and nip the presidential hindquarters even if he had.

Wolf packs are ruled by a strict social hierarchy that recognizes a pack leader that is usually referred to as the "alpha" wolf by scientists. The pack leader manages and controls the various moves of the pack, and the other wolves are programmed to watch him and follow his lead, thus making the pack an efficient hunting organization. The sheepdog is predisposed to accept the shepherd as the alpha wolf. The dog frequently looks to the shepherd, who needs only to teach him a few commands to tell him what to do next.

Manipulating Genes and Behaviors

It may seem odd, but you can manipulate behaviors more easily by using selective breeding when the behaviors are relatively complicated and multileveled. Much of the genetic programming of fundamental movements and reflex responses appears to be fixed and immutable. Thus, aggression, which is complex, has been genetically manipulated and aggressive behaviors vary widely across different breeds. Although we can increase or decrease aggressive tendencies through controlled breeding, we can't change the fact that all dog breeds fight in the same way. Their basic patterns of attack, their biting and defensive moves seem to be unalterable aspects of the basic genetic code of canines. Such regular and predictable specific behaviors, which are not dependent upon learning in order to appear, are called "fixed action patterns." When we genetically manipulate aggression in a dog breed we are making a *quantitative*, not a *qualitative*, change. We do not alter the basic behavior patterns, but rather their likelihood and how easily they can be triggered in the dog.

Consider care-giving behavior in mother dogs. While this complex behavior is not a fixed action pattern, a number of its major aspects are. The female dog having her first litter is preprogrammed to know what to do. Her maternal behaviors will start about twenty-four to forty-eight hours before she delivers, when she automatically starts "nest building" to prepare a place to have her litter. Immediately after the birth of each puppy, the mother removes the birth sac and cuts the umbilical cord. This behavior is so fixed and stereotyped that we can predict with relative certainty that the cord will be cut using a carnassial tooth (the upper tooth right before the molar). Next the puppy will be licked dry and, if necessary, the umbilical cord will be trimmed shorter. Licking is a vital fixed action pattern serving to stimulate various muscle reflexes, including those involved in breathing. It also triggers elimination behavior. For the first two weeks of life newborn puppies can't eliminate waste voluntarily and so the mother licks and grooms the puppy's anal and genital regions to stimulate urination and defecation. She then eats the waste products, which helps keep the nest clean. Obviously if we had to teach every dog to do these things, instead of relying on genetically encoded instructions, the survival of the species would be at risk.

It is a remarkable testimony to the stability of fixed action patterns that even with more than fourteen thousand years of domestication, and despite concerted efforts to alter dogs genetically, so few changes have occurred in the ancestral patterns of behavior. Our genetic manipulations have only minor effects on *which* specific behaviors a dog uses, but have a strong effect on *how frequently* such behaviors are expressed. Thus, while we cannot selectively breed dogs so that they can produce human speech sounds, we certainly can produce dogs that bark more frequently, as in the case of terriers. What we are really manipulating is the animal's readiness to act. If we increase this readiness to a high enough level, then the fixed behavior patterns can be triggered by stimuli other than those that the original genetic programming intended; thus terriers bark at anything that raises their excitement level.

The automatic nature of these "prewired" behaviors, given the appropriate stimulus, is quite remarkable. For example, the urinary-marking behaviors of an intact adult male dog simply depend upon having the right stimuli present. Thus a vertical surface that has already been marked by another dog is often enough to initiate the distinctive leg-lifting behavior. Sometimes it appears as if the dog is a slave to these events. When my beagle Darby was young and initially began to lift his leg to urinate, it seemed almost as if he was surprised by his own actions. The first time that I observed him leg lifting, he also twisted his head around to watch this strange contortion of his body, which caused him to hop unsteadily on three legs while urine flowed out in a stream. He appeared to be quite curious, and perhaps a bit puzzled, as to what was "happening to him" rather than showing any understanding of what he was actually doing. Leg-lifting behavior does not seem to be something that dogs voluntarily choose to produce. It is almost as though it is an action that forces itself upon the dog when the conditions are right. In this way leg-lifting shows another feature that is common to fixed action patterns, in that it is very difficult to bring under voluntary control. Even though a male dog lifts his leg many times during the day, which ought to give many opportunities to selectively reward this behavior and bring it under outside control, it turns out to be very difficult to train a dog to do this on command, as animal trainers who have tried to get dogs to do this on cue for a movie or TV role can attest. Some patterns of behavior are under such a primitive, instinctive level of control that they simply cannot be easily modified by subsequent learning.

Breed Differences in Behavior

The set of behaviors that distinguish dogs of different breeds represent clear examples of human genetic manipulations. In sporting breeds, for example, we have the classic pointing behavior of pointers and setters and the barely restrainable retrieving urge in many retrievers. In an interview on *The Tonight Show* with Johnny Carson, Truman Capote, author of *In Cold Blood* and *Breakfast at Tiffany's,* told a story about a blind date a friend of his once had. When his friend arrived at the woman's apartment, she wasn't quite ready to leave and asked him to wait in the living room. When he sat down her friendly Labrador retriever carried a ball over to him and dropped it in his lap. Capote's friend took the ball and amused himself while he waited by tossing it to the dog, who gleefully retrieved it. The dog was excited and seemed totally focused on his retrieving, so the friend began to throw the ball a little harder to give the dog more of an opportunity to chase it. Then, by accident, he threw the ball and it flew out of an open window across the room. Totally focused on retrieving, the dog went after it, flying out of the eighteenth-story window and disappearing from sight. When his date finally returned to the living room, Capote's friend did not say a word about what had happened, later telling Capote that he hoped there would be no second date where he might have to broach the subject.

When Capote finished his story, comedienne Elaine May suggested that the friend might have said, "You know, your dog seemed very depressed to me . . .' "

While this story has always seemed suspect to me, I did experience one instance that almost convinced me that it might be true. I was walking with my flat-coated retriever Odin along an embankment by the flood-swollen Vedder Canal, not far from our farm in British Columbia.

Suddenly Odin saw a very large stick floating in the water, and since I often threw things for him to fetch from the water, his retriever instincts went into overdrive and apparently he assumed that it was an object that he should return to me. While I gasped in horror, he leapt over the forty-foot-high (12 meter) embankment into the flood. The swift current dragged him nearly a quarter of a mile (half a kilometer) downstream before he was washed close enough to the bank so that I could drag my exhausted dog to shore. As I sat there gasping for breath, my heart pounding from concern over him, he looked mournfully at the stick, which was disappearing around a bend, and gave a couple of frustrated barks.

Because breed-determined characteristics are often specific and easily identifiable, purebred dogs make wonderful subjects for studying how behaviors are genetically determined. Jasper Rine of the Department of Molecular and Cell Biology at the University of California at Berkeley noticed some behaviors of border collies and Newfoundlands that were quite contradictory. For example, Newfoundlands love water and seek it out, but border collies are quite indifferent to it. Newfoundlands bark somewhat frequently and carry their tails high, while border collies are relatively quiet and carry their tails low. Finally, of course, border collies show the various components of herding, such as crouching, staring, and making hard eye contact, all of which are absent in Newfoundlands.

To learn more about the genetic control of breed-specific behaviors, Rine cross bred a border collie and a Newfoundland. In that first generation of puppies all of the dogs showed the crouching and glaring behaviors of the border collie as well as the water-loving behavior of the Newfoundland. The rate of barking, however, was somewhere in between, since these dogs were noisier than border collies usually are but quieter than Newfoundlands normally are. When a second generation was generated by mating these crossbred dogs to each other, strange mixtures of behaviors began to emerge, but different combinations of traits appeared in different individuals. For example, there might be a dog that crouched and carried its tail low (collie traits) but loved water and barked a lot (Newfoundland traits), while its littermate might be exactly the opposite, never crouching, holding its tail high, hating water, and seldom barking. Preprogrammed and genetically coded behavior characteristics apparently sort themselves out in various random combinations. Obviously, if you encounter a mixture of behavior traits that is special and useful and try to preserve it, then you are really trying to create a new kind of dog—perhaps a new breed if those characteristics can be passed on reliably from parent to offspring.

Genetically Determined Language

Canine communication demonstrates some of the most interesting and complex genetically determined behaviors. As with other complex behaviors, communication contains sets of fixed action patterns. For example, very young puppies do not have to learn the basic care-seeking signals, such as whining for attention, tail-wagging with the head held low, yelping, licking their mother's (or any adult's) face, nose, and lips, jumping up to make face contact, pawing, and following adults.

Later on other social signs and signals will spontaneously appear, even though the puppies may have never seen adults demonstrate them. These include innate dominance signals, such as standing over a littermate while holding the head and tail high and arching the neck, placing the head over a rival's neck or upper back so that the dogs form a sort of "T," standing with the forepaws on the littermate's back, wide-eyed staring, or shoulder and hip bumps and mounting (with or without pelvic thrusts).

Moving from dominance to threat involves the preprogrammed "showing of weapons" by snarling while showing the incisors and canine teeth. A subtle threat is wagging only the tip of an upright tail, and as the threat escalates the hackles will be raised and the tail will fluff out stiffly. Circling a littermate with tail held high and wagging stiffly while moving with a stiff-legged walk is another threat.

Submission signals are also instinctive, such as tail between the legs, ears held flat against the head, head held low, and eyes turned away to avoid eye contact with the dominant dog. Licking the air or lips, and a submissive "grin" with the corners of the mouth retracted back, are signals that come as part of the dog's submissive signal programming. A nondominant dog will also automatically freeze and remain stationary while a dominant dog circles or gives other dominance signals. The extreme submissive gestures, such as rolling onto the back, lying on the side to lift the leg to show the genital area, and perhaps releasing a trickle of urine are also instinctive.

Certain play signals, including the play bow, with elbows on the floor and hips and tail held high, and even mock hunting, such as stalking other pups with head and tail down while the hindquarters are raised and the ears are held erect, are instinctive and are usually triggers for the equally instinctive chasing or wrestling play behaviors. If the play gets too rough, the animal that accidentally acted too aggressively will immediately produce another play bow as if to say, "Excuse me! That was just done in play!"

All of these body language signals appear without any intervening learning, and they also seem to be interpreted without benefit of experience. Learning will make the signals more subtle and will shape the situations where they are used and how they are responded to, so that very sophisticated "conversations" can take place. However, the basic "language" is instinctive and would be understood regardless of whether a dog was bred in North America, China, or France.

The Sounds of Dogs Speaking

A dog's response to certain sounds is also preprogrammed. In human language, sounds are fairly arbitrary and no set of word sounds has a common meaning for all members of our species. Thus "caballo," "cheval," "Pferd," and "horse," all mean the same thing, yet there is not even a shred of a common sound pattern linking these words. Some people have tried to create a "universal language"—Esperanto is probably the best known of these—but none has gained wide acceptance. The sounds that canines use to communicate with each other, however, are mostly predetermined and have quite a bit of similarity even across different species. As in the case of body language signals, the ability to interpret them is innate. This universal language code of animals, or "Evolutionary Esperanto," allows not only various groups of dogs to understand each other's vocal signals but also allows other species (including humans) to extract a good deal of the meaning from these signals. For instance, low-pitched sounds (such as a dog's growl) usually indicate threats, anger, and the possibility of aggression. Low-pitched sounds basically mean "Stay away from me." In general, high-pitched sounds mean the opposite. They indicate "I'm no threat," "It's safe to come closer," or ask, "May I come closer to you?"

The evolutionary language used by dogs focuses on three dimensions: the pitch of the sound, its duration, and the frequency or repetition rate of the sounds. Eugene Morton, a naturalist working at the National Zoological Park, analyzed the sounds of fifty-six species of birds and mammals and found that all use the same "Rule of Pitch." Just as dogs have a low-pitched rumbling growl, so do elephants, rats, opossums, pelicans, and even chickadees. All of these growls seem to mean "Keep your distance," "You are annoying me," or "Stop that." The same whimpers and whines that we find in dogs are also heard from rhinoceroses, guinea pigs, mallard ducks, and even wombats. These high-pitched sounds all have the general meaning of "I mean no harm," "I hurt," or "I want." Psychologists have shown that humans unconsciously use this aspect of universal language in their speech. When a person is angry or making a threat, the pitch of their voice tends to drop to a lower register. Conversely, when a person is trying to be friendly and inviting someone to come closer, his voice tends to rise in pitch.

There is an element of physics behind the Rule of Pitch, since big things make lower sounds. You can demonstrate this by tapping first a large and then a small empty water glass with a spoon. The bigger one gives a lower-pitched ringing sound. Similarly, a longer string on a harp, a longer organ pipe, and larger animals (because of their longer windpipes and larger mouths) all make lower-pitched sounds. During their evolution the animals that avoided other animals making low-pitched sounds (which were apt to be large and dangerous) were also more likely to avoid fatal encounters. These animals survived to pass on the genes that programmed their offspring to do the same. Conversely, animals evolved to respond to high-pitched whines, whimpers, and peeps, usually made by small, nonthreatening creatures, including their own puppies, which might be signaling a need for adult care or protection.

The marvel of evolution is that, over time, this physical sound cue for size became genetically coded and is now used as part of canine communication behaviors. To cause another animal to move away or back down, dogs automatically produce lower-pitched signals, like growls, to suggest that they are larger and more dangerous. A high-pitched signal, like a whine, suggests that the individual producing the sound is small and safe to approach. Yet even large animals will whimper or whine to signal that they are not contemplating doing anything harmful. Obviously, changing the pitch of a sound signal does not change the size of the animal making it, but the evolutionary pressures on animals suggest that responding to sound quality is important. An animal growling in a low-pitched voice is definitely one that should be avoided, regardless of his size. Little teeth in an angry mouth can cause wounds that may be just as dangerous as large teeth. By responding to these genetically coded pitch signals, dogs avoid confrontations and the social harmony in the pack is improved.

The "Rule of Duration" is the second important feature of the universal evolutionary language. Sound duration combines with pitch to modify the meanings of sounds. Generally speaking, shorter sound durations are associated with higher-intensity fear, pain, or need. If you shorten the high-pitched whining sound of a dog it becomes a yelp, which may mean that the dog is hurt or terrified. That same whining sound when lengthened in duration becomes a whimper, which can mean pleasure, playfulness, or invitation. The underlying rule seems to be that the longer the sound, the more likely that the dog is making a conscious decision about the nature of the signal and the behaviors that are about to follow. The long-duration, low-pitched growl of a dominant dog indicates that he has every intention of holding his ground and not backing down. Growls that are given in shorter bursts, and sustained only briefly, usually indicate that the dog is fearful and worried about whether it can successfully get away with a full attack without injury.

The third dimension in this genetically determined language is the repetition rate of the sound. The "Rule of Repetition" says that sounds that are repeated frequently, at a rapid rate, indicate a degree of excitement and urgency. When vocal sounds are spaced out or not repeated, they usually mean that that the "speaker" is not all that excited or is indicating a passing state of mind. A puppy that looks at something happening and gives one or two barks is only showing mild interest in the event. If the puppy is barking in multiple bursts and repeats them many times a minute, however, he shows that he is in a heightened state of emotion and that he feels that the situation is important, perhaps even a potential danger to himself or the pack.

Sophia Yin conducted research at the University of California at Davis in which she recorded and analyzed dog barks and found that they were predictably related to the situation that the dog was in. When dogs were disturbed or threatened, they produced barks that were lower in pitch (also harsher sounding) and were longer in duration. Higher-pitched sounds of short duration were associated with invitations to play. She also noted that sometimes, when dogs were very excited, their rate of repetition increased and they might fuse together three or four barks to form what she called a "superbark."

People Talking to Dogs

Since dogs are born with a predisposition to make and respond to certain sounds, it would seem reasonable that human beings can use particular sounds to communicate with dogs and control their behavior. Note, we are not talking about learned sounds, such as the familiar obedience commands "Sit" or "Down" but rather preprogrammed sound interpretation on the part of the dog. For example, dog trainers often stress that when you are interacting with a dog, *what* you say is not as important as *how* you say it. Some dog-training manuals insist that a particular command must be given in a "firm, but not threatening, tone of voice" or in an "exciting and inviting manner." I took some training with the well-known dog trainer and writer Barbara Woodhouse around 1970. She was in her sixties at the time, at the peak of her career. During the training session, she took me aside and explained how I should modify my voice, especially on the "Come!" command, since she felt that any hint of a demand in voice tone would actually make it less likely that the dog would have any desire to come to me.

She then told me, "You know, there are some people who bring their dogs to me for training whose main problem is that they don't know how to speak to their dogs. For those clients I insist that they have to first have a session of voice training with me, without the dog present, before I will agree to work with them."

Patricia McConnell, of the Department of Zoology at the Madison campus of the University of Wisconsin, researched whether some common human sounds produced consistent responses in dogs. She reasoned that animal trainers have honed their knowledge about communicating with dogs based upon what seems to work and what does not. Thus, unconsciously perhaps, they may have tapped into the basic makeup of dog language. If animal trainers use consistent sound signals, these might give us some insights as to how to best communicate with dogs. To eliminate any biases that might creep in if she studied only one language, Dr. McConnell interviewed and recorded a large number of animal handlers (104 in total) who were native speakers of many different languages, including English, Spanish, Swedish, German, Polish, Basque, Peruvian Quechua, Finnish, Chinese, Korean, Arabic, Farsi, Pakistani, and the North American Indian dialects of Navajo, Shoshone, and Arapaho.

McConnell was most interested in the kinds of signals that were used to change the dog's activity level, either exciting him to increase activity or causing him to slow down and inhibit his activity. She found that the trainers, regardless of their language and culture, used signals that reflected the dog's genetically programmed rules of duration and repetition in a fixed combination: short sounds that were repeated several times increased a dog's activity level, while long, drawn-out, single sounds tended to slow activity or get the dog to remain still. Nonword signals included repeated hand claps, hand slaps against the trainer's thigh, finger snaps, tongue clicks, lip smooches, or kissing sounds to get a dog moving, especially when coming toward the handler. Vocal signals might include "Fetch it up!" or "Be quick!" since each involves several short sound signals. Out of 2,010 signals that McConnell analyzed, these kinds of repeated short signals were never used to stop activity or to get the dog to stay in place. To slow or stop a dog's activity, longer, single signals were used, such as "Down," "Stay," or "Whoa" in English. In telling the dog slow down or stop, each word was pronounced with the vowel sounds drawn out for a longer duration than might be used in normal conversation. In whistle signals used by shepherds, two short, sharp whistles might get a dog to run out toward the herd of sheep and one long whistle gets the dog to stop or lie down. Once the dog is moving toward the herd, the short sharp whistle can also be used to speed up the dog.

What about the Rule of Pitch? Do human trainers fail to use that? No, we use it, except it is a bit more subtle, according to McConnell's research. She has found that human signals to dogs vary in the number of different pitches in the signal (technically referred to as the "bandwidth" of the sound). Claps, tongue clicks, and kissing sounds have a broad bandwidth with both low- and high-pitched sounds. If a sharp sound like "k" or "t," or a hissing sound like "ts," "sh," or "ch," is part of a word, especially at the end, it also adds a strong dose of higher-frequency components. So phrases like "Take it," "Let's go," or "Go back" fit the pattern of multiple-broadband sound bursts. Contrast this to a word like "Down," which has a narrower bandwidth, with a much smaller contribution from the higher-pitched sounds. So, it appears that dog trainers naturally resort to more complex sounds with higher pitches to get dogs moving and lower pitched sounds to slow or stop them.

Had you taken that voice lesson from Barbara Woodhouse, she would have demonstrated this by using inflections on common words. To get a dog to come, she demonstrated calling the word "Come," which was modified so that it came out as if it were a two syllable word with a rising pitch at the end. To get the dog up and moving for a walk, she used the artificial word "Walkies," with that same rising tone in the second syllable. Commands for stay and down used what she called "my grandfather's voice," which was low-pitched and drawn out in duration. She also noted that using a dog's name is useful if you want your dog to do something, but the name should not be used if you want the dog to stay in place. Obviously, adding the dog's name adds a few extra sound bursts (such as "Lassie, come"), while eliminating the name can keep the command structure as one drawn-out sound (such as "Staaay").

Breed Dialects and Idioms

Since aspects of dog communication are genetically controlled, it is possible there will be breed differences in dog signaling. Deborah Goodwin, John Bradshaw, and Stephen Wickens, researchers from the Anthrozoology Institute at the University of Southampton in Great Britain, studied ten different breeds of dogs and found that they seem to have different dialects. There were systematic differences in the number and pattern of communication signals that each breed produced. Before we can understand those differences, we must first understand the way in which domesticated dogs differ from wolves.

Perhaps the single most important difference between domestic dogs and wolves involves *neoteny*, the condition in which certain juvenile features and behaviors are retained in the adult. Put simply, this means that the adult domestic dog resembles a wolf puppy more than an adult wolf. Physically, some specific wolf puppy characteristics are a shorter muzzle, a wider and rounder head, and in many breeds the floppy, puppy-like ears, rather than the upright, pricked ears of the adult wolf. Behaviorally, dogs also act more like wild canine puppies. They have a greater interest in playing, are more friendly, and more likely to take guidance and instruction from those who seem to be in positions of dominance than will an adult wolf.

Neoteny seems to be a natural consequence of domestication. In the distant past, when dogs and humans first established contact and well before people were actively trying to breed dogs as companions and workmates, dogs appear to have begun the process of domesticating themselves. This came about because the evolutionary principle of "survival of the fittest" works regardless of the environment in which it is applied. Our association with dogs began when early canines decided to hang around human settlements in the hopes of getting food scraps without the need to risk life and limb while hunting large dangerous animals. For such opportunistic scavengers, the "fittest" canines would be the friendliest and least threatening, since they were the ones most likely to be allowed to get closer to the campsite and any available food resources.

The evolutionary pressure for dogs to be friendly actually increased when humans began to try actively to domesticate canines by controlling their breeding. Any newly domesticated dog that was vicious or fearful of humans would not fit well into village life. Unsociable creatures would not be kept or tolerated but would be driven out of the settlement or, most likely, simply killed. The dogs that were friendly toward people would also prove to be much more trainable and hence more useful. These dogs would be kept and nurtured and would go on to parent the next generations of dogs.

Genetically, certain things tend to be linked, and sometimes the linkages are surprising. Sociability and friendliness are puppy-like mental traits, and they seem to be linked to certain physical conditions. In effect, by selectively breeding for pleasant, easygoing canines, we also selectively breed in a slowing of the maturing process. This produces dogs that may never reach the full adult stage of physical development but demonstrate neoteny by keeping some puppy characteristics. In addition, it is possible that early men and, perhaps to a greater degree, women may have thought that the more puppy-like of their newly domesticated dogs (which might be smaller with bigger eyes and rounder, flatter faces) were simply more appealing and they were apt to care better for the ones with the greatest puppy "cuteness" factor.

The research team from the University of Southampton started with the observation that all domestic dogs do not show the same degree of neoteny. The best physical indicator of how much or how little neoteny a breed has is probably how similar the individuals are in their appearance to an adult wolf. Thus, dogs that look a lot like wolves, such as German shepherd dogs and Siberian huskies, not only have more adult physical characteristics but show fewer juvenile behaviors. The flip side of this is that dogs that look more like puppies, such as the Cavalier King Charles spaniel or the French bulldog, should not only have more juvenile characteristics physically but should also act more like puppies.

As a first step, these researchers ranked ten different breeds of dogs on the basis of whether they looked puppy-like or more like adult wolves. These were, starting from the most puppyish: Cavalier King Charles spaniel, Norfolk terrier, French bulldog, Shetland sheepdog, cocker spaniel, Munsterlander, Labrador retriever, German shepherd, golden retriever, and Siberian husky. They then looked at fifteen communication signals, concentrating on those that show dominance and submission. Their results are consistent with the notion of neoteny, not only for body shape but for dog language. The least wolf-like of the dogs, the Cavalier King Charles spaniel, has the most limited social vocabulary and consistently shows only two of the fifteen social signals. The signals they produced are care-soliciting signals that appear very early in wolves (normally in a three- or four-week-old puppy). It seems as though the social vocabulary of this breed stalls at this level. The wolf-like Siberian husky, however, produced all fifteen of the social communication signals, thus demonstrating a behavioral vocabulary similar to that of an adult wolf. In between these two extremes, the more wolf-like a breed is, the greater the number of social signals it uses and the more likely its gestures are to be those of a mature wolf. All of the dogs still do respond to these same signals when given by other dogs, so the ability to decode these genetically shaped social signals is still there, but the likelihood that they will produce these signals themselves is affected by the same genes that make dogs more puppy-like.

Although genes shape much of a dog's behavior, they do not shape all of it. Every dog still has much to learn if he is to function in the world. Furthermore, some of his later learning may even contradict his genetic programming, and this can cause a variety of behavioral difficulties. The dog will begin a lifelong process of learning new behaviors and adapting to the outside world, virtually from the moment that he leaves his mother's womb, as we will see next.

CHAPTER 9

Early Learning

BELIEVE IT OR NOT, an important clue to dog behavior can be learned from research done on geese and ducks. Before we get to that point, however, we must be clear that while there is a lot of behavior that is genetically coded in dogs, many of their most important behaviors are *epigenetic*, which literally means "above the genes." The young dog's experiences and interactions with the environment will have a great deal of influence on the adult dog's behavior. Some of this influence will involve learning that rewards or punishments accompany specific behaviors. Other influences will involve special forms of learning that have not been found in humans. Still other influences will involve experiences that we might not call learning at all but that nevertheless physically shape the dog's brain.

If you look at the brain of a day-old puppy, who will eventually grow up to be a sixty-five pound (30 kg) dog, you will notice that the brain is extremely small, perhaps about 10 cubic centimeters, about the size of an average adult's middle finger from the tip to the first joint. That brain has a lot of growing to do. When the pup reaches the age of eight weeks, his brain will have increased to five times its original size and will now be close to 60 cubic centimeters. After another eight weeks of growth, it will be about 80 cubic centimeters and it should reach its full size of about 100 cubic centimeters sometime between the age of nine months and one year of age. This means that the day-old pup has only ten percent of his adult brain!

In addition to being very small, the new puppy's brain is still quite immature in its structure. It looks almost jellylike, since the fibers that connect neurons to one another have not yet fully developed the fatty white sheath (called myelin) that speeds communications between locations in the brain and electrically insulates each nerve cell so that its messages are not interfered with by the action of its neighbors.

The dog's brain, however, was already being shaped by its environment even before the puppy emerged from its mother's womb. Research has shown that if a mother is stressed while she is pregnant, her offspring will grow up to be relatively fearful animals. If the mother is stressed in the final third of her pregnancy, her pups will show reduced learning ability, may show some extreme or exaggerated behaviors, and will be extremely emotionally reactive. This is probably a direct result of the production of stress-related hormones (corticosteroids) by the mother.

Another possible prenatal influence on the puppy's brain is its littermates developing in the womb beside him. Data show that if there are a lot of male pups in the womb, then enough male hormones (androgens) leak out into the embryonic fluid to affect all of the pups. Females born in mostly male litters tend to act in more masculine ways, suggesting that the hormones from her brothers affected the shape and function of her developing brain in the womb.

Once the puppy is out of the womb, however, his experiences cause major changes in his developing mind as it does in other species, including geese and ducks. In 1935 the Austrian ethologist Konrad Lorenz observed that shortly after birth young goslings begin to follow their parents around. Strangely enough, however, if geese are hatched by humans in a setting where there are no adult geese to interact with, the goslings will often start to follow their human caretakers around. Furthermore, when they grow up, these geese will treat humans the way normally reared geese treat other geese. In fact, the males may even perform mating dances for the human, completely ignoring available female geese. Lorenz called this process *imprinting* and suggested that it is a form of learning that occurs very rapidly. It is based upon the first moving objects that stimulate the animal's senses (which will normally be its parents), and this experience will shape the animal's behavior throughout the rest of its life. Lorenz felt that one of the unique characteristics of imprinting is that it involves learning the characteristics of an entire species. In this case, imprinting determines in the goose's mind what constitutes another goose. This early experience results in the animal directing most of its social behaviors toward members of the species upon which it has imprinted.

One of Lorenz's most important observations was that there is a limited period of time when the animal is most susceptible to imprinting, called the "critical period." The exact timing of the critical period depends upon the species. For example, mallard ducklings are most susceptible to imprinting at about fourteen hours of age. At that time, exposure to another duck for as little as ten minutes will imprint the duckling. If, however, he encounters a chicken, a bouncing blue balloon, or a human such as Dr. Lorenz, then the ducking will identify with the chicken, balloon, or ethologist. In its mind the goose effectively says, "I am just like that. I can fall in love with that. I can mate with that," and so forth. Many species refuse social contact with any animal except one of the same species on which they are imprinted.

Another important feature of critical periods is that they close down after a particular age. For the mallard duck, the critical period ends after about two days of age. After that it is virtually impossible to achieve imprinting. Animals that miss this window of time may never have an appropriate concept of what their species is and may never appropriately interact or mate with other ducks.

Lorenz and the ethologists and psychologists who did research on critical periods also found that there are different critical periods for different behaviors. For example, songbirds actually learn their songs by a process that resembles imprinting. If they are exposed to particular songs after they are a few days old, but before they are about a year old, they will imprint that song, even though they might not actually start singing until much later in their lives. For example, a twelve-day-old nightingale was kept in the same room with a black-capped warbler for about one week. The next spring the nightingale began singing, but he sang a typical black-capped warbler song instead of a nightingale song.

Very early imprinting, with rigidly defined critical periods that permanently fix behaviors for the rest of an animal's life, seems to be most common in "precocious" animals, such as geese, ducks, sheep, and cattle, where the young animal is born at a fairly complete stage of development, advanced enough so that it can move around and stay with the flock or herd within a few hours of its birth. Such animals need to develop species identification quickly, so that the newborn will stay close to its own kind and not wander off to be caught by predators. "Altricial" animals, where the newborn is quite helpless and requires continuous parental care and nurturing (such as dogs and humans), don't really need this kind of quick learning. Newborn pups don't even have fully functioning vision and hearing and are not capable of wandering off on their own for a couple of weeks.

In the 1950s J. Paul Scott, who was then director of the dog research facility at Bar Harbor, Maine, extended the concept of critical periods to dogs. He defined a critical period as a special time in life when a small amount of experience will produce a large effect on later behavior. The difference between the amounts of effort needed to produce the same effect at different ages is a measure of just how "critical" the period is. For example, if a small amount of experience will easily produce a behavior at about three weeks of age, but at a later age no amount of experience will establish the behavior, then we are looking at a rigid, inflexible critical period similar to those that Lorenz saw in his geese. However, if at this later age, by investing a lot of patient effort for hours, weeks, or months, we can eventually reproduce the behavior that would have developed during the critical period, then that period of time is still very important but probably should not be called "critical," since some changes can occur after it (although with difficulty). In cases where learning at one age is very easy but there is still some small degree of flexibility later on, scientists have come to prefer the label "sensitive periods." The research at the Bar Harbor facility would clearly demonstrate some important sensitive periods in the development of the young dog.

Neonatal Period (0 to 12 Days)

The first sensitive period lasts just under two weeks after birth. The newborn puppy is still blind and deaf, but other sensory systems are working and the pup can taste and smell, it is sensitive to touch, pressure, movement and temperature changes, and to pain. In fact, it is likely smell that gives the puppy its first imprinting experience.

I have already mentioned that shortly after birth the mother licks and grooms the pups. The gentle massage of her tongue causes the pups to urinate and defecate; however, the mother's saliva also gives the pup one of its first outside messages. It says to the pup, "Remember, I am your mother and this is what my saliva smells like." Learning this scent appears to be quite critical for the pup's survival since now, much the way geese and ducks follow the first moving objects they see, the pup follows the scent trail of his mother's saliva. Since lactating mothers tend to lick their own nipples, this provides a scent marker for the pup to aim at. Research has shown that if the mother's nipples have been washed in soap and water, the puppies can't find them. This is also why it is difficult to get a pup to suckle on an artificial nipple, even if you put the nipple in its mouth. It simply lacks the smell stimulation. However, coating that nipple with the mother's saliva causes the pup to actively go toward it and to start to suck when he gets there.

For the first week or so the puppy's behavior is mostly driven by outside stimulation. As long as he keeps against something soft and warm (its mother and littermates), he will lie quietly for hours. The pup needs stimulation not only to eliminate but also to feed properly. Newborn pups will attempt to nurse only when they are stimulated by their mother.

At this point, the pup's brain is still so immature that it is virtually impossible to discriminate whether the pup is sleeping or awake based on the electrical activity in his brain. Yet that brain is capable of learning, and during this period the puppy's experiences have a lasting influence on his mind.

Most of the puppy's behaviors during the first days of its life are designed to solicit care-giving (technically, *et-epimeletic* behaviors). If the pup is taken away from its mother and placed on the floor a short distance away, it begins to crawl slowly, throwing its head from side to side, using the scent of its mother's saliva and his "heat-seeking" nose receptors to try to find her. It is also whining or yelping as it moves along, making plaintive sounds designed to trigger care-giving and attract the mother to the pup.

When most of us look at these immature and obviously helpless little beasts, we naturally try to protect them from any stress or disturbance, but this is exactly the wrong instinct to act upon. Research has clearly shown that mild stress—physical handling, touching, and stroking, as well as changes in temperature—is actually a great benefit to the developing puppy during this early time. Puppies that have been handled and mildly stressed during this sensitive period grow up to be more confident, less fearful, and better problem-solvers. They also explore their world more and seem less likely to be shaken by unexpected events, loud sounds, and bright lights later in life. A lot of handling is not required, since as little as three minutes a day for the first three weeks of their lives gives significant improvements. These effects are reliable enough so that some dog breeders (including the U.S. Army Veterinary Corps) provide such stimulation routinely for pups of this age, and they report remarkable improvements in emotional stability, stress resistance, and learning ability.

Rather than leaving the pup alone at this time (as some books on dog-rearing advise), or just assuming that the mother will provide adequate stimulation, human handling of the puppy by humans is very beneficial during the neonatal period. A simple stimulation routine that works during this sensitive period is to take each puppy in the litter in turn and hold it in both hands with its head higher than its tail for about ten seconds. Next, change the pup's position so that its head is lower than the tail for another ten seconds, and then repeat this gentle slow rocking once more with head up for ten seconds and head down again for another ten. Next, hold an ice cube in your closed fist for about ten seconds to cool down your hand, then slip the cold hand, palm up, under the pup. He may wiggle a bit, but since your hand will quickly warm to body temperature, you are really providing only a mild stress for a short period of time. An alternate way to do the same thing is to place the pup on a cool surface for a few moments each day. Next hold the pup on its back and cradle it for a minute while you gently stroke its belly, head, and ears with your fingers. Finally, take a cotton swab and gently spread the pads of the feet and tickle the pup between the toes. This series of activities should take about three to five minutes at the most, although there is no harm done in handling the pup for a longer period of time.

This simple set of handling activities during the neonatal period is psychologically beneficial and also stimulates physical improvements. Puppies that are handled and mildly stressed actually show faster maturing of the electrical pattern of their brain activity, often grow more quickly, and show earlier coordinated movement activities.

Transition Period (13 to 20 Days)

As its name suggests, this period is one of rapid transition and change. It is the time when the puppies begin to move around more, feed themselves more reliably, and pick up greater amounts of information about their world. The helpless patterns of behavior that were typical of the neonatal period evolve into behaviors that will be more typical of later puppyhood and adult life. Yet this whole process takes only about a week. A neonatal puppy is difficult to feed by hand and only sucks half-heartedly at a bottle. By the time it is two weeks of age, however, it becomes quite adaptable at feeding itself. It will readily nurse from a bottle and can even lap up soft food or milk from a dish. It is not a pretty sight, however, and the pup will often end up splattered with food and occasionally choking. By three weeks of age, however, the pup can stand and drink and eat from a bowl in a reasonably efficient manner. Also during this week, the pups stop crawling on their bellies and begin shaky attempts at standing and walking.

Most important, the rest of the pup's senses now come into action. The transition period begins with the opening of the puppy's eyes at around thirteen days. You can tell that the eyes are functioning at this time because shining a light into them causes the pupils to contract, indicating that the light is being received and responded to. It may take a while longer, however, for the eyes to respond to shapes and distances accurately and reliably. The end of the transition period is marked by the opening of the ear canals at about twenty days. The best evidence that the ears are functioning is that the puppy will now respond to a loud noise, such as a metal pot struck by metal spoon. In addition, the pup's brain responses, as measured by electrical recordings (EEGs), begin to show more distinct patterns indicating sleep, waking, and degrees of arousal.

It is now that the pup displays its first deliberate social responses. He is beginning to engage in play fighting, during which he will wag his tail, bark, and even growl. He also becomes socially conscious, and his littermates are now valued companions and not merely soft heat sources. If he finds himself outside of the group in an unfamiliar environment he may yelp in distress, even if he is well fed and warm.

The transition period is a brief interlude between two sensitive periods. The person trying to influence the puppy to develop into "the perfect dog" should continue the handling behaviors of the neonatal period, only now make sure that it includes lots of stimulation provided by the human voice. Talking to the dog as you pick it up or stroke it will familiarize it with human sounds. Having the radio or television on to provide additional sounds also helps steady the growing pup. During this time you can gently introduce the pup to new sources of stimulation. Introduce toys or objects that can be manipulated or investigated into the nesting area. Take the pup to different areas of the house, where the floor textures are different, the lighting is different, and there are different things to look at. This kind of stimulation will help make the pup more emotionally stable and a better problem solver later on. Let him explore and sniff around at his own pace during these early trips.

Socialization Period (4 to 12 Weeks)

The socialization period, which is approximately the next nine weeks, is probably the most influential time in a puppy's life. This interval comes the closest to being a critical period, and some events that happen—or stimulation that does not happen—during this period will shape the dog's behavior forever. Undoing any negative behavioral effects that result from experiences during this period of life may be extremely difficult and perhaps impossible.

Socialization is to the process by which an individual learns about his social world. He learns what his "society" expects of him and basically learns all of the rules and behaviors that allow him to become a functioning member of a particular society. A wolf pup has to learn only that he is a wolf and then how to act around other wolves in a wolf society. Because dogs are domesticated and will live their lives with humans, however, their socialization is more complicated. A dog must socialize to dogs in order to learn that he is a dog and how to function in a canine society, but he must also learn how to act and behave in a society of people, meaning that he must socialize to humans. This is a delicate balance, because dogs must come to accept and respond to humans while not altering their sexual preferences for dogs or acting in ways that would cause them to be rejected by their own species. They must welcome both dogs and humans as acceptable members of their family or pack.

Dogs can actually be socialized to any of a number of different species. For example, I received an e-mail that included photos of a mixed-breed terrier puppy named Flash who had been rescued at just under four weeks of age and then reared in a home in Philadelphia. Because he was so young, his owners put him in with their cat Mildred, who had just had a litter of kittens, in the hope that the kittens would provide him with some company. Flash was the same size as the kittens and Mildred adopted him as if he were one of her own. She even washed Flash with her tongue just like she did the kittens. By the age of sixteen weeks, Flash's behavior was more that of a cat than a dog. His favorite toys became cat toys, like a squeaky mouse and a ball with a bell in it. He even learned cat mannerisms, such as the typical cat postures in stalking and pouncing when playing with his adopted feline family. Perhaps most surprising was the fact that he also learned the typically feline habit of washing his paws with his tongue and then using them to clean his face and ears. When given a choice, he would select the company of cats over that of other puppies. Flash's case is not unusual. In laboratory studies, puppies have been socialized to rabbits, rats, cats, and monkeys.

It is vital for a puppy to have adequate contact with dogs during the socialization period of four to twelve weeks of age so that of canine socialization can occur. To illustrate this, J. Paul Scott, at the Bar Harbor Laboratory, directed a rather extreme but scientifically useful study. In this experiment a puppy was removed from its litter at the age of twenty-one days and then completely isolated from the company of other dogs. It also had only limited contact with humans, since although it was carefully fed and watered, its caretaker was not allowed to play with or even speak to it. This means that by the time it was sixteen weeks of age the puppy had not had any contact with other dogs except for the first twenty-one days of its life, and had had only minimal human contact (except for a caretaker who barely acknowledged the pup's existence when she fed and watered it). At four months of age, the experimental puppy was once again placed with its littermates. It did not recognize them, either as littermates or as animals that were the same species as he was. The puppy's isolation during the critical socialization periods, with its complete separation from the companionship of other dogs and humans, had distorted its character to such an extent that it would never adjust to the society of either. This unfortunate puppy had passed beyond the age of adjusting socially to any living things, and once the patterns were set in his brain, he would not get another chance. This dog would tend to avoid its own species both socially and sexually for the rest of its life.

The dog's ability to modify its socialization to include other species is vital to some important functions we require of dogs. Herding dogs provide a wonderful example of the importance of socialization. There are two types of herding dogs that grow up in the same environment, and both are required to respond to the same environmental stimuli, namely sheep. One type, particularly the collies, herd the sheep, while another, like the Maremma, Great Pyrenees, or Kuvasz, guard the sheep. Behavioral scientists once thought that herd-guarding behavior, like herding, was also genetically prewired. Research by Raymond Coppinger, a professor of biology at Hampshire College, has shown that that is not the case.

Many of the herd-guarding breeds of dogs, even those coming from long lines of successful herd guards, turn out to be useless at their job. They either run away from the flock or attack or harass the sheep. The difference between the successful herd-guarding dog and the unsuccessful one seems to have less to do with genetics than with the dog's early history and socialization.

The traditional way to produce a herd-guarding dog is to rear it with the sheep that it will ultimately be asked to protect. The puppy lives with the sheep from about four or five weeks of age up to sixteen weeks of age. Except for a daily ration provided by the shepherd, the puppy has to fend for himself among the sheep. His social interactions are mostly with sheep. He grows up with the herd and will live with it for the rest of its life. When a predator, such as a wolf or coyote, approaches the herd, the guarding dog will rush toward it. Whether this is due to an urge to defend the flock that the dog has now socialized to, or whether it is simply to check out this strange new animal, is unclear. In either event, the predator's usual stealthy hunting approach has been disrupted, and it might respond aggressively by snapping at the herd-guarding dog (which will cause the dog to act more hostilely if it encounters this species of predator again) or it might take flight and run away. Either event protects the herd and prevents loss of livestock.

Some people suggest that since the dog was reared with the sheep and socialized to sheep, it now thinks that it is a sheep and thus must defend its own kind. This is not really the full story, however. Herd-guarding dogs know that they are dogs. Although they socially interact with sheep, the behaviors that they direct toward them are actually dog behaviors, which are quite different. For example, sheep threaten a dog or another sheep by stamping their feet, whereas dogs threaten sheep by showing their teeth and growling. Growling is a social communication strategy in dogs. Dogs growl at animals that they want to communicate with and will stop growling if the animal responds appropriately. Dogs usually don't growl at their prey when hunting, since that would only serve to warn them and give the intended victim a chance to escape. So when we observe a herd-guarding dog growling at sheep, this tells us that this dog has developed a social relationship with the sheep. It is much like when you communicate with your dog using human language and social behaviors. Obviously you don't think that you are a dog, although you feel that you and your dog have a social relationship and that he can understand what you are trying to say.

Herd-guarding dogs socialize to three different species. Typically, livestock-guarding dogs spend their first sixteen weeks not just with the sheep but also with one or two of their littermates, a few adult dogs (which usually includes their mother and other breeds of dogs that actually do the herding), and of course the human shepherd. This gives the dog the opportunity to accept dogs, sheep, and humans as appropriate targets for social contact and social interactions. The trick is that this has to be done during a critical period that extends from three to twelve weeks of age or the socialization will not be successful.

The scientific research that established that there was a sensitive period for socialization in canines came from what has been labeled "The Wild Dog Experiment." This was a study that was conducted at the canine laboratory at Bar Harbor. It involved rearing litters of puppies in large, open fields so that they had the regular company of their mothers and littermates but only limited contact with humans. Each animal was restricted to one week of interactions with humans. During this week each dog would be brought into the laboratory every day and would be handled, played with a bit, and spoken to for a while. What was varied was the age the pup when he got that week of human contact. Some got their week of human interaction when they were two weeks old, others at three, five, seven, or nine weeks. One group got no human contact until it was tested at fourteen weeks.

The researchers noticed that when they took the pups out to give them their initial contact with humans, the two- and three-week-old pups were only mildly attracted to a person sitting quietly near them, while pups that were five and seven weeks were quite happy to approach the person. The willingness to approach a stranger decreased again at 9 weeks. Furthermore there appeared to be a gradual increase in signs of fearfulness of the strange human, and that fear reached a moderately high level at nine weeks.

The most important test of the effect of the age of the puppy's contact with humans happened when the puppy was brought in from the field and put on leash at fourteen weeks. He was then taken on a walk through the laboratory building and up a set of stairs (which for many puppies was the most frightening part of their journey). A puppy that has never been on a leash often becomes alarmed and fearful, partly because it is in a new place and partly because its movements are now restrained. A puppy that walks well on a leash and stays near the person at the end of it shows that he is comfortable and feels safe with the human nearby. This "good behavior" on a leash also shows that the pup is willing to accept people as leaders and to interact socially with people by watching them and following their movements. A puppy that does not accept social interactions with humans will not follow and will balk or resist attempts to move. Resistance is usually greatest when passing through doorways or when out in a wide open area. Such pups will often fight the leash, run as far as the leash will allow in order to increase their distance from the human, or whine, whimper, howl, or growl at being restrained.

Puppies that had had a chance to socialize with humans between five and nine weeks had the fewest problems on the leash. They followed fairly happily, or required only a bit of coaxing, resisted or balked only occasionally, and even then were easily calmed. The puppies that had had their week of human contact before the critical socialization period began were considerably less controllable on the leash, while the pups that had had no human contact until testing at fourteen weeks were the worst. The puppies that had had their human socialization too early or too late also showed the greatest levels of fear and anxiety. They whined and whimpered fearfully, and when offered a treat at the end of the leash test, they were often too overwhelmed by their anxiety to accept and eat it. Further research confirmed that full socialization to humans is only fully effective if it occurs after the beginning of the third week and before the end of the twelfth week.

What happens if there is no human contact during the socialization period? The Bar Harbor researchers took one such dog that had not had human contact before fourteen weeks and tried to make it a pet and to get it to socialize with humans. A researcher took the dog home with him but found that the pup was extremely fearful. Therefore, he adopted the procedure that is usually used to tame wild animals. First the puppy had to be confined so that it wouldn't run away. Next he resorted to hand-feeding it. Hand-feeding forces the puppy into human contact for each mouthful of food that it gets. Eventually the researcher and his family were able to calm the dog and get it to accept close contacts with people. Even with all of this intensive care, attention, and social contact, however, this was not a well-socialized dog. It proved to be difficult to control for the rest of its life and was very timid and fearful around strangers. Furthermore, whenever it was given a choice to make contact with humans or with dogs, it always chose the dogs.

The amount of contact that a dog needs is really not all that much. Some studies have shown that as little as twenty minutes a week of human contact throughout the four- to twelve-week period can achieve adequate socialization. Some social interaction is vital during that time, and more concentrated and active social interaction produces the best effects. Spreading the interaction out over several days during the week is also important. Increasing the amount of time with humans makes puppies more confident around people and less fearful of strangers, and it forges a stronger emotional bond with the humans that will be its caretakers and family later in life.

Learning to Communicate

Socialization also includes learning the rules that govern the societies in which the dog will live. The dog has to learn to interpret social signals from others and to respond with appropriate signals himself. Some of these skills are learned by interacting with adult dogs, but a much more important aspect of social learning comes from interactions with littermates. The litter serves as a sort of miniature pack, and the puppies respond to each other with playful, aggressive, and sexual behaviors. They may try to show their dominance over their littermates with prewired behaviors such as stares, by rearing over their backs, or by mouthing. They work out patterns of social behavior by learning which responses are evoked by their actions. Mouthing is an important example of the way this works, since the puppy learns *bite inhibition* at this early age—he learns to mouth without biting hard enough to actually hurt the other individual or break his skin. The puppy first learns this from the mother, when he bites too hard on the nipple while nursing and is punished for his transgression, and the lesson is repeated when littermates respond negatively when his bite hurts them. There is good evidence that puppies that have been weaned too early or removed from their litter at too young an age will tend to bite with greater force and with less provocation than those that have been kept in the litter until around eight weeks of age.

Puppies also learn their basic communication skills at this time. For instance, puppies do not wag their tails when they are very young. Typically the first episodes of tail wagging will not appear until some time during the third week of life. On average, even around thirty days of age, only about half of all puppies are using tail wagging as a social signal. Communicating with tail wags is usually not fully established until around forty-nine days of age.

Why does it take so long for the puppy to start wagging its tail? The answer comes from the fact that puppies begin tail wagging when they need it for social communication. Until they are about three weeks of age, puppies mostly eat and sleep. They are not interacting significantly with their littermates other than when curling up together to keep warm when they sleep or crowding together to nurse. They are physically capable of wagging their tails at this time, but they don't. Soon, however, the puppies are interacting socially, mostly in play. Now communication becomes more necessary. Since the pup is in the process of learning bite inhibition, at times he may still bite too hard. When this happens, the puppy soon finds out he is apt to be bitten back, and perhaps the game that he was playing might be terminated by his now angry littermate. Here is where that newfound communication ability becomes useful. Obviously, once the hard bite has been given it is too late to inhibit it, so tail-wagging and a lowered body can be used to indicate submission rather than threat, and that may help to smooth matters over with an annoyed littermate.

Feeding time is another arena with a lot of opportunity for conflict and social learning. When a puppy wants to suckle its mother, it must come very close to its littermates as it crowds in to find her teats. This puppy is now coming close to the very same individuals that might have been nipping, jostling, or chasing him a few minutes earlier. To indicate that this is a peaceful situation, and to calm any fearful or aggressive response by the other puppies when they are pushing toward their mother's nipples, the puppies begin to wag their tails. Tail-wagging in the puppy then serves as a truce flag to its littermates. Later on, puppies will begin to wag their tails when they are begging food from the adult animals in their pack or family. When soliciting food, the puppies come close in order to lick the face of the adult and they signal their peaceful intentions by tail-wagging. Thus it seems that the reason that very young puppies don't wag their tails is because they don't need to send appeasement signals to other dogs yet. When they have to communicate with other dogs, however, they rapidly learn to display the appropriate tail signals.

Dogs that have been hand-reared from birth by humans, without any other dogs, show much less tail-wagging. In addition, the subtleties of other dogs' tail wagging are often lost to them. Thus they seem to have more difficulty discriminating the meanings of the high tail carriage and small, quick tail movements that mean dominance and threat versus the broader, lower tail wags that contain no challenge. These dogs will sometimes inappropriately rush up to a dog that is using its tail to express dominance and warning others to keep their distance. These socially deprived dogs may inappropriately snarl or growl at a dog that approaches them with broad tail swings who is trying to signal a friendly greeting. Because the learning of this form of canine communication needs to occur during the critical period, and that window of time has been missed, these dogs do not learn the correct interpretation of canine tail signals from their later encounters with other dogs. Instead, they seem to blunder through their lives, continually getting into spats with dogs that normally do not show any hostility. In most instances they are the source of their own problems, since they are not responding appropriately to clear social signals given by other dogs.

A pivotal influence on the social and personality development of the puppies occurs somewhere during the fourth or fifth weeks of their lives, when the mother starts to walk away from the pups when they try to nurse. This signals the end of their care-seeking and dependency phase of life and the beginning of a social life that will be concerned with self-maintenance and dominance and submission issues. The specific behaviors that the mother uses to discourage nursing not only have an immediate effect on the puppies, they also have long-term effects on their social interactions and emotional well-being.

Erik Wilsson of the Department of Zoology at Stockholm University studied six hundred German shepherd dog puppies and their interactions with their mothers during weaning, including the length of nursing, the number of inhibited bites, growls, and mouth threats that the mother used to prevent further nursing, and the mother's nibbling and licking of her pups. Some mothers used many more threatening behaviors to punish the pups when they tried to nurse. These punished puppies started to show passive submission behaviors by lying on their backs to be licked, and these submissive behaviors occurred earlier than they did in puppies whose mothers were not so threatening. Some of the mothers were extremely aggressive and continued to punish or threaten the pups even after they had backed away from her. Other mothers were gentler; they used fewer aggressive threats and rather attempted to paw their pups into submission. When the puppy finally gave a submissive signal, these mothers would often groom the pups by vigorously licking them afterward.

The severity of the mother's behavior during the weaning process has a lasting effect on how her puppies will ultimately behave with humans. Puppies from the litters that had been severely punished and threatened were less socially gregarious with people and were less likely to approach a stranger. The puppies from the gentler mothers were friendlier and also seemed less fearful in general. The puppies from the gentle mothers were also more likely to retrieve a tennis ball for a person during a "fetch" test. This is an important indicator of the ultimate trainability of the dog. Puppies that do not retrieve, or at least make a start at retrieving by running out after the ball, picking it up, and carrying it a few steps, are often much more difficult to train as adults. In fact, when Clarence Pfaffenberger was developing a set of puppy tests to select guide dogs for the blind, he found that retrieving was the best single test to predict whether a dog would eventually successfully complete the training program for visual assistance dogs.

The technique that the mother uses to change a puppy's behaviors from a dependency relationship to one oriented toward dominance and submission will clearly affect the mind of the growing dog for the rest of its life. Yet learning about dominance and submission is absolutely necessary for the pup's later social life. It can be argued that what a puppy is really learning when his mother nips or growls at him when he tries to suckle is not simply fear of a larger and stronger individual, but rather compromise. He is learning his place in the social order and learning to play the role appropriate for his abilities and rank. Research shows that if puppies are reared under completely nonpunishing conditions up to week ten of their lives, they prove to be virtually impossible to train. Thus a balance must be struck. The pup must be taught to respect authority and to understand the meaning of threats, but it must not be punished in an abusive manner, where his emotional responses will swamp his behaviors and interfere with his ability to interact with people and dogs later on in life.

The Juvenile Period

Earlier research suggested that the socialization period comes to a close at around twelve weeks of age, and the juvenile period begins next and extends to about six months of age. This is the time when the dog's social behaviors begin to take on adult form. However, we have come to understand that the end of the socialization period is not is clearly defined as we used to think. There are even some systematic differences among dog breeds, with some having more extended socialization periods. The degree of neoteny predicts some aspects of the socialization process. Dogs that appear to be more wolf-like, with longer narrower faces and pricked ears, seem to have more sharply defined socialization periods, while dogs that are more puppy-like, with shorter faces, large round eyes, round head, and floppy ears, seem to have longer socialization periods that don't end abruptly. For all breeds, the winding down of the socialization period is associated with an increasing fear of new places, new individuals, and new events. This fearfulness of unfamiliar things typically rises to a peak between twelve and fourteen weeks of age, makes the pups less willing to interact at that time, and seems to end the socialization period.

Although socialization to dogs and people may have been accomplished by four to twelve weeks of age, it is not yet fully set and it can be improved. Dogs that are well socialized at twelve weeks of age, but are then removed from the regular presence of humans and other dogs during the juvenile period, may well lose their socialization over time. A dog that was properly socialized but then denied opportunities to interact socially for a prolonged time will start to act just like a dog that was not socialized in the first place (although the chance of improving the behavior at a later date will be better). The socialization process needs to start during the critical period, but it must be strengthened by repeated periodic social encounters until the dog is six to eight months of age.

During this "late socialization period" the dog must be exposed to a variety of living things that it will encounter in its life. As a person you recognize that children, men with beards, men or women wearing hats, people in floppy raincoats, people wearing sunglasses, senior citizens, and people with canes, crutches, or wheelchairs are all humans. To a dog, however, each of these appears very different, moves differently, seems larger or smaller, with odd outlines and perhaps unreadable expressions. In the dog's mind, then, each of these unknown beings might be potentially dangerous and the dog may think its best course of action is running away, or he may prepare to defend himself. The dog must learn that each is human and not a threat. He needs to encounter farm animals, other pets, things that move but are not alive, such as floor fans, lawn sprinklers, and motor vehicles, and anything else that will be part of his daily life. He needs to be exposed to different environments and situations that require different social responses. For example, a dog jumping up to greet a person might be permitted in the friendly surroundings of your own living room, but it is not permissible social behavior when walking on the street.

Think of socialization, then, as a process that has several levels. The primary level is when the dog learns who and what he is in terms of his species and thus also learns with whom he should be socially interacting. This primary level must occur within a narrow window of time to be effective. The second level involves the dog learning about his social world, how to act in that world, what his society expects of him, and all of the rules and behaviors that allow him to become a member of a particular society. This second level is complex and probably will continue to evolve and strengthen throughout the dog's life if he is given proper exposure and experience—much the same way it does for us humans.

CHAPTER 10

The Personality of Dogs

DO DOGS HAVE PERSONALITIES? Are there predictable breed differences in personality? I can already sense some of my scientific colleagues cringing at the very thought of using the word "personality" when speaking about dogs. They might agree that some dogs are more or less excitable, aggressive, dominant, sociable, emotional, and so forth, but they would prefer to refer to these characteristics as differences in "temperament," leaving the word personality exclusively in human territory. Yet when these same scientists discuss the personality of a human being, they might summarize a person by using the same words—thus they might refer to Fred as being dominant, aggressive, and excitable, while Susan is sociable, unemotional, and passive. Whether we use the words temperament or personality, we are simply summarizing behavioral tendencies that emerge in a variety of different situations. Thus what we are saying is that we would expect Fred to be pushier and more likely to try to control situations than Susan. Personality is an interesting aspect of a dog's mental processes because the final product is a combination of both genetic influences and the individual's learning and personal history.

Dissecting Personality

Trying to find a meaningful way to describe a dog's or a human's personality has proven to be more difficult than one might imagine. There is a long history of psychological classification of people into personality types. Hippocrates, the Greek physician who lived around 400 B.C., categorized people into four personality types: the "sanguine" personality, which was cheerful and easygoing; the "melancholic" personality, which was depressed and moody; the "choleric" personality, which was aggressive and excitable; and the "phlegmatic" personality, which was calm and unresponsive. These four personality types seemed to make sense, and the labels have survived in our language to this day. Thus to be sanguine about something means to be comfortable and optimistic, melancholy is used to mean sadness and depression, phlegmatic is used to describe a person who doesn't say much, while the slang phrase "hot under the collar" comes from the phrase "hot and under the choler," which is used to describe a person who is angry and irritable.

Unfortunately, people (and dogs) usually don't fit into nice, discrete categories simply because their behavior patterns are too complex. Even trying to categorize someone as smart or dull is not unambiguous because many people have specific areas in which they show brilliance and others in which they appear to be almost witless. Take the case of Albert Einstein. Although a brilliant theoretical mathematician, a fine philosopher of science, and even a talented musician (he played the cello), he also had areas of mental incompetence. His weakness was simple arithmetic, and his addition and subtraction skills were so bad that his personal checkbook was always completely out of agreement with the records of the bank. I have also known an extremely brilliant research chemist who couldn't follow a simple recipe to bake a cake and a renowned clinical psychologist who can't figure out the first steps in housebreaking his dog. Depending upon the circumstances, then, all of these individuals have a combination of tendencies toward intelligent and inept behaviors.

Today behaviorists tend to measure a large variety of specific behavioral predispositions and assign a score to each. We can't call these predispositions abilities, since they are behavioral tendencies rather than skills, so they are called "personality traits." These traits tend to form natural and meaningful clusters or groupings of behaviors that psychologists refer to as "personality factors," but you can think of a factor as a general personality characteristic. Something as simple as describing how "sociable" an individual is has at least three separate aspects, namely: (1) being gregarious and inclined to seek out the company of others; (2) being friendly and pleasant to others; or (3) offering opportunities for informal social interaction. Each of these traits may exist to a different degree, and the combination of the three gives us the strength of the sociability characteristic in a person. When talking about dogs, we might want look at sociability in other situations, such as the way the dog interacts with (1) family members, (2) children, (3) strangers, and (4) other dogs. Each of these traits has important consequences and affects the strength of the general canine sociability characteristic.

This analysis of personality-specific traits combines to give us a general score that indicates how strongly any individual will show a particular personality characteristic. Thus rather than trying to sort dogs or breeds into separate categories (such as sociable or not sociable), we could rank order them. For example, we might say that golden retrievers are more sociable than boxers, who are more sociable that Akitas.

Canine Personality Traits

Several scientific studies have used this trait approach to rank different dog breeds on particular personality characteristics. The first major problem in measuring the personality of dogs is how to collect the data. Earlier studies tried to isolate commonly observed behaviors that might reflect personality differences in dogs. They then surveyed groups of professionals who work with dogs and have presumably had opportunities to observe these characteristics in the various breeds.

Probably the classic study based on collection of data from professionals who know dogs was conducted in 1985 by Benjamin and Lynette Hart, now with the Center for Animal Behavior at the University of California at Davis. When attempting to collect their data, however, they found that not all dog experts could provide the needed information.

The Harts initially decided that the best judges of dog personality would be dog obedience judges, dog show (conformation) judges, professional dog handlers, and veterinarians in small animal practices. But in preliminary interviews, they found that the conformation judges were reluctant to rate breeds against one another because they felt that this might create a perception of bias later on, when they would be called to select winners from groups of different breeds. The professional dog handlers also were not that helpful, since most tend to handle only a few closely related breeds and felt that they did not have the kind of broad overview that the researchers needed. In the end, the Harts collected data from forty-eight dog obedience judges and forty-eight veterinarians, who were asked to rate the fifty-six most popular dog breeds (according to American Kennel Club registrations).

Each expert was asked to rate the dog breeds on thirteen different personality characteristics, namely: general activity, excitability, excessive barking, aggression toward other dogs, snapping at children, dominance over its owner, territorial defense, watchdog barking, destructiveness, playfulness, demand for attention, trainability, and ease of housebreaking. An example was given to make it clear what each characteristic represented. For instance, data on excitability was asked for in the following way: "A dog may normally be quite calm but can become very excitable when set off by such things as a ringing doorbell or an owner's movement toward a door. This characteristic may be very annoying to some people. Rank these breeds from least to most excitable." There was generally a good degree of reliability and agreement on rating the various breeds on most of the behavioral tendencies, although the agreement on ease of housebreaking, destructiveness, and demand for attention was low. The data then was subjected to extensive computer analysis and several important findings emerged.

One of the more interesting results was that some personality differences depended upon the sex of the dogs, and these transcended any breed differences. Overall, male dogs were more likely to show dominance over their owners and more aggression toward other dogs; they were more playful, had higher general activity and territorial defense, and were more likely to snap at children. On the other hand, females were better at obedience training and ease of housebreaking, and they also were more demanding of affection. Males and females showed no differences in excitability, watchdog barking, or excessive barking.

Below is a brief overview of the ratings of various breeds for eleven of the thirteen personality characteristics (we'll talk about trainability issues later). It lists those dogs that are highest (top 10 percent) and lowest (bottom 10 percent) in each characteristic. Within each grouping, the breeds are also listed from higher to lower.

The first dimensions that we'll consider are associated with activity and excitability.

General Activity

High: silky terrier, Chihuahua, miniature schnauzer, fox terrier, Irish setter, and West Highland white terrier

Low: basset hound, bloodhound, bulldog, Newfoundland, collie, and Saint Bernard

Excitability

High: Scottish terrier, Yorkshire terrier, silky terrier, miniature schnauzer, West Highland white terrier, and fox terrier

Low: bloodhound, basset hound, Newfoundland, Australian shepherd, Chesapeake Bay retriever, and Rottweiler

Excessive Barking

High: Yorkshire terrier, cairn terrier, miniature schnauzer, West Highland white terrier, fox terrier, and beagle

Low: bloodhound, golden retriever, Newfoundland, Akita, Rottweiler, and Chesapeake Bay retriever

In these activity and excitability traits we find a large number of terrier breeds scoring in the high range, whereas hounds and the big blocky dogs like the Newfoundland tend to score in the low range. This dimension of personality seems to be very important to the quality of the human-dog bond in families. A recent survey of dog owners in Melbourne, Australia, suggested that the most commonly reported behavior problems about which dog owners complained were overexcitement (listed by 63 percent of owners) and a specific behavior associated with overexcitement, namely jumping up on people (listed by 56 percent of dog owners). Rushing at people and excessive barking were two other indicators of the same high degree of excitability that dog owners complained about.

Next let's consider some traits or behavior characteristics that seem to be associated with dominance and aggression.

Aggression Toward Other Dogs

High: Siberian husky, West Highland white terrier, Scottish terrier, chow chow, fox terrier, and miniature schnauzer

Low: golden retriever, Newfoundland, Brittany spaniel, bichon frise, Shetland sheepdog, and bloodhound

Snapping at Children

High: Scottish terrier, miniature schnauzer, West Highland white terrier, chow chow, Yorkshire terrier, and Pomeranian

Low: golden retriever, Labrador retriever, Newfoundland, bloodhound, basset hound, and collie

Dominance over Owner

High: fox terrier, Siberian husky, Afghan hound, miniature schnauzer, chow chow, and Scottish terrier

Low: golden retriever, Australian shepherd, Shetland sheepdog, collie, Brittany spaniel, and bloodhound

Territorial Defense

High: Doberman pinscher, Akita, miniature schnauzer, Rottweiler, German shepherd, and chow chow

Low: basset hound, bloodhound, Brittany spaniel, golden retriever, pug, and bichon frise

Watchdog Barking

High: Rottweiler, German shepherd, Doberman pinscher, Scottish terrier, West Highland white terrier, and miniature schnauzer

Low: bloodhound, Newfoundland, Saint Bernard, basset hound, vizsla, and Norwegian elkhound

Destructiveness

High: West Highland white terrier, Irish setter, Airedale terrier, German shepherd, Siberian husky, and fox terrier

Low: bloodhound, bulldog, Pekingese, golden retriever, Newfoundland, and Akita

While the traditional guarding dogs, such as the Doberman pinscher, Rottweiler, and German shepherd, appear to have relatively strong aggressive and dominance traits, several terrier breeds also show up with these characteristics, even though they are fairly small in size. The breeds that seem to show the lowest aggression and dominance traits in the Harts' data set are the hounds, retrievers, and large working dogs like the Newfoundland. Some people might wonder why the so-called "pit bull terriers" do not show up in these groupings, given the current popular beliefs about such breeds. At the time that this study was conducted, they were simply not that popular, and so they were not included.

This research did not specifically isolate a sociability trait, but did measure two characteristics that are associated with sociability, namely, playfulness and demand for affection.

Playfulness

High: standard poodle, Airedale terrier, cairn terrier, miniature schnauzer, English springer spaniel, and Irish setter

Low: bloodhound, bulldog, chow chow, basset hound, Saint Bernard, and Alaskan malamute

Demand for Affection

High: Lhlasa apso, Boston terrier, English springer spaniel, cocker spaniel, toy poodle, and miniature poodle

Low: chow chow, Akita, bloodhound, Rottweiler, basset hound, and collie

Finally, this study rated the trainability of various dog breeds. We will deal with these important characteristics later on, when we specifically discuss learning and intelligence in dogs.

Some two decades after the Harts' study, I conducted a similar piece of research, rating dogs on twenty-two behavioral dimensions. The purpose of that research was to see if there were characteristics in different breeds that would make them more or less compatible with particular human personalities. My research used information from ninety-six dog specialists, including veterinarians, dog trainers of several sorts, dog judges of all kinds (obedience, conformation, field trials, search and rescue, tracking, terrier trials, and so forth), several writers of dog books, some canine psychologists, and behavior analysts. This study tried to include all of the breeds that the American Kennel Club and Canadian Kennel Club had recognized in 1995, so that I could make a broader comparison of breeds. All of the professionals did not rate all of the breeds, but at least twenty rankings had to be obtained for a breed to be included in the data analysis. In the end this gave me useable data on 133 breeds of dogs.

I isolated the breeds that had the highest rankings on a composite set of traits that could be called dominance, aggression, and protectiveness. For convenience, let's just call these "highly dominant dogs." Since this is larger than the Harts' list, we will present the breed names alphabetically.

Highly Dominant Dogs

Akita
American Staffordshire terrier
Belgian Malinois
Belgian sheepdog
Belgian Tervuren
Boxer
Briard
Bull terrier
Bull mastiff
Chesapeake Bay retriever
Chow chow
Doberman pinscher
German shepherd
German wirehaired pointer
Giant schnauzer
Gordon setter
Komondor
Kuvasz
Maremma sheepdog
Puli
Rhodesian ridgeback
Rottweiler
Schnauzer
Staffordshire terrier
Weimaraner

There is a good deal of overlap between this list and that of the Harts. The major difference is that my sample of professionals tended to rate the smaller terriers as being less dominant, aggressive, and protective than in the earlier study. This could be because more breeds were rated here. It is certainly the case that many of the smaller terriers ranked well above average for these personality traits, but they were not in the top grouping.

This research specifically addressed a number of characteristics that dealt with sociability, including friendliness and affection displayed toward family, children, strangers, and dogs. The top breeds on this trait are:

Sociability

Airedale
Beagle
Bearded collies
Bichon frise
Border terrier
Brittany spaniel
Cavalier King Charles spaniel
Clumber spaniel
Cocker spaniel
Collie
Curly-coat retriever
English cocker spaniel
English setter
English springer spaniel
English toy spaniel
Field spaniel
Flat-coated retriever
Golden retriever
Irish setter
Keeshond
Labrador retriever
Miniature poodle
Newfoundland
Nova Scotia duck toller
Old English sheepdog
Portuguese water dog
Pug
Soft-coated Wheaten terrier
Standard poodle
Tibetan terrier
Vizsla
Welsh springer spaniel

Again the group is larger than the Harts' simply because the breed sample is larger. Perhaps the most interesting aspect of this data is that there is no overlap between the breeds rated as highest in dominance and those rated highest for sociability. This suggests that the professionals that I surveyed probably viewed protectiveness and aggressive tendencies as being the opposite of sociability. This might even suggest that in the minds of my judges this was one single dimension, with dominance at the one pole and friendliness at the other.

While such rankings by knowledgeable authorities are useful, the fact that one set of experts can give a somewhat different interpretation of dog personality than another suggests that outside factors may influence personality assessments. These may well involve the circumstances and situations in which these professionals interact with dogs, because situations do affect the appearance of personality traits. Thus a German shepherd might be quite dominant and pushy at home around his own family but much less so at work or around strangers. An example of how different judgments can be is shown in rating the trait of excitability in the Old English sheepdog, which was ranked 5 by obedience judges and much lower, at 35, by veterinarians. For excessive barking, German shorthaired pointers were ranked 4 by obedience judges but only 43 by veterinarians. For territorial defense, Dalmatians were ranked 6 by obedience judges but a very low 53 by veterinarians. Thus, as with people, the personality traits shown by dogs may vary depending upon the situation in which they find themselves.

Testing Personality Objectively

A number of researchers have been trying to get more consistent and perhaps more objective personality ratings of dog breeds by testing dogs under controlled and uniform conditions. Such test results are difficult to obtain and involve a lot of time and expense. Imagine trying to test fifty dogs of each of the approximately one hundred and sixty breeds registered by the American Kennel Club. That means that there would be eight thousand dogs to test. Testing four dogs a day for five days a week (with no time off for vacations) would involve more than seven years of research!

Fortunately, temperament testing of dogs has been conducted for many years by centers that are involved in the selection of service dogs—specifically police dogs, explosive and drug detection dogs, search-and-rescue dogs, guide dogs for the blind, hearing-assistance dogs, and so forth. It is our good luck that records have been kept of all of the dogs tested by some of these centers. Probably the largest such data bank was assembled by the Swedish Working Dogs Association from 235 test locations over the period 1997 to 2000. In total, standardized behavioral tests were given to 15,329 dogs representing 164 breeds. This data was then statistically analyzed by two ethologists, Kenth Svartberg at Stockholm University, and Bjorn Forkman at the Royal Veterinary and Agricultural University in Frederiksberg, Denmark, and this research gives us the best picture that we have of dog personality to date.

The assessment they used is called the "Dog Mentality Assessment Test," which was developed mainly as a tool to assist people who were trying to improve the breeding of working dogs. The idea was that by using the test results, the behavioral reactions of the puppies could be compared to that of their parents to see which personality characteristics were passed on genetically. The test was soon adopted by many breed clubs in Sweden, who use it as a general test of dog temperament.

The procedure involves exposing the dogs to several different, novel situations. The dog's reactions are then evaluated by specially trained observers using a standardized score sheet. Ten subtests are given in a fixed order so that each dog has the same experience and the data can be compared across breeds and testing centers. Each test is set up in advance at different stations along a path in a wooded area, which allows many dogs to be tested in a short period of time. For each test, a judge observes and scores the dog, and several assistants are also needed to perform various functions.

The complete battery includes tests of sociability, such as the social contact test, in which the dog's reaction to meeting a stranger is assessed. Playfulness is measured by the dog's willingness to play with a friendly stranger. The dog's chase instinct is tested by noting its reaction to an erratically moving furry object. The dog's response to passive restraint is tested by tying him on a leash 10 meters (33 feet) away from his handler for three minutes. The dog's boldness and self-confidence are measured in several tests: In one, a human-shaped dummy suddenly pops up in front of the dog; in another a chain is drawn across a sheet of metal to make a loud metallic sound in a location near the dog; in another there are gunshots; and in the "ghosts" test the dog is approached by two slowly moving people with white sheets over their heads. In each of these tests the dog can show a variety of different reactions, including being momentarily startled, being fearful and avoiding, being aggressive or threatening, or being confident and exploring the strange objects and situations that it is presented with.

The most important finding that emerged from the data analysis was that the personality structure of dogs seemed to be described by five basic personality traits: sociability, curiosity versus fearfulness, playfulness, instinct to chase, and aggressiveness. There was one quirk in this classification: in retrievers and spaniels, playfulness and sociability seem to merge into a single trait.

Using the breed groups of the Federation Cynologique International (FCI), certain comparisons could be made across groups of dog breeds. Companion dogs and the sheep-and cattle-herding dogs (excluding the livestock-guarding dogs) got the highest scores for playfulness. The least playful dogs were the so-called *primitive breeds,* those dogs that seem to be closest to wolves or other wild canines in both their physical and behavioral characteristics. The most common of these are the spitz breeds, which include the majority of the Nordic sled and hunting dogs. (It is often said that if you take a northern wolf and curl its tail, then you effectively have a gray Malamute or a Siberian husky.) The second group of primitive dogs includes the Basenji, Carolina dog, and Canaan dog. Because the primitive dogs are close to the "wild-dog type," it is not surprising to find that they are not playful. These dogs are also quite low in sociability. They seem to be very high in their chase instinct and also in overall aggressiveness. In contrast, the northern spitz types are quite sociable in spite of a low playfulness rating.

There was a lot of overlap between the traits, so these researchers conducted a further statistical analysis and found that you could combine all of the traits, except aggressiveness, to form a broad personality characteristic that they called the "shyness-boldness continuum." Dogs that are high on this personality trait are bold dogs, who are usually very active, interested in other dogs and people, curious, and relatively fearless when faced with novel objects and strange situations. Dogs that score low for this trait are shy dogs that tend to be uninterested in play, who are timid, cautious, and evasive in unfamiliar situations. Other research has shown that this shyness-boldness continuum is also found in wolves, which suggests that our efforts at domesticating dogs have simply moved various breeds up or down along a temperament trait that has remained "evolutionarily stable." When we consider different dog breeds along this continuum, we find that the boldest were the Belgian Malinois, commonly used as police or detection dogs, the Labrador retriever, and the flat-coated retriever. It was somewhat surprising to find that pinschers, along with the smooth-coated collie, and the Rhodesian ridgeback, were among the shyest of the breeds.

The importance of this personality dimension was demonstrated in a separate piece of research in which Svartberg concentrated on German shepherds and Belgian Tervurens (which are very similar to the Belgian Malinois, only with a longer coat). Here he was studying whether an individual dog's personality characteristics, specifically its standing on the shyness-boldness continuum, could predict the dog's performance on tasks that are necessary for dogs used for military and police work. Among such required tasks are tracking, searching, carrying messages, and protecting the handler. One interesting result of this research is that it verified that the males were bolder than the females. The results also showed a breed difference, with the German shepherds being the bolder of the two breeds. The main finding, however, was that the dogs with the highest boldness scores, regardless of their sex or breed, tended to do the best when trained for service work. Bold dogs seem easier to train as working dogs.

Genetics and Personality

The studies just discussed point out that there are breed and sex differences in personality. Sex and breed are genetically determined, so we must assume that personality is also genetically determined, at least to some extent. Breeders who claim that they are breeding for temperament as well as for looks and soundness of structure work on this assumption. Sometimes this is done quite casually, such as in the case of Mrs. L. M. Wood of Victoria, British Columbia, who began the Melita kennel line of cairn terriers. Cairns are an interesting breed of small terriers that sometimes display a tendency to be pushy and a bit dominant, which can make them somewhat confrontational at times. Mrs. Wood did not like that trait in her dogs. Since she kept them in large group kennels, she could observe them interacting. She would selectively breed only the dogs that were fairly easygoing and did not show any spontaneous aggression against the other dogs. Over the approximately forty years that her kennel was in operation, she eventually developed a line of cairn terriers that were quite prized by cairn terrier fanciers—not only for their looks but for their placid, amiable personalities.

More systematic data showing a genetic determination of dog personality has come from several other sources. One interesting study was conducted by Anthony Podberscek of the Department of Clinical Veterinary Medicine at Cambridge University and James Serpell of the School of Veterinary Medicine of the University of Pennsylvania, who were specifically studying aggression in English cocker spaniels. Although this breed has been quite popular, in the early 1980s it suffered from some negative publicity that focused on its aggressive tendencies. At the same time, Roger Mugford, founder of the Animal Behaviour Centre in England, published some reports in which he noted that English cocker spaniels were the third most likely breed to be referred to his clinic for behavioral problems. Perhaps the most interesting aspect of his report was that 74 percent of the cockers with aggression problems were red or golden solid-colored dogs. This is particularly interesting because coat color is clearly genetically determined.

Podberscek and Serpell decided to test Mugford's clinical observations systematically. They obtained data on 1,109 English cocker spaniels and were able to confirm that coat color was linked to personality in this breed. They found that solid-colored dogs were likely to be more aggressive in a variety of situations than varicolored or particolored dogs. Among the solid-colored cockers, the reds and goldens were much more likely to be aggressive than the blacks. Males were also more likely to be aggressive than were females. These results clearly link genetically determined characteristics of dogs to the personality trait of aggression.

A team of researchers from the Institute of Animal Genetics, Nutrition and Housing at Berne University were also interested in whether various temperament traits were genetically transmitted. They used a sample of 3,497 dogs, tested over the period of 1978 to 2000 by the

Swiss German Shepherd breeding club. This club had also been using a standardized test to select dogs that had the stability, self-confidence, and resilience that would make them good service dogs. The club obviously believed that there was a strong genetic determination of the dog's personality because members used the scores on these tests to determine which dogs would be allowed to breed, believing that the breed would be strengthened by controlling the genetic contribution of dogs with undesirable traits.

These Swiss researchers confirmed that genes contributed significantly to all of the personality traits that they measured. Furthermore, the selective-breeding program for personality seemed to be working. Over the twenty-two years when this data was being collected and used to determine which dogs would be bred, a modest but steady improvement occurred in most of the personality characteristics measured. In recent years, the rate of improvement dropped off, perhaps because the earlier improvements may have reached a ceiling. Thus, today, only about 8 percent of the dogs are failing the test, which means that any changes made in the gene pool by selecting breeding dogs on the basis of test scores will be small.

Mix-and-Match Personalities

In an earlier chapter we mentioned Jasper Rine of Berkeley, who is working on the dog genome project, mapping the genetic code of dogs. Rine began his research with a border collie named Gregor (after Gregor Mendel, the nineteenth-century monk credited with inventing the science of genetics) and a Newfoundland named Pepper (because she is black), who then were bred to each other. Gregor and Pepper, along with their seven offspring (scientifically labeled as the F1 generation), along with 23 grandchildren (the F2 generation), are part of an extended attempt to identify canine genes using the most up-to-date techniques for investigating DNA.

Rine chose border collies and Newfoundlands for two reasons. First he wanted dogs that were, behaviorally and physically quite different. Second, the dog genome project wanted to have its puppies cared for by volunteer families living in and around Berkeley, so the pups would have to be appealing in some way. Each family that adopted one of these pups had to agree to raise the puppy properly and keep it for the dog's lifetime (or return it to Rine). In addition, if the pup was a female they had to agree to let her have litter of her own with a father selected by the members of the project.

In personality, the breeds are very different. Newfoundlands are easygoing and affectionate dogs, protective of people, loyal, not easily startled by noises or distracted by things going on around them. They are not overly active and would rather walk than run. Border collies are much the opposite. Although they can be friendly enough, they are much more devoted to their work than to the people around them. They are intense and focused but can easily be upset by sudden, attention-grabbing events going on around them. When you enter a room, a Newfoundland will nudge you, demanding that you give it attention and affection, but a border collie is more likely to acknowledge your arrival with a glance and then return to its task of trying to herd the cat.

When Gregor and Pepper were mated, their puppies (the F1 generation) were rather a blend of the five personality indicators that the project studied: demand for affection, excitement barking, startle response, sociability with other dogs, and likelihood of staring or "showing eye," which is a dominance behavior used to exert influence over other animals and people. In general, the puppies fell somewhere between their parents, more affectionate and easygoing than their border collie father but more intense and excitable than their Newfoundland mother. However, when members of the F1 generation were mated to each other (to create the F2 generation), the personality traits began to sort themselves out in unique, unpredictable mixtures. One of the F2 puppies seemed to be very demanding for affection and not easily startled (both Newfoundland personality characteristics) but was not very sociable around other dogs, seldom barked, and used lots of threat stares (border collie personality traits). Another pup was very affectionate with people and sociable with other dogs (Newfoundland characteristics) but made lots of dominant eye contact and startled easily (collie traits). His barking at home was still a mixture of the characteristics of his grandparents, more than a collie but less than a Newfoundland. The twenty-three members of the F2 generation exhibited just about every combination of the personality characteristics of their grandparents. These characteristics had averaged out in a sort of a mishmash in their F1 parents, but as the genes recombined, some personality emerged in recognizable form and strength again, only in combinations never seen in the purebred grandparents.

Although modern studies like this one may eventually tell us which genes make a Newfoundland affectionate and which make a border collie startle easily, the practice of manipulating dog personality has been around for quite a while. I once saw an eighteenth-century manuscript from a monastery in France that was known for the quality of dogs that it bred. The manuscript specified rules for breeding in terms that seem quaint today. Specifically, the monks were instructed to focus their selective breeding efforts on those dogs that showed the highest degree of "Christian traits," such as loyalty, affection, cooperation, and, most important, obedience.

Looking for the Perfect Guide Dog

Clarence Pfaffenberger, one of the most important figures in the development of training and selection programs for guide dogs for the blind, demonstrated beautifully how systematic and selective breeding can produce dogs with particular personality traits. In the mid 1940s, when he first became involved in guide dog selection and training, only 9 percent of the dogs enrolled successfully finished the training program. Pfaffenberger was disturbed by this low success rate and began to develop a series of tests of learning and problem-solving ability to predict which dogs would best learn the complex obedience tasks associated with guiding the blind. He found, however, that intelligence was not enough. Dogs that passed, or even excelled, in learning and problem-solving intelligence were still failing the course. He then discovered that personality factors were equally important. To be a good guide dog, the animal had to have not only adequate intelligence but also an appropriate set of personality characteristics.

Pfaffenberger applied these concepts by selecting and breeding for *both* personality and intelligence. By the end of the 1950s, he had raised the percentage of dogs that successfully completed the program from 9 percent to 90 percent! The appropriate pattern of personality traits allowed some dogs to apply their full range of intelligence in such a way that they became excellent working and obedience dogs, while other dogs had certain personality characteristics that interfered with their ability to achieve a useful level of functioning.

Pfaffenberger kept careful records during his systematic breeding program for guide dogs. Since each dog and its parents were tested for both intelligence and personality (particularly fearfulness, aggression, sociability, and motivation to work), this gave him objective information about the genetic transmission of both. His records show that many personality characteristics, including the willingness to work for humans, are carried genetically. He demonstrated that the personality of a litter was directly predictable from the personality of the sire and dame. His scoring system for willingness to work used a scale that ran from a low score of 0 to a high score of 5. In one instance he took a German shepherd named Odin, who achieved the highest possible score of 5 on this dimension, and mated him with a female of the same breed named Gretchen, who had achieved a score of 4, expecting that all of the resultant puppies would have temperaments that fall between these values. When he administered tests to the six puppies in the litter, four of them scored 5 and the remaining two scored 4. Thus the personalities of the parents were passed on to the offspring.

The genetic component in dog personality also explains certain regional differences in dog breeds. Doberman pinschers and Rottweilers that have been bred in North America tend to be somewhat calmer and less likely to initiate aggressive action than dogs that have been bred in Europe. This seems to be the result of a deliberate attempt on the part of North American breeders to tone the breeds down a bit, to make them more acceptable as pets, while some European breeders seem to prize and select for what is sometimes called "temperamental fire," a euphemism for a willingness to display aggressive tendencies.

When Personality Goes Wrong

Perhaps the best evidence for a genetic contribution to the personality of dogs comes from looking at personality extremes. Dogs are actually being used to study the genetic basis of a number of personality disorders. Karen Overall of the Veterinary School at the University of Pennsylvania and Gregory Acland at Cornell University feel that dogs and people share a number of psychological problems based upon disordered personalities. For example, fearfulness and separation anxiety in dogs are very similar to certain social and attachment anxieties in humans. Fearfulness also shares some characteristics of certain "generalized anxiety disorders" in people. Furthermore, dogs respond to some of the same kinds of treatments that work for humans.

Panic disorders, irrational fears or phobias, impulse control disorders that lead to aggression, and obsessive and compulsive behaviors appear, not only in people, but also in dogs. The DNA of dogs and humans is sufficiently alike that scientists feel that if they can map the location of the genes that produce certain personality defects in canines, this may help identify the genes for the human counterparts to these psychological problems. Along the way, we may also learn something about the genetic nature of normal personality.

Selective breeding allows us to create dog breeds that will have physical and behavioral characteristics we desire. This process sometimes requires a great restriction in the size of the gene pool. For instance, we choose a dog that has the qualities we want and mate that dog with another with similar qualities, but which also happens to be the daughter or sister of the chosen sire. Obviously, this kind of inbreeding will often perpetuate the traits that we want, but this inbreeding also allows the effects of harmful recessive genes to emerge. Often, after several generations of inbreeding of lines of purebred dogs, the pups will start showing genetically based behavioral and physical problems that had not been in evidence before.

For the psychologist and the geneticist, any extreme or abnormal behaviors are a special opportunity to study how heredity plays a part in complex behaviors. It is easier to study these issues in dogs because they are far more genetically homogeneous than virtually any human population. This research is also greatly helped by the fact that dogs produce many more offspring than humans, hence the chances are greater of eventually producing dogs with the characteristics researchers want to study. The task of sorting out the genetics of complex traits is not simple, but it is a lot easier when you can study them in populations that can be inbred and crossbred in the laboratory.

The line of research that looks at the genetic contribution to personality problems in dogs began in the 1940s. A well-known clinical psychologist, Frederick Charles Thorne, studied a basset hound named Paula, who could be described as shy, easily frightened, and nervous, and who would try to bite any stranger who extended a hand toward her. The human equivalent of such behaviors would be considered evidence of *social phobia* and *generalized anxiety disorder*. Nonetheless, Paula, who was handsome by basset hound standards, was frequently bred and produced a large number of offspring. It also became clear that this "fear-biting" dog had passed on her extreme and undesirable personality traits. Of fifty-nine dogs that were genetically related to Paula, forty-three (that is, 73 percent of them) were shy, unfriendly, and avoided social contact with humans. Thorne's analysis suggested that this was the result of a dominant gene and felt that this personality trait would not be responsive to modification using the usual training and learning techniques.

Since Thorne's report, the most researched line of dogs with a personality disorder has been the progeny of Appalachian Annie, an English pointer who produced a line of so-called "nervous pointers." Annie was so fearful that she could not be used to hunt, was not a good house companion, and seemed to be subject to fear and panic attacks whenever she was approached by humans. A group of psychiatrists and psychologists at the University of Arkansas at Fayetteville and the Veterans Administration Hospital in Little Rock acquired Annie and began to selectively breed a line of fearful pointers in the hopes that they could use these dogs as test subjects in studies that might eventually lead to a cure for neurosis. Although the usual behavioral treatments did not work, the line has been kept going because it provides what is called an "animal model" for this behavioral disorder.

These poor creatures are truly fearful dogs. I got to visit one of them named April. She was in a large kennel where she and her littermates were being studied. When I entered the kennel the dog first acted startled, but unlike a normally startled dog who will dash away and try to hide, April just froze in place. Her pupils dilated, the muscles around her jaw tightened, and the muscles on her sleek flanks constricted to such a degree that she began to tremble. Her front legs were widespread, her back somewhat arched, and her tail was tucked well under her body in the perfect example of canine panic. Having been around many frightened dogs before, I used all of the techniques that usually work to calm a dog. Frozen in fear, April did not move when I gently stroked her head and silky ears. Even after I left her and ducked around the corner to observe her while staying out of sight, she remained immobile. It was several minutes before she slowly turned her head to check out her kennel and probably to verify that I had really gone. A blood sample taken immediately after this interaction verified that she had high levels of cortisol in her system. This is a hormone released by the adrenal glands in response to major stresses.

Not all of the pointers in April's litter have her problem, since she is the result of mating dogs who themselves were the result of mating normal and nervous dogs. Like the other personality traits that we have discussed, the recessive fearful genes that were carried by her grandparents or great-grandparents will show up only in some individuals. Most of April's littermates, who had been reared in this same laboratory setting, acted quite normally and demonstrated the usual friendly English pointer temperament. They ran toward me when I approached, responded with jumps, licks, and barks when I fondled and stroked them, and followed me around as I moved among them. They clearly wanted to continue playing and seemed disappointed when I exited their kennels, with one or two of them giving plaintive "come back" barks to try to entice me to return.

There is a high likelihood that the selective breeding process used to create good pointers is what led to the existence of these nervous, panic-frozen dogs. Pointers have been selected to point, to find a bird, look directly at it, and then remain motionless in that posture. At the behavioral level, psychologists recognize that pointing behavior is similar to an "orienting response" that becomes frozen. An orienting response (sometimes called the orienting reflex) can be thought of as a "What is it?" reflex. It involves a collection of bodily responses that assist in "receiving" the stimulus and "taking it in" to be processed further. The head and eyes turn toward the stimulus. If the ears can move, they turn in the direction of what has caught the dog's attention. The dog's nostrils flare to suck in more scent and he is tuned to observe and monitor any changes that occur in or around the target of interest. The pointing trait may actually represent the selective breeding of dogs that have an abnormal orienting response. Pointer breeders have known for years that, even in the best lines of hunting dogs, some with the best and earliest pointing behaviors can be too nervous and fearful to become reliable hunting dogs. This is the fact that eventually leads us to back to Appalachian Annie and April. It seems likely that the genes that produce the pointing behavior and the genes that produce nervousness may be linked. A normal dog will orient toward a bird, rabbit, or other prey and then either chase it or simply turn away and go back to its original activity. A neurologically normal dog (other than a pointer) does not stay frozen in an orienting posture with head and eyes pointed directly at the object being hunted. It appears that the very act of breeding for a dog that will freeze to point at a bird also makes it more likely it may also freeze in panic in response to many other events.

Rage Syndrome

Many breeders do not recognize that when you choose to breed for a specific feature, whether a behavioral or a physical characteristic, you may also be selecting some unwanted and unexpected traits. For example, some springer spaniels appear much more likely to bite without warning than other dogs. These bites occur most commonly in social situations, and the dog's owners claim that they happen with no advance warning. Such behavior is unusual, since in most cases of dominance-related aggression dogs gradually increase the level of threat, giving clear signals at each step along the way. They usually start with a stare, moving to a growl, then to a lip curl, next to a warning snap usually with no contact or a greatly inhibited bite, and only at the end of this sequence do the dogs finally resort to biting. This usually gives the target of the threat plenty of time to retreat and for both individuals to avoid actual physical conflict. In springer spaniels, however, the dogs seem to move from the first-level threat stare (often later described as a "glazed look") to the full-blown attack, skipping all of the intermediate stages. As with human beings who show aggressive outbursts without warning, this is thought by psychologists to be evidence of a lack of impulse control, which leads to a behavioral overreaction. These aggressive outbursts are startling, violent, and unexpected and they have received the label "Springer Spaniel Rage Syndrome."

When rage syndrome in dogs was studied by Ilana Reisner, who is now at the Veterinary School of the University of Pennsylvania, she found that the most severe cases could be traced back to a common bloodline, suggesting a genetic component. This seemed to be confirmed in part by the findings that the biochemistry of these aggressive dogs was different. Many of the dogs she studied seemed to have abnormally low amounts of serotonin in their systems. In humans, low serotonin levels have also been found in violent mental patients and prison inmates with a history of violent assaults on others. Serotonin, one of the neurotransmitters found in certain pathways of the brain, seems to have a calming effect on mood. Research suggests that, in most mammals, increasing the amount of serotonin decreases the amount of aggression that appears during dominance conflicts.

When you look at the dogs that descended from the bloodlines that have demonstrated rage syndrome, you cannot help being struck by how elegantly they move and how self-assured they seem. This may be the problem. Springer spaniel breeders want dogs that strut in the show ring, holding their heads far to the front while moving with a body posture that suggests that they are virtually lunging forward. Several genes seem to have to work together to produce this appearance and gait. The desired movement pattern looks similar to hunting and attacking motions, so it may well be that the very genes that give the dog this elegant strutting posture also supported active offensive physical onslaughts in the dog's evolutionary history. Thus to get a breed with a desired movement pattern, we may have fostered a race of springer spaniels that are subject to impulse-driven aggression.

A myth that is probably traceable to Jack London's books—for instance, *Call of the Wild*—suggests that northern dogs, like the malamute or Siberian husky, have an aggressive temperament because they are "primitive dogs," similar to wolves in nature. The truth of the matter is that the northern breeds that are used to pull sleds need a sense of cooperation and teamwork, so not surprisingly they score quite highly on objective tests of sociability. On long journeys, the dog that has started in the lead position is routinely rotated to another position (or even out of the harness for a while) to keep the animal from exhausting itself. Socially dominant and aggressive dogs would find this unacceptable and might fight if they felt that their status was being challenged by being shifted out of the lead position. Sled dogs were bred to work cooperatively and to show deference to anyone who assumes or is placed in a position of leadership. In the case of some Siberian huskies, selectively breeding a dog for deference can lead to exaggerated shyness.

A line of shy Siberian huskies has been maintained by Gregory Acland of Cornell University. They are descendants of a handsome dog named Earl who was donated to Acland's research project by the breeder, who found the dog to be painfully shy. Earl could be comfortable with his owner, but around strangers he became fearful and avoided social contact. Acland used selective-breeding techniques to see if this shyness was, indeed, genetically based. First he mated Earl with a female beagle, then a shy female from that litter was mated with an unrelated male beagle. In that second generation litter there were two very shy males, confirming that this personality characteristic was genetically transmitted. Successive breedings showed that different offspring varied in their degree of shyness, however, which means that several genes are probably involved and these pool their effects in a sort of average to produce this personality profile.

The shy huskies show different patterns of anxiety from the nervous pointers. Rather than the virtual freezing in panic of the nervous pointers, the huskies seem to have the same kind of fearfulness and submission that might be found in any other dog, but to an exaggerated extreme. When I met one such shy Siberian husky, whose name was Cinder, he immediately skittered to the back of the kennel, turning his head away to avoid any eye contact and to avoid any suggestion of challenge. This is much like the behavior of a very submissive dog when threatened by a dominant one. Even though I moved very slowly with soft, high-pitched, reassuring words, the dog still avoided me. He slicked his ears down and lowered his head when I reached for him, and then tried to hide in the corner of the kennel, pushing backward against the wall, head still turned away, but now a nervous stream of saliva began to dribble from a mouth that appeared to be tightly clenched. He was obviously frightened and unhappy but not frozen into immobility the way that April had been.

Evidence suggests that the basis of the unusual behaviors in both the pointers and huskies is similar to that of extreme anxiety disorders in humans. If they are given a small amount of lactic acid, a harmless substance that gives milk its sour taste and accumulates in our muscles to make them ache after exercise, it triggers a massive anxiety attack for both the nervous pointers and the shy huskies. This is exactly the same response that humans with certain panic disorders exhibit when given the same substance. Over time, with daily contact, a person can develop a more comfortable relationship with the shy huskies (although their first response to strangers will always be fearful). The nervous pointers, however, remain virtually unapproachable and seem never to be comfortable with anybody, no matter how familiar they might be.

Studies of dogs with rare and extreme personality disorders such as these are important because they demonstrate the degree to which a dog's personality is controlled by genetic factors.

Puppy Personality Testing

Since there is a large genetic component in a dog's personality, observations of a puppy's behavior should be able to predict his later adult behavior. In fact, puppy temperament tests are used by some breeders to select dogs that would most suitable for a particular family or a specific environment. Much of the data supporting the accuracy and usefulness of early puppy personality tests was based upon small or selected samples, but some of the results are quite intriguing. For example, Pfaffenberger claimed that a young puppy's willingness to retrieve playfully thrown objects was the best single indicator of whether he would grow up to be a good working dog, and he used this as one of his tests in selecting dogs that would be trained as guide dogs for the blind.

The first systematic, large-scale attempt at evaluating the personalities of puppies to predict the behaviors they would have as adult dogs was the Fortunate Fields Project, which operated in Switzerland in the 1920s and 1930s. This was a philanthropic organization whose objective was to develop the perfect service dog—not only for use as a guide dog, but also for other purposes. The only dog breed tested was the German shepherd, but the project created an elaborate testing system that included a number of personality tests suitable for any breed of dog.

The well-known animal psychologist William Campbell (who was one of the founders of the American Society of Veterinary Ethology) extended the work of Pfaffenberger and the Fortunate Fields Project and eventually created a simple set of tests that could be used by breeders and dog owners. Campbell looked at four personality traits. The first was *excitability vs. inhibition,* where a more excitable dog is very responsive to any form of stimulation while an inhibited dog is much more self-controlled. The second was *active vs. passive defense tendencies,* where an active response to a threat is biting while a passive one is less confrontational and involves freezing or running away. The remaining two dimensions indicated whether the dog was *dominant vs. submissive* in social settings and a *sociability* factor that measured whether a dog sought to make contact with people or was independent and more of a loner.

Perhaps the most popular personality test for puppies was developed by the talented and innovative dog behaviorists Joachim and Wendy Volhard. Their "Puppy Aptitude Test" took elements from of its predecessors (Fortunate Fields, Pfaffenberger, and all of Campbell's tests) and added two tests suggested by Elliot Humphrey and Lucien Warner for working dogs, one for *sound sensitivity* (a sound-sensitive dog becomes fearful around loud sounds such as gunshots or shouted commands) and *touch sensitivity* (a touch-sensitive dog can be difficult to train, since any collar or leash correction can set off the dog's defensive reactions). The Volhards integrated these into one system with an easily interpretable scoring system. Although some dog behaviorists have modified the testing procedures or scoring for some special purposes, the Puppy Aptitude Test remains the most popular personality-testing procedure in North America and is used by many breeders and prospective dog buyers who are evaluating puppies before choosing one from the litter.

Recent scientific studies have questioned the usefulness of puppy temperament testing. The largest test of whether puppy temperament tests predict adult behavior was conducted by Erik Wilsson of the Department of Zoology at Stockholm Univerity and Per-Erik Sundgren of the Department of Animal Breeding and Genetics at the Swedish University of Agricultural Sciences. They used records from a set of objective behavioral tests originally developed by the Swedish Army School and later standardized by the Swedish Dog Training Center—one of Europe's largest centers for training and breeding service dogs since the 1930s. It produced and trained most of the police dogs, guide dogs, protection dogs, and narcotic detection dogs used in Sweden.

As part of the selection process, all puppies were tested to see if they had the temperament that would make them good service dogs. The test focused on personality characteristics that vary considerably among eight-week-old puppies and which seem to be part of most other puppy tests—sociability, independence, fearfulness, competitiveness, general activity, and exploration behavior. It also included a retrieving test similar to that used both by Pfaffenberger and the Volhards. Following testing, the puppies were placed in private homes and brought back to the center for further testing (and perhaps selection for one of the training programs) between the ages of fifteen and twenty months. Data were collected from 630 German shepherd pups, and the temperament test scores from the test given at eight weeks were compared to those given at approximately a year and a half. The result was rather disappointing, since there was no evidence that the puppy scores predicted the adult personality. Several other studies using smaller samples have arrived at much the same conclusion.

When Personality Testing Works

The reason for the seemingly surprising failure of early puppy personality testing is that, although a feature may be genetically determined, it may take some time for it to show itself. A clear physical example of this is the pattern of human male balding, which is genetically determined but may not be measurable until a man reaches the age of thirty and in some men not until the age of fifty or older. The same sort of delayed appearance occurs in some dog personality traits. Although the genes that may cause a certain adult pattern of behavior are present, they might not show themselves clearly enough to be measurable in a puppy.

A stable personality pattern in dogs seems to take time to emerge. The genetic research on personality characteristics of German shepherds at the University of Berne noted that even some of the more clearly displayed genetic traits, such as self-confidence, continued to change over the dog's lifetime. In their data they saw a steady increase in the self-confidence of dogs between the ages of eighteen and thirty months. In fact, the dog might not reach his final, stable level of self-confidence until almost five years of age. This makes predictions based upon puppy testing considerably less reliable for this aspect of personality.

Research by Michael Goddard and Rolf Beilharz at James Cook University in Australia focused on fearfulness in dogs, which seems to be an exception in its predictability, since it can be predicted by temperament testing as early as twelve weeks of age. Fearfulness is a particularly important personality trait, since it is the most common reason why dogs are disqualified from guide dog programs. Predictions are much more reliable, however, if they are taken at six months of age. In other words, although this aspect of temperament can be detected in early puppy testing, testing an older dog gives a better picture of what the adult personality characteristics will be.

In the large study of Wilsson and Sundgren, which found that puppy testing at the Swedish Dog Training Center did not accurately predict adult personality, the researchers went on to test 1,310 German shepherd dogs and 797 Labrador retrievers on ten personality dimensions. However, these dogs were somewhat older, between fifteen and twenty months. This age is important since the dogs were out of the puppy stage, when so many changes occur so quickly, and by then much of their personality has likely been set. With this later testing, the results are quite different and much more useful and reliable. Personality tests given at this age turned out to be good predictors of how these dogs would perform as service dogs. The predictions were sufficiently reliable to allow the researchers to determine which combinations of personality traits would help the dogs to succeed (or fail) when assigned to learn a specific job. These same test results, when taken from these adolescent or young adult dogs, can also determine which would become the most successful as human companions.

Personality Is More Than Genes

Even though personality tendencies have a large genetic component, a dog's adult personality is also shaped by his early experiences. Clarence Pfaffenberger demonstrated that the conclusions of early puppy temperament tests can be invalidated by the presence or absence of adequate socialization. He began by testing a large group of puppies for their personality traits and then selected a group of 154 pups that all passed the tests at around seven weeks of age. If the test results were valid predictors, these are the dogs that should have had the genetic personality predispositions to successfully complete the guide dog training program.

Prior to testing, all of Pfaffenberger's dogs had been kept in a kennel, with very little extended contact with people. Each dog that passed the puppy test, however, was placed in a home for about a year. There they were socialized, learned basic obedience commands, and developed emotional bonds with people. At seven or eight weeks of age, when the testing was completed, the puppy would be right in the middle of a sensitive stage where contact with people is vital if they are to avoid becoming shy or insecure around humans. Unfortunately for the dogs, it was not always possible to find a home for each dog immediately after evaluation of their test. Pfaffenberger discovered that when all of the dogs were later brought back for training, it was their early socialization experiences that predicted whether they had the temperament to complete the program successfully. Of the puppies that had passed their tests and had been placed in homes within a week of their assessment (they would be around eight weeks of age), 90 percent completed the training program and went on to become guide dogs. Those dogs who were in the kennel more than one week and less than two weeks after testing (at between nine and eleven weeks of age) fared almost but not quite as well, with about an 85 percent success rate. In those dogs left at the kennel more than two weeks but less than three (they would be about twelve weeks of age), there was a massive drop in their ability to make it through the program, and only a bit more than half of them would be able to finish and be placed as guide dogs. Finally, of those who were in the kennel more than three weeks after the tests (older than twelve weeks), less than one-third would make it through the training and graduate as guide dogs. The usual reasons for rejection were fearfulness, overexcitability, shyness, aggression, or lack of cooperation.

The importance of this study is that every one of these dogs had already passed a puppy temperament test that concluded that they had the basic personality to do the job for which they had been bred. Their life history, not their genetic heritage, ultimately determined what their true personality would be. Breeds and breeding make a difference, but they merely favor or predispose a dog to achieve a certain temperament. There is more difference between individual dogs in any given breed than there is between breeds and bloodlines.

Does this mean that one cannot predict the personality of a puppy at all when they are still young and in the litter? This is one of those yes-and-no answers that scientists are wont to come up with. All other things being equal, the heritability of many personality traits means that observing the personality of the sire and dam should give you a good idea of the predisposition and the potential of the personality of the pups. This, at least, can guide you to the *litters* that are most likely to have the perfect puppy to meet your requirements. As for selecting among the puppies in the litter, the sex of the puppy will make a difference. Research shows that males are more likely to be stable and less easily frightened and to have a higher drive and stronger motivation to accomplish tasks. At the same time, males are also apt to be more socially dominant, to have a higher defensive tendency, and to be more likely to respond to threats with aggression.

Looking more closely at the differences among the pups, research shows that the larger puppies in the litter are apt to be more dominant, have higher drive, be less likely to overreact to negative events, and also have a stronger defensive reaction as adults. Although these size differences predict for both sexes, their importance is even greater in female pups. Finally, the pups that are most excitable and most fearful while still in the litter are likely to grow up to be the most excitable and fearful as adults. How extreme any of these differences are, however, will depend upon the early rearing conditions and degree of socialization that the pups receive once they are out of the litter and in their new homes. In essence, although genes will bias a puppy toward a particular personality pattern, the breeder and the puppy's new owner will ultimately get to shape much of the dog's personality by the experiences and socialization that they provide for it in the early days of its life.

CHAPTER 11

Emotional Learning

As a psychologist, I know that it is impossible to talk about the mind of a dog without also dealing with the issue of learning. As a trainer, I also know that it is more important to understand how and why dogs learn rather than to understand any one training technique.

A lot of fine books give step-by-step instructions on how to train a dog. Yet, glancing through them will show you that there is no consensus on the best way to teach Lassie to sit or Rover to follow a scent trail. Fifty or sixty years ago, most dog training was based upon jerking on the collar to correct errors and praising for appropriate performance. We have come a long way since then. Today's training techniques include "click and treat," "motivational-drive training," "play training," "behavior capture training," "physical prompting," "lure-reward," "autotraining," "shock collar training," and many others. All of them work, at least to some degree, and their effectiveness depends upon how efficiently they incorporate the basic laws of learning.

If you know how and why dogs learn, you do not need to be tied to any one training technique. You can try different approaches to different problems and settle on the methods that work best for your dog and your situation. For this reason I will try to give you some idea of the basics of canine learning, including some data that suggests that the ways that dogs learn may be much more similar to the ways that people learn than has been hitherto suspected. In these discussions I will try to avoid as much technical and scientific jargon as possible (which may greatly annoy some of my scientific colleagues) in order to give you a clearer picture of what is actually happening. Where it seems relevant, however, I will use the appropriate vocabulary.

Breeds and Learning

There is a general consensus that all breeds of dogs do not learn at the same rate, at least as measured by their responsiveness to human attempts to train them. The study by Benjamin and Lynette Hart that measured personality characteristics also asked ninety-six experts (veterinarians and dog judges) to rank fifty-six breeds of dogs from the easiest to the most difficult when it came to obedience training. According to their results, the breeds in the highest and lowest 20 percent when it comes to trainability (listed in order from most trainable down) are:

High: Australian shepherd, Doberman pinscher, Shetland sheepdog, standard poodle, German shepherd, miniature poodle, English springer spaniel, golden retriever, collie, Chesapeake Bay retriever, Labrador retriever

Low: Pekingese, Pomeranian, pug, Chihuahua, West Highland white terrier, beagle, basset hound, Afghan hound, fox terrier, chow chow

Approximately ten years later I conducted a larger survey that looked at 110 different breeds of dogs. In this study I ranked the working and obedience ability of dogs, which corresponds to what most people would call "trainability." According to my experts, 199 dog obedience judges (approximately half of all the dog obedience judges in the United States and Canada), the top 20 percent in trainability were (moving down in rank):

High Trainable:

Border collie
Poodle
German shepherd
Golden retriever
Doberman pinscher
Shetland sheepdog
Labrador retriever
Papillon
Rottweiler
Australian cattle dog
Welsh corgi (Pembroke)
Miniature schnauzer
English springer spaniel
Belgian Tervuren
Schipperke
Belgian sheepdog
Collie
Keeshond
German shorthaired pointer
Flat-coated retriever
English cocker spaniel
Standard schnauzer

While the bottom 20 percent were:

Low Trainable:

Dandie Dinmont terrier
Petit basset griffon
Vendeen
Tibetan terrier
Japanese chin
Lakeland terrier
Old English sheepdog
Great Pyrenees
Scottish terrier
Saint Bernard
Bull terrier
Chihuahua
Lhasa apso
Bull mastiff
Shih tzu
Basset hound
Mastiff
Beagle
Pekingese
Bloodhound
Borzoi
Chow chow
Bulldog
Basenji
Afghan hound

The results of these two studies overlap to a remarkable degree, especially when you consider that the second study ranked nearly twice as many dog breeds. Some general trends: retrievers (the poodle is also a retriever), herding dogs, and working dogs appear to be the most trainable, while hounds and terriers appear to be the least trainable.

Little data exists beyond expert rankings about the learning ability of various breeds. Nonetheless, some data can be gleaned from the results of obedience trials and competitions held by various kennel clubs. The number of obedience titles awarded to each dog breed appears to be consistent with the experts' rankings. However, one must be cautious in interpreting the data, since a breed that is more popular would also be expected to win more titles than a less popular breed simply because there are more dogs out there to compete in obedience trials.

As a casual experiment, I selected a breed that scores high on both my experts' rankings and those of the Harts and also a breed that scores low, but with the restriction that both breeds had to have roughly the same number of registered dogs in the American Kennel Club. It turns out that the golden retriever and the beagle fit these criteria. Randomly choosing two months from the current year, I counted the number of obedience titles awarded to each breed, using obedience titles rather than actual performance scores since any one dog can earn a title only once. In this comparison, golden retrievers were awarded 29 obedience titles while beagles received only 3. That means that a golden retriever is nearly ten times more likely to win an obedience title than a beagle, although there are approximately the same number of dogs of each of these breeds in the country. In addition, for the current year I found that, of the 25 top-scoring dogs in the country, 11 were golden retrievers, and according to the records that I have available (which go back over fifteen years), there has never been a beagle in the top twenty-five obedience dogs in the U.S.A.

Please note that I am not picking on beagles out of any dislike of the breed. In fact, I currently live with a wonderful, pleasant beagle, Darby, and would not give him up for any reason. He is difficult to train, however. His problem, and perhaps the problem for many of the other dogs ranked low on the trainability list, has more to do with personality, I believe, than intelligence. Most dogs that are lowest in trainability are breeds that are easily distracted and have been genetically programmed to place a higher priority on certain behaviors that may interfere with their being taught new skills. For my beagle, Darby, which is a breed that has been bred to respond to and follow smells, a fascinating scent wafting from the ground will dominate his consciousness more effectively than the sight and sound of his trainer. Once his attention is captured by an interesting smell, he is more apt to wander off in the direction his nose takes him, rather than keep his mind on learning the obedience task at hand.

Although breed differences in learning ability certainly exist, all dogs are trainable. Some will require more work, however, because of cognitive or personality predispositions, but with adequate effort and appropriate training techniques the vast majority of dogs can learn enough to adapt to their environment and to successfully integrate themselves into the human and canine worlds. For some dogs, however, their ceiling or maximum performance may be limited by the simple practical consideration that an owner has only so much time and effort to devote to any one dog's education. Genetic considerations will also define which kinds of skills a dog is most likely to learn easily. To give the beagle his due, he will learn to track better and more quickly than a golden retriever, even though his performance on obedience exercises that depend on quick responses to human signals may be considerably inferior to that of his blond counterpart. Regardless of any one breed's predispositions or abilities, the basic principles that form the foundation for learning are the same for all dogs.

Kinds of Learning

When talking about learning, we are really talking about some form of relatively permanent change in behavior that comes about as a result of the dog's experiences in the world. This change can be the deliberate result of training or just the end product of the dog's interactions with his world. More than two hundred years ago, the philosopher John Locke concluded that we learn by association—a connection that we mentally establish between events that occur in some sequence. For example, if you see and smell chocolate and then eat some and find it satisfying, the next time you see and smell chocolate you will expect that eating it will be satisfying again.

You can form two types of associations. The first is the association between two stimuli or sense impressions, while the second is the association between some action or response that we perform and its outcome. These two forms of association come about because of different types of learning. An example of learning the association between two stimuli is the case where our experience is that a flash of lightning is always followed by a loud crack of thunder. After a while, a flash of lightning makes us tense in anticipation of the noise that is to follow. This kind of learning is called "classical conditioning." The word "conditioning" is just psychological jargon for learning, and "classical" is applied because it was the first form of learning to be that was systematically and scientifically studied.

"Operant conditioning" is learning the association between a stimulus and a response. For instance, we learn that pushing a button on a vending machine causes a candy bar to be delivered to us. It is called operant conditioning because we learn what happens when we perform certain operations or actions. Although we must consider each a separate kind of learning, both kinds are often involved in the same task.

Learning the Meaning of Stimuli

Classical conditioning was first systematically studied by Ivan Petrovich Pavlov, a Russian physiologist who devoted the first twenty years of his scientific career to the study of the digestive system, including the role that saliva played in the early phases of digestion. This work was so important that it won him a Nobel Prize in 1904. Despite the prestige associated with this great award, he is most remembered not for his studies of digestion but for his experiments on learning, which he conducted for thirty years after winning the Nobel Prize.

Pavlov's learning research started with a casual observation. He was studying the salivary secretions in dogs and knew that when he put food into an animal's mouth it would always salivate. He also observed that when he worked with the same dog on several occasions, the dog would begin to salivate when he observed things associated with food, such as the food dish, the sight of the person who normally brought him food, or even the sound of that person's approaching footsteps. Pavlov could have dismissed this observation simply by saying, "It is nothing more than the fact that the dog is now expecting to get some food, and that expectation causes his mouth to water." Instead, he recognized that the dog's response showed a special form of learning and involved a response that couldn't be controlled voluntarily. For example, if I would say to you, "Make your mouth water," you would find it virtually impossible to set up a constant flow of saliva simply by willing it. Pavlov realized that something special had occurred: An involuntary action (salivation) that is usually triggered only by a certain class of stimuli (food) was now being controlled by a new stimulus (the sight of the experimenter). In other words, an association had been formed between the sight of the experimenter and food, and the visual impression of the experimenter has come to produce much the same effect on the dog's behavior as food itself.

Pavlov studied this process using a simple procedure. During training he presented a neutral stimulus (one that doesn't cause the dog to salivate), such as the sound of a bell, immediately before he propelled a bit of meat powder into the dog's mouth with a puff of air to trigger salivation. A few repetitions of the sequence "ping—puff—slobber" would then be followed by a test with just the sound of the bell. Sure enough, the sound of the bell, which originally had no effect on the dog, would now cause the animal to salivate. What the neutral stimulus was made no difference; it could be a click, a light, a drawing of a circle, a touch on the rump, or anything else. The important thing was that now the dog was responding to it as if it were the meat powder—by salivating. The dog doesn't have to want this to happen, or participate actively in the learning process; it will just happen on its own.

You can demonstrate a simple classical conditioning experiment with a willing friend. Have your friend sit down. Stand or sit close enough to his face so that you can gently blow a puff of air into his eye. When you do this, his eye should blink. Now take a spoon in one hand and tap it against a cup. This pinging sound is a neutral stimulus, so the eye should not blink. Now set up a training sequence in which you tap the cup and then immediately puff some air into the person's eye, giving you the training sequence "ping—puff—blink." Repeat this a number of times and then simply tap the cup without puffing any air. After a few repetitions, the person's eye will most likely blink in response to the tap on the cup even though the person may have no awareness of any conscious intention to blink. You have just classically conditioned an eye blink.

Emotional Learning

Why should we care about training our dogs to drool on cue, when many of us are already bothered by the amount of drooling that they do naturally? The truth of the matter is that we are not interested in drooling or eye blinking but rather in another class of behaviors. The real importance of classical conditioning is that it is the way in which we learn to attach emotional responses to things.

The most famous example of how classical conditioning can produce learned emotional responses was provided by John Watson, the founder of the school of psychology known as Behaviorism. At Johns Hopkins University, Watson conducted an experiment that would never make it past the ethical review panel in any of today's research institutions. He took an eleven-month-old baby named Albert and showed him a white rat. Albert demonstrated no fear of it at all. Next Watson showed Albert the rat while behind the baby a hammer was banged against a piece of metal to cause a loud clanging sound. This startled Albert, frightened him, and caused him to cry. After a few repetitions of this sequence of "rat—clang—fearful cry," just the sight of the white rat would cause him to cry and try to crawl away. He not only acted afraid of the rat, but now Albert seemed to be afraid of any furry objects, including white rabbits, stuffed toys, fur coats, and even a Santa Claus beard. Watson concluded that he had classically conditioned the emotion of fear and attached this emotion to furry objects in Albert's mind. Notice that Albert did not have to want to learn, or actively participate in trying to learn this fearfulness; it happened automatically simply due to association of the stimuli with something that triggered his emotional response. A sad footnote to this story is that Albert's mother became so upset that he had now learned a new set of fears that she removed him from the experiment before Watson could complete the process, which would have involved removing those learned fears.

While the strength of most classically conditioned behaviors tends to increase if there are a number of repetitions or practice trials, when the strength of the emotion or the intensity of the stimulus is strong enough, this form of learning can sometimes occur after only a single event. For example, to a naive dog the sight of a porcupine is neutral. But if he runs up to it and gets a face full of quills, then this very traumatic event causes great pain and fear. After that single sequence, "porcupine—quills—pain and fear," it is likely that the sight of a porcupine will cause signs of stress in the dog, and he is also likely to try to avoid them for the rest of his life.

In his classic book on training herding dogs, *The Farmer's Dog*, John Holmes gives another example of classical conditioning of a fear response with only one exposure. Holmes was walking across a field with one of his border collies when the dog dashed ahead to go through an open gate and collided with another dog coming toward him. So now we have the sequence "dog and gate—collision—pain and fear." Even though there was no malice intended by the other dog, from that time on this border collie would never go through that gate if that dog were visible.

An interesting application of the principles of classical conditioning is a procedure used to prevent wolves from preying on sheep. A freshly killed sheep is laced with a chemical that causes nausea and stomach cramps and then it is put out where wolves can find it. They eat some of the chemically spiked meat, which makes them nauseous. Given the sequence "sight, smell, and taste of sheep—eating—discomfort and nausea," and given the intensity of the physical symptoms, the next time the wolves see and smell a sheep, just the thought of eating it is apt to trigger those same twinges of stomach upset, which will cause the wolves to avoid them. This same technique has sometimes been used successfully to stop domestic dogs from killing livestock.

Learning Good and Bad

Classical conditioning of emotions explains why reward-based training procedures seem to work better and establish a stronger bond between the dog and his trainer than punishment-based systems. Every time you give the dog a treat or some other reward, you set up the event sequence "sight of you—treat—pleasant feeling." Even if your timing is off and you are not a very good and knowledgeable trainer, there is no harm being done in this case. Every instance of reward makes it more likely that the dog will feel better about you because you are actually conditioning the emotional response "sight of you—pleasant feeling."

The flip side of this coin is the use of punishment of harsh corrections. The sight of you, or your hand, or the training leash and collar immediately followed by pain or discomfort will ultimately come to be associated with negative feelings and avoidance. This was demonstrated to me when I visited a facility that trained protection dogs. The technique that the trainer was using was rather harsh and unpleasant, the idea being that dog should ultimately develop a distrust and antipathy for any strangers. This was accomplished by presenting the dog with a series of negative encounters with people he did not know, in order to classically condition the dog's aggressive feelings toward anyone with whom he was unfamiliar. I also noticed that when the trainers approached the dogs' kennels with the training collar in their hand, the dogs would retreat to the far wall and try to avoid having the collar put over their head. Clearly the trainers and the entire training scenario had come to be conditioned to produce unpleasant feelings. As I looked at these behaviors, I could not help but think of my own dogs, who have been reward trained (perhaps to excess) and who dance merrily around me and mill in front of the door with tails batting and eyes full of eagerness when they see me pick up the bag that contains their training gear or when I reach for their leashes. My dogs may not be the best trained or the most perfect performers in the obedience ring, but they do their exercises with joy because their numerous rewards and classical conditioning have caused everything associated with their training to produce positive feelings.

Classical conditioning also explains why some people think that dogs feel guilt. Consider the following scenario: A dog owner comes home and Lassie looks at him and slinks away and hides. The owner assumes that this is a guilty response and looks around the house for a transgression. Sure enough, Lassie has knocked over the garbage bin and refuse has scattered over the kitchen floor. A common response to this is to grab the dog, show her the mess, and punish her. What this does is to set up the classical conditioning sequence "sight of you and garbage on the floor—pain from punishment—fear." This means that the next time that you come home and both components are present (the sight of you and garbage on the floor), the dog will show its conditioned fear. It is fear that makes the dog slink away, not guilt. If you have a dog with this problem, you can demonstrate that the response is fear, not guilt, by tipping over the garbage yourself and letting the dog see it on the floor. Under these conditions a dog that has been punished for raiding the garbage will cringe and try to run. Obviously the animal feels no guilt for your actions, but the sight of you and that mess has conditioned him to produce a strong negative emotion.

There is an interesting practical application of classical conditioning to one of the most difficult common problems that dog owners have—namely, a dog that chews and destroys objects of value. The reason why this problem is difficult to deal with is that it usually occurs when the owner is away, so there is no one there to stop the dog and correct him. Punishing the dog after the event has little effect, since his transgression occurred well in the past and he is unlikely to associate the punishment with his actions. Punishment would just teach the dog to have negative emotions associated with the person who punishes them (via conditioning based on the sequence "trainer—punishment—pain and fear"). We can use a similar set of learned negative feelings, however, to solve the chewing problem if we attach those negative emotions to the proper objects.

Suppose that your dog has developed the problem of chewing your shoes when you are away. Your task is to make the sight and smell of your shoes (without you in them) trigger a negative feeling, much like the chemical in the sheep meat triggered nausea in the wolves. However, you have to find some way to make this work even when you are out of the house. Here is where classical conditioning of emotions works. You start when the dog does his first damage. Call the dog over to you and have him sit next to you. You may have to slip the dog's leash onto him if he frightens easily. Then show him the item that he chewed, or one that you don't want him to chew. Next (this will sound odd), while the dog watches, you angrily punish the *item*, slapping the shoe itself and yelling "No!" and so forth in a sham display of displeasure. Dogs tend to watch what we do and also to respond to our voice, motions, and other actions that signal our state of mind. This loud, angry display will cause a negative emotional response in the dog, but since his eyes are on the object you are hitting, that feeling is attached to the thing that you want the dog to leave alone and not to you. Thus the sequence of events is "sight of object—angry behavior—fear." You may have to repeat this several times over the next few days, but eventually it will produce the conditioned sequence "sight of object—stress and avoidance" in your dog. It does work, only I suggest that you don't do it when someone who has not read this book is around, since it may be difficult to explain why you are spanking your shoe while your dog looks on!

Teaching Love

Classical conditioning is the most powerful means of establishing a positive emotional bond with your dog. This works really well with young puppies that you want to socialize, with any newly adopted dog, or simply with a dog that you have had for a while with whom you want to strengthen your bond. There is no formal "teaching" involved. All that you have to do is to hand feed your dog for at least one meal a day. It will only take five minutes or so to do this, even though you are dispensing his food one kibble at a time. The process is quite simple. Take your dog's bowl up off of the floor. Talk pleasantly to him, show him a kibble, reach out and touch his body or tug his collar, then give him the bit of kibble. If he knows any basic commands, such as "come," "sit," "down," and so forth, you can mix these in, with a kibble for each performance. What you are doing is establishing an emotional bond using the sequence "your voice, sight of you, and touch—food—positive emotional response." Each piece of kibble then becomes a stimulus that triggers a good feeling in the dog and associates that good feeling with your presence. After a while it will require only your touch, the sound of your voice, or the simple sight of you walking into a room to give the dog a positive emotional feeling. I can't say that you have effectively classically conditioned your dog to love you, but you certainly will end up with a dog that wants to be around you because it makes the animal feel good.

CHAPTER 12

Skill Learning

WHEN MOST OF US THINK of learning we think of acquiring skills, such as learning to ride a bicycle, to solve arithmetic problems, or to be polite in social situations. These skills are acquired using a form of learning that links an individual's action to its outcome, called "operant conditioning." Most actions or responses are triggered by things that we perceive, so we are really looking at learning the sequence "stimulus—response—result." The action or behavior can be simple or complex, and the result can be something that we want or want to avoid. Learning to ride a bicycle gets you to where you want to go, learning arithmetic earns you good grades, and learning not to poke our fingers into candle flames keeps us from getting burned.

The basic principles behind operant conditioning are quite simple, but that does not mean that they are simple to apply to training a dog. After all, the basic principle behind playing the piano is simple—just press the keys corresponding to the notes that you want to hear—but years of study may be required before it is mastered. The basic principle behind operant conditioning is that any behavior that is rewarded will be strengthened and the likelihood that it will appear will increase, while any behavior that is not rewarded will be weakened and the likelihood that it will appear will decrease. That's it! To train a dog you do not have to understand the underlying neurological or chemical events, or know which brain centers and pathways are involved, but the "tricky" part is getting the animal to perform the behavior so that you can reward it. You also have to get that reward to him at the right time, so that the appropriate behaviors will be strengthened. This process sometimes requires a fair bit of time and effort. There are four main strategies commonly used in operant conditioning, all of which can be successfully applied to dog training. These are "behavior capture," "luring," "physical prompting," and "shaping." Each has its strengths and weaknesses.

Behavior Capture

The easiest form of training is sometimes called "autotraining" (because the dog seems to be training himself) but is more accurately called "behavior capture." In theory this technique is incredibly simple. You merely wait until the dog spontaneously performs the behavior that you want and then you reward it. To see how behavior capture might work, suppose that we have a puppy with the highly original name of Lassie. All that would be required is that you watch the puppy's activities carefully when you are interacting with her. As she begins to move toward you, say "Lassie, come" and then quickly follow it with a reward (perhaps a food treat or a pat). Similarly, when she begins to sit you say "Lassie, sit" and give her a reward. Make sure that you give the dog her reward at the end of each action, just as if she initiated the action at your command. The reward strengthens the association between the command words and the dog's actions. With a few repetitions, the command word will come to signify and trigger the action in the dog's mind.

A drawback to behavior capture training is that it might take a bit of time before you actually get the behavior that you want. Once the dog knows that there is a reward waiting if she engages in some kind of behavior, however, she will treat the experience as a pleasant game. It may take her a few "guesses" to deduce which behaviors produce the reward and which don't. Along the way the dog will make many mistakes, but this should not distress you. Although we normally focus on the importance of getting the response we want and then rewarding it so that it becomes stronger, the second aspect of the operant-learning principle, namely that unrewarded actions tend grow weaker, is equally valuable. Think of it this way: The more errors that your dog makes, the more she learns what is *not* rewarding. Ultimately she will eliminate the unprofitable options and start repeating the actions that you reward. Dogs really seem to enjoy this game, and it is simple enough that you can even get young children to join in the training process. This technique also works particularly well on fearful, shy, poorly socialized, and aggressive dogs, since it seems to focus their attention and calm them down.

Timing the reward can be difficult. Suppose that Lassie is coming toward me and I say "Lassie, come." I next have to rush out to give her a bit of kibble. My sudden movement may stop her approach, or she may even stop to wait for the kibble to arrive near her mouth. This means that the reward has actually interfered with or stopped the behavior that we want the dog to perform. The desired sequence of events is "the dog coming toward you—the reward—the positive strengthening effect on the approach behavior." Instead, we have "the dog stops because a reward is coming—the reward—the positive strengthening effect for the dog stopping or stopping at a distance from you." This is because the basic principle of operant conditioning is that it is the behavior that occurred *immediately before the reward* that is strengthened. What we need is a reward that doesn't stop the behavior, that can be precisely delivered to coincide with the behavior that we want to strengthen, and that can be delivered from a distance.

The creation of this special reward turns out to be straightforward and uses the classical conditioning of emotions to create "instant rewards." The reward will actually be a signal that makes the dog feel good and will not interfere with the ongoing behaviors. After all, it is the positive emotion associated with a reward, not the reward itself, that really strengthens the behavior that came before it.

To create a new reward, you must first decide what kind of signal you want to be rewarding. Over the past few years a click from a small handheld clicking device has become popular, but the signal can be nearly anything: a whistle, light, tone, word, or specific action. I prefer using my voice, since that leaves both of my hands free for other things. Words such as "Good dog!" or "Yes!" said with great enthusiasm work well.

Next we "charge" that signal with a positive emotional value via conditioning. The easiest way to do this is by using food. For instance, to make the phrase "Good dog" rewarding, you simply say "Good dog" immediately before giving the dog a bit of food. Now repeat this many times, setting up the classical conditioning sequence "Good dog—food—warm and happy feeling." After a few repetitions the dog will perk its ears and wag its tail happily at the words "Good dog." This means that you have classically conditioned this sound to produce a positive emotion in the dog, and it now can be used to reward new behaviors.

Technically you have created a "secondary reward," as opposed to a primary or unlearned reward, such as food. In a training situation you will often hear this referred to as a "secondary reinforcer," since this learned reward can be used to strengthen (reinforce) a behavior that you want the dog to learn. Most of the rewards used to control human behaviors are secondary rewards. Primary rewards are biological, such as food, drink, and sex. Secondary or conditioned rewards include money, grades in schools, praise, promotions, medals, awards, and titles. At first glance it may be difficult to see how these secondary rewards were learned, but if you trace back far enough you can find classical conditioning of emotions at the root. Working for good grades or awards is an example. When a mother feeds a baby she usually talks to the child. As she puts the food in the baby's mouth, she typically says something like "that's a good boy" or "good girl." The conditioning sequence is "praise ('good')—food—positive feeling." Being told that you are "good" thus becomes a conditioned reward that produces a positive emotion in you. Later you are told that you are "good" when you get a high grade on a test. Now the conditioning sequence is "grade—'good'—positive feeling." Soon the high grade itself will produce a positive emotional response. Notice that we are using a secondary reward to create a new secondary reward. This process is sometimes referred to as "chaining," and it explains why awards, titles, and public recognition all make us feel good and why we are willing to work for them. It may be quite a long chain of secondary rewards that ultimately leads back to the initial classical conditioning based on a primary reward. In the same way that people will work and learn to achieve these conditioned secondary rewards, dogs will work and learn for a happy "Good dog" or a click if these have been conditioned as secondary rewards and produce a positive emotional response.

Once we have created our secondary reward, the words "Good dog" or a click can be used to reward the dog while it is performing an action that we want it to learn. In the early stages the secondary reward will be followed by a primary reward to strengthen the association. As Lassie starts to move toward us, we say, "Lassie, come," quickly following it with the secondary reward, "Good dog." We will then follow the secondary reward with a treat after she actually gets to us. Some animal trainers call this conditioned sound a "bridging stimulus" because it serves to bridge the time gap from the instant that the animal performs the correct action to the moment when we can actually deliver the treat. These trainers often think of the secondary reward as a sort of an IOU or a message that tells the dog that "there is kibble in the bank waiting for your arrival." However, because of classical conditioning, the very sound "Good dog" is rewarding and produces its own positive emotion. It is useful to keep the secondary reward signal "charged" by maintaining an association between the sound and the food, but you don't have to continue to reward the dog every time you say "Good dog."

As the dog becomes more reliable, you can stretch things out so that she has to do several correct things before a primary reward. During the early stages of learning, giving a secondary reward followed by a primary reward every time you get the desired behavior seems to be most effective. The true importance of the secondary reward is that it can be used very precisely. You can say "Good dog" at exactly the moment the dog is performing the action. Since the reward is a sound, you don't have to be at arm's length (as you must to deliver a treat) and the dog does not have to stop her action to chew and swallow.

Behavior capture is particularly useful in teaching the dog activities that are difficult or impossible to enforce. For example, when housebreaking my dogs, I walk them down a familiar route. As soon as the dog begins to squat to eliminate I say, "Be quick," and repeat it once or twice during the elimination process while alternating with my secondary reward, "Good dog." The dog is then rewarded with a treat after the action is finished. After a couple of weeks, using "Be quick" as a command begins to cause the dog to sniff around to choose a place to eliminate. In this way, some aspects of the dog's elimination can be placed under control.

Lure Training

Lure training is another hands-off method of training your dog. It has one major advantage over the behavior capture method, in that you actually induce your dog to perform the actions that you want to reward, so there is not so much waiting around for something to happen. The lure in most cases is a bit of food, but it could be a toy or something else the dog wants. If the lure is something that the dog desires, then he will look at it, turning his head to follow its movements. If you can move the dog's head, then you can move the dog's whole body, so you can use lure training to teach body positions (such as sit, down, and stand) or to control the direction of the dog's movements (come, roll over, spin, go right, go left), and even to get him to focus his attention on specific objects or people that you want the dog to attend to.

To see how lure training works, suppose that you want Lassie to sit on command. If you can lure her to move her nose, the rest of her body will follow. First show the dog a treat, then slowly lift the food lure upward and backward. The path you are following with the lure is to move directly over your dog's nose and then take a high path between the eyes and move toward the back of the head. As Lassie looks up to follow the movement of the food, her rear end will naturally lower into a sitting position. Then, just as in capture training, you say, "Lassie, sit," followed immediately by "Good dog" and a treat. Then, release your dog with a happy "OK" or "All done" and a quick pat (these will automatically come to be the release command for any behavior). It is important that you give the treat and secondary reward before the dog gets up, so in the early stages of training you will have to be fast. Repeating this a few times, sometimes when the dog is at your side and sometimes when she is in front, will quickly give you a good reliable sit command.

Once your dog is performing reliably, you can begin to phase out the lure. First, mimic the luring movements with your hand but with no food visible, while still giving the verbal command. When the dog does what you want, she still gets the secondary reward of "Good dog," followed by the food treat. Next begin gradually to make your movements smaller, and soon the dog will be responding to the verbal command alone. When the dog is performing well, you should start to phase out the food—sometimes the dog will get only the conditioned words of praise, while at other times the animal will get both the "Good dog" and the food. Gradually wind down the number of food rewards, only randomly giving a treat for performing, but never wind down the secondary rewards. Those words of praise should be there virtually every time the dog does what you ask, since they evoke the same good feelings that an actual food reward does.

I particularly like both the capture and the lure-training methods because you train your dog without any assistance from the leash. This sets in the dog's mind the idea that he still benefits from obeying your commands even when he is not physically connected to you by the lead and even when you are some distance from him. This mindset is very helpful and gives you much more reliable control over your dog.

Physical Prompting

The most traditional way of training dogs has depended on leashes, collars, and *physical prompting.* For most people the first images that pop into their mind when they hear about dog training is the sight of someone popping or jerking on the leash to get the dog to heel, or tugging up on the leash while pushing down on the dog's rump to make him sit. This physical prompting seems like an easy way to get the dog to do what you want. It seems rational, since the learning principle is that the last behavior that the dog performed before it was rewarded is what will be strengthened, and prompting is forcing the dog to do what we want so that we can reward it. The truth is that physical prompting is really quite complicated and takes an experienced person to do well. Good timing, expert leash handling, and absolute consistency are needed, and most people need a lot of practice before they can master it.

When done properly—and that means with good timing, and in a *gentle*, *patient,* and *nonthreatening* manner—physical prompting can work. A side benefit is that, when done well, it involves direct handling of the dog, and with the trainer's hands all over their pet as part of the training, the bond between the owner and the dog will strengthen. Unfortunately, especially when used by novice trainers, it is seldom done well.

Let us be quite honest and recognize that a sharp jerk on the leash is unpleasant. Thus if we use leash tugs as prompts, we are conditioning unpleasant emotional responses to the sight of the leash and collar and perhaps also to the general setting associated with training through the process of chaining. If we combine an unpleasant leash jerk upward with a hard push down on the dog's rear, we are conditioning a negative emotion to our hand touch as well. Giving the dog a treat once he has actually achieved the sit position in this case may not be rewarding the act of sitting, but rather the act of his bracing or resisting our efforts when we try to get the dog into that position. In other words, we may really be rewarding the dog for trying not to sit. Finally, since the dog must be restrained by the leash throughout, we are not promoting good off-leash control but rather telling the dog that he only needs to respond to commands when we are physically connected to him because that is the only time that you can actually enforce your will and that is the only time that he gets any rewards.

The Ethics of Reward

Before moving on to other aspects of learning, I want to address the controversy that has arisen about the use of food in training. Inevitably, someone will object to the use of food, arguing that "If I use food for training my dog will only obey commands when I have food, and if he's not hungry he won't respond even if I have treats." Actually, food is given for every correct response by the dog only during the early stages of the training. Remember that you will replace the food lures with hand signals or verbal signals. You will also reduce the number of food rewards over time and replace them with secondary rewards such as "Good dog," which may sometimes be followed by a pat, and perhaps an alternative reward such as tossing a ball or some other occasional opportunity to play.

Another common objection asks, "Isn't using food just bribing your dog?" and this is often combined with "Shouldn't dogs obey you simply out of respect for you?" I recommend the use of food because it can be so many things—an effective lure, a reward, and a component in classically conditioning positive feelings. The word "bribe" used in this context has always bothered me, since it seems to imply something immoral. Giving politicians money to ignore ethical and legal considerations and support a proposal that might earn you a lot of money is certainly bribery, but how is it unethical or immoral for your dog to sit when you command him to do so? I look at food reward as payment for the work the dog has learned to do. Because you receive a paycheck at the end of the week, would it be fair to say that your boss had bribed you to work? Suppose your boss told you that you were no longer going to be paid for your work, since he expected that you would do your job simply out of respect for him. How long would you stay in that job? Food in training is simply the canine equivalent of a paycheck.

I suppose that the strangest objection that I hear to the use of food for training runs something like, "Isn't it demeaning to use food treats during training?" To me the word "demeaning" suggests that the dog must be embarrassed or shamed by receiving treats for his performance. Yet I have never had a dog appear unhappy or submissive simply at the prospect of receiving a treat as a training reward. My dogs seem to love the idea of food rewards and dance merrily around with tails gaily batting, and perhaps drooling a bit, when I bring out their training gear. If they feel that I am being stingy and giving treats that are too tiny or unappealing, they might show some unhappiness, but their behavior never suggests that they feel in any way demeaned.

In my mind the final word on using food to control a dog's behavior is probably also the first word. Think about how we domesticated dogs in the first place—they originally hung around the camps of our prehistoric ancestors simply to feast on the scraps of food that we considered garbage. Ultimately they were lured into the camp, not by yelling or displays of force, not because our hairy ancestors were charismatic and commanded respect, but because our ancient forefathers tossed bits of food to induce the ancestors of dogs to come close and stay with them. It might not be far-fetched to say that the contract that we humans have with dogs to obtain their loyalty and assistance is signed in food. By giving our dogs food treats for their obedience and their service, we simply honor that ancient contract.

Shaping

Some behaviors are unlikely to occur spontaneously, so they can't be capture-trained and they are too complex or have too many steps to lure the dog or physically prompt. To teach these we use a method called "shaping" or training by "successive approximations." To demonstrate the principle behind shaping, the famous Harvard University psychologist B. F. Skinner, who is credited with doing the research that led to our basic understanding of how operant conditioning works, used the example of how to train a dog to ring a bell on a distant wall.

First you must establish exactly what your target behavior will be. Here it would simply be pushing against the bell to make it ring. Next you break the behavior down into as many simple parts as is practical. Each of these simple behaviors will be trained by behavior capture and rewarded with the secondary reward (we'll stick with "Good dog") followed by a bit of food. The list of behaviors that have to be captured might look like this:

1. The dog turns its head away from you.
2. He turns his head away and in the general direction of the bell.
3. He turns his whole body in the direction of the bell.
4. He takes a step in the direction of the bell.
5. He takes several steps in the direction of the bell.
6. He moves one-quarter of the way to the bell.
7. He moves halfway to the bell.
8. He moves three-quarters of the distance to the bell.
9. He moves all the way to stand near the bell.
10. He goes to the bell and looks at it.
11. He brings his nose near the bell.

12. He touches the bell with his nose.
13. He pushes hard enough against the bell with his nose to make it move.
14. He pushes hard enough against the bell to make it give a sound.

Each step or behavior must be mastered before going on to the next one.

Several conditions must be met if the dog is to succeed. To begin with, each change in behavior has to be in small enough increments that the dog has a chance to succeed and to get his rewards. The secondary reward has to occur as soon as the dog makes the response that you want and before he moves on to something else. The real difference between good and great trainers is the precision of their timing of the secondary reinforcer. Good trainers must also be good observers; otherwise, they might miss behaviors that should have been rewarded. Training is a dynamic process. If the dog seems to be having difficulty with one step, then go back a step or two so that you can keep the momentum going. If the animal still has difficulty with one step, see if you can break it up into simpler parts that he can master. Each step should receive enough training to make sure that it is a reliable platform on which the next step can be built. However, once the dog masters a step, you must start on the next approximation to your target behavior, gradually fading your reward for the previous step and insisting that the animal move to the next behavior.

This kind of learning often moves very quickly at first but may slow down as the requirements become more complex. Flexibility on the part of the trainer is the key. The dog must receive enough rewards to keep him from getting frustrated or quitting. If any signs of anxiety appear, go back to a step that the animal has already perfected and then start moving on from there again. It is also important always to end a training session on a positive note, with the dog achieving a reward for whatever the approximation of the behavior he has achieved.

There is still some controversy about when you should introduce the actual command for the behavior. For simple behaviors like "Sit" or "Down," which don't have to be shaped, the command is given just as the dog is starting to perform the correct behavior. In the case of shaped response sequences, you often wait until the dog is reliably performing the action before starting to add the command. So when the dog dashes toward the bell and you know he is going to ring it, you would add the command, "Rover, ring it." I like to use a command from the beginning, such as an arm motion to prompt the dog to start moving, and then, when he is actually doing what I want him to do, I add the spoken command. In the final stages of learning, the dog will only get a reward when he performs the action on command, not spontaneously.

The Truth About Punishment

I am not a fan of punishment as a means of controlling a dog's behavior, not because it doesn't work, because it does if done right, but rather because it is so difficult to make it work correctly. The improper use of punishment can lead to some very negative psychological outcomes for the dog, and it can completely undermine the bond between the owner and the dog. In the nineteenth century punishment was the preferred means of training dogs; in fact, dog training was called "dog breaking." In his classic 1894 book, *Practical Dog Training,* which actually called such practices into question, T. S. Hammond described the situation this way:

> Nearly all writers upon the subject of the dog agree that there is but one course to pursue; that all knowledge that is not beaten into a dog is worthless for all practical purposes and that the whip, check-cord and spike-collar, with perhaps an occasional charge of shot or a vigorous dose of shoe leather, are absolutely necessary to perfect his education. (p. 1)

Punishment is simply defined as the opposite of a reward, namely something unwanted that happens when the dog performs a particular behavior. The early belief was that by punishing something we weakened the behavior and made it less likely to occur. The notion was that if you punished the dog for doing things that you did not want him to do, he would stop doing them. Today psychologists, behaviorists, and trainers use more effective ways to get rid of unwanted behaviors. One means is simply to remove the rewards associated with those behaviors, thus eliminating or technically *extinguishing* them. An alternative method is to teach the dog a behavior that is incompatible with the behavior that we want to eliminate, so that if he is doing what is rewarded, he can't simultaneously be doing what we don't want.

For example, if a dog jumps up when greeting a person, he is often simply seeking social attention. We inadvertently reward such behaviors by saying something to the dog, looking at him, touching him, and so forth, all of which constitute social attention and thus provide a reward and strengthen the likelihood that the dog will jump up in the future. Some dog-training books suggest painful punishment techniques to stop this behavior, such as kicking the dog in the chest as he jumps up or grabbing his front paws to hold him up and then treading on his hind paws to punish him. Many people who have tried these techniques can verify that all that they got as a result is bite marks on their hands and a dog that still jumps up.

To stop a dog from jumping, remove the reward and train an incompatible behavior. To remove the social reward, as the dog jumps up you simply turn your back and walk away without saying anything or making any eye contact. This effectively removes any possibility of a social reward for the moment. The dog will probably be puzzled and run around in front of you, and as he does so you simply say "Sit" to the dog. (Presumably, you have already trained him to sit on command.) After he is sitting in front of you, you can bend down, give him a pat, and say nice things to him. The sitting behavior is incompatible with jumping, since you can't sit and jump at the same time. Furthermore, you are rewarding the sitting behavior but not the jumping. After a while, you can anticipate the possibility that the dog might jump with an early "Sit" command as you enter the house. As the behavior of "sitting to say hello" becomes stronger (since it is systematically rewarded and jumping is not), the probability that the dog will greet you by sitting and waiting to be petted increases, without chest kicking, toe treading, or other punishment.

Most research has shown that what punishment does most effectively is that it momentarily stops behaviors. This can be useful if, during that lull in behavior, you can substitute another behavior that you want and reward it. One critical factor is the intensity of the punishment to use. Most people start with a mild punishment and simply continue escalating the intensity when that doesn't work. The problem with this is that dogs build up a resistance to the punishment and, starting with a low level, virtually guarantees failure unless your dog is particularly soft. The punisher must be sufficiently intense to reliably halt the behavior so that another behavior can be substituted. Starting gradually simply lets the dog build up a resistance to the punisher, and in the end you will need an even more intense punishment to be effective. However, nothing about punishment is easy. If the punisher is very strong or very frequent, not only will unwanted behaviors be suppressed but virtually all of the dog's behaviors will come to a grinding halt. A punished animal will cringe, cower, or freeze; it might even run away and try to evade the person doing the punishing. If the dog is not doing anything because it is immobilized by fear, then obviously we cannot capture and reward a better behavior until he starts to engage in active behaviors again. This means that the punishment has actually reduced our ability to effectively modify the animal's future actions. Furthermore, the dog may become so focused on, or swamped by, his negative feelings that he loses all understanding about which activity actually triggered the punishment, which completely defeats its use as a training aid.

Why Punishment Fails

For punishment to work it must not only be of the correct severity, but it also must instantaneously follow the unwanted behavior. Pamela Reid, a dog trainer and author from Toronto, describes an experiment that demonstrates what happens when the punishment is delayed even a little bit. A dog was allowed to enter a room in which there were two bowls of dog food on the floor and an experimenter sitting midway between them. One bowl contained a generic dry dog kibble and the other a meaty, very desirable canned dog food. There were three groups of dogs, each of which was allowed to eat the dry dog food but was punished for eating the canned dog food by being given a resounding smack with a rolled-up newspaper. The only difference between the groups was that in the first one the dogs were punished the moment they put their faces into the bowl of better food, while the second group was hit five seconds after they started and the third group had their punishment delayed by fifteen seconds. All of the dogs quickly learned to avoid the canned dog food. For the testing phase of the research the experimenter left the room and observed the dogs through a one-way mirror. On each day of the test period the dogs were again permitted to enter the room which contained both the desirable and less desirable bowls of dog food (but no visible experimenter), and each was allowed to do whatever it wanted for ten minutes. The dogs that had been immediately punished when they started to eat waited on average for about two weeks before succumbing to the temptation and eating the more savory food. The dogs whose punishment had been delayed for only five seconds after they began to eat the forbidden food succumbed in roughly half the time, at about eight days. However, the dogs whose punishment had been delayed by just fifteen seconds waited on average only three minutes before going to the better bowl of food.

Compare these results to the following situation: A person comes home and finds that his new white carpet now has areas of yellow and brown from Lassie using it as a lavatory. Lassie is dragged in, shown the evidence of her misbehavior, and soundly punished. How long ago had her bad behavior occurred? Most likely it happened hours ago, and yet the research suggests that punishment that is delayed by only fifteen seconds is virtually ineffective. A psychologist would refer to this as "noncontingent punishment," since there is virtually nothing to connect the punishment that the dog is now receiving to the behavior that triggered the punishment. Most probably, all that Lassie's owner did was classically condition a negative emotion to his walking in the door.

Yet some people insist that noncontingent punishment works. An example of this that still makes me wince when I read it comes from none other than William Koehler, a highly respected dog trainer in the 1950s and 1960s. He was the chief animal trainer for the Walt Disney Studios and also was an instructor for the U.S. Army K-9 Corps. In 1962 he wrote:

> If you come home and find your dog has dug a hole, fill the hole brimful of water. With the training collar and leash, bring the dog to the hole and shove his nose into the water; hold him there until he is sure he's drowning. If your dog is of any size, you may get all of the action of a cowboy bull-dogging a steer. Stay with it. I've had elderly ladies who'd had their fill of ruined flower beds dunk some mighty big dogs. A great many dogs will associate this horrible experience with the hole they dug. (p. 200)

Koehler really doesn't seem to care about establishing a contingency between the dog's action and the outcome, as becomes clear when he continues:

> It is not necessary to 'catch the dog in the act' in any of the above instances of correction. Be consistent in your corrections and your dog will come to find the smell of freshly dug earth quite repugnant. (p. 200)

It is in this last statement that we see what is really happening. Obviously pushing the dog's nose into the muddy water will not be connected to digging in the dog's mind, but as Koehler himself points out, the desperate fear of drowning in that place will certainly classically condition a fear response when he next encounters the smell of freshly turned soil. Clearly the intensity of the conditioned negative emotion when dealt with using harsh methods such as this will cause the dog to avoid a place, or an object, that is closely associated with these events. Of course, the owner is also associated with this event, and some of negatively learned emotion is bound to carry over and weaken the human-dog bond. As a result of such inhumane treatment, a sensible dog may try to escape and evade further contact with his owner or at least with his owner's hands. Another negative outcome is that it establishes the fact that aggression is not only possible but permissible between the dog and what he considers to be the rest of his pack. Thus such treatment may well turn an otherwise sound dog into a fear biter.

To my mind punishment, used by itself as a training technique, is at best very inefficient. A reward gives the dog explicit information, telling him "What you just did was correct." Punishment simply tells the dog that the particular behavior he tried was wrong and gives him no guidance or direction that might tell which behaviors are acceptable. This makes it a very ineffective way of teaching. While Thomas Edison, the inventor of the electric light bulb, could boast "If I find 10,000 ways something won't work, I haven't failed. I am not discouraged, because every wrong attempt discarded is just one more step forward," rest assured that your dog *will* be discouraged and will most likely simply quit trying. It is much more efficient, quicker, and more pleasant for you and your dog to capture a correct response on a single try and reinforce it with a reward, rather than to punish the dog dozens of times for errors committed without giving him a clue as to what he *should* be doing.

Time Out

Having dismissed punishment as a way of training, let me note there is one form of punishment that works for certain aspects of behavior control in dogs but which avoids many of the problems that I have mentioned. Up to now we have been talking about what is technically defined as "positive punishment," meaning that when the dog does something wrong, something bad and unwanted happens to him. Another form of punishment, technically called "negative punishment," is where inappropriate behavior causes something desirable to be taken away. In dogs what we take away is the opportunity for further rewards.

The actual technique will be familiar to some people who have had to deal with the behavior problems of children. It is called "time-out." It simply involves taking the dog out of the situation and putting him in a safe, quiet place by himself for a period of time. Dogs are very social creatures and just being around others, whether dogs or people, is rewarding for them. This means that a brief period of forced social isolation can be unpleasant and can be used to control their behavior. Socially isolating the dog removes any opportunities for play, affection, and social interactions. Besides all of the lost social benefits, taking the dog out of a training situation will also deprive him of any chance to earn additional rewards, such as treats or petting, that he might have gotten if he had been permitted to stay.

To be most effective, we will need a bridging stimulus that you can view as a conditioned or secondary punisher. I use the word "Enough!" although I have heard others use the phrase "Time-out." As with conditioned or secondary rewards, the exact sound that you use is unimportant, since whatever the chosen sound may be, it assumes its punishing quality by becoming associated with social isolation. Each time the dog shows the unwanted behavior, you immediately use your secondary punisher, "Enough," and then grasp the leash or collar firmly and haul off the dog to the time-out room. Speed is important, since you want to form a connection between the undesired behavior, the secondary punisher, and the time-out consequence.

The time-out room can be any place that is safe and quiet, such as a bathroom or even a large closet. *It should not be the dog's kennel or crate*, however, since you do not want to associate that with punishment. To convince the dog that this is special treatment, I prefer to anchor the leash on the door knob or to pinch it in the doorjamb, leaving enough slack for the dog to lie down comfortably but not enough for him to wander around the room. I like to keep the dog in a time-out for two to three minutes. If the animal complains, I say "Enough" loudly and give a sharp rap on the door. He must have been quiet for about fifteen seconds before he is let out. When he is released from his time-out, he is taken back to the original situation and given something to do (perhaps just a few obedience commands, such as "Sit" and "Down" followed by a reward). Then you can proceed with your normal activities. If the dog goes back to his bad behaviors, you repeat the time-out.

Time-out is particularly effective for social transgressions, including rough play, jumping up, mouthing, excessive barking, food begging, and so forth. These behaviors are often difficult to deal with in other ways, and time-out is a nonaggressive means of controlling them.

In this chapter, I have tried to outline the basic principles by which dogs learn skills and to give you a sense of how dogs' minds can be deliberately shaped by our attempts to teach them and control their behaviors. Technical knowledge of psychology and even a university degree in behavioral sciences does not necessarily make you a good or even a competent dog trainer. Those who most effectively manage to teach dogs are often people with a particularly sharp sense of observation, a great sense of timing, and a lot of patience. Remember, a lot of dog training is simply watching to see when the behavior you want comes along and then trying to capture it with a net made of rewards. If you are effective in doing so, not only will the dog learn, but he will enjoy the process of learning. To tell the truth, training dogs is easy—training trainers is hard.

CHAPTER 13

The Social Secret of Learning

CONSIDER HOW YOU LEARNED much of the important knowledge that you use to guide your life. Often that knowledge was simply gained by observing other people, such as teachers, parents, or friends. You learned language by listening to someone speak it and repeating those sounds. You learned how to tie your shoelaces or button your blouse by watching as your mother demonstrated how it was done. You learned how to fry an egg by observing another person doing this same thing. These behaviors were not captured, lured, shaped, or classically conditioned, but came about because we extracted information from the deliberate or casual actions of other human beings and used it to guide and shape our own actions. Psychologists call this "social learning," not because it involves learning social manners, customs, or communication, but because it refers to a type of learning that is socially transmitted or socially facilitated. This kind of learning and performance seems to be unique to the most evolutionarily advanced animals, who live in a complex social environment.

Learning by Observation

Only a few years ago, scientists did not believe that dogs had the capacity for social learning, including imitation, behavior modeling, and observational learning. As recently as 1996, Pamela Reid, who holds a Ph.D. in psychology, spent only two paragraphs on the issue in *Excel-erated Learning,* a book about dog learning. She finished by saying:

> . . . there is virtually no evidence that animals, except for humans and the great apes (gorillas, orangutans, and chimpanzees), are capable of pure imitation. Some researchers have devoted their entire professional lives to devising ways to demonstrate imitation, without success. Sorry to rain on your parade, but dogs just don't seem to be able to manage learning by imitation. (p. 169)

Science, however, marches on, and while that statement might have been defensible in 1996, a vast amount of new data has appeared since then which suggest that observational learning and imitation are quite possible in dogs. In fact, dogs may have some special abilities that make them uniquely tuned not only to benefit from watching the behaviors of other dogs but also to extract information from the behaviors of humans.

Long before this research appeared in the scientific literature, however, the idea that dogs learn by observation had been well established among people who work with dogs. The standard practice, for instance, in training a herding dog is to put the animal to work with a dog that already knows the job. The young dog seems to pick up the complexities of keeping a flock of sheep together and even the meaning of the shepherd's signals through the simple act of observing another dog who already knows the job. In fact, shepherds claim that this practice works far better than having the shepherd train the dog himself.

Sled dogs are also initially trained by hitching them up with a team of dogs that already knows the job. In the interior of British Columbia, I got to watch a group of five-month-old Siberian huskies first being introduced to their future job as sled dogs. This particular trainer had ten or eleven pups that had never been asked to pull before. He took out a box of small harnesses and put them on the young dogs and then put them in tandem on a towline. At the front the line were several old, experienced leaders with years of sled-dog racing in their history. In this case there was no sled, but rather the towline was attached to an all-terrain vehicle. The trainer explained that "The four-wheeler is just there for the weight, and because it has a good set of brakes that can control their speed."

Going very slowly, the operator of the vehicle allowed the lead dogs to begin moving. They were going at a pace that was slower than a human walk. It was interesting to watch the puppies' reaction. Most looked around as if trying to figure out what was happening. The pups that were farthest forward focused intently on the experienced team leaders, who were leaning into their harnesses. In a few minutes these pups also were pressing forward and pulling in the same direction. Farther back along the towline, however, there was more confusion. One of the puppies near the rear kept sitting down, only to have the towline move him forward every minute or so, while another was straining and trying to pull against the forward movement. In the middle the puppies seemed to be observing. It was not clear how well they could see the actions of the adults who knew the work, but they could see the puppies directly in front of them pulling forward. One by one, in a wave moving from the front nearest the experienced dogs and going backward toward the end of the line, the pups began to lean into their harnesses and pull in the direction that the dog in front of them was moving. It was a noisy cavalcade, with the puppies yelping, barking, whining, and moaning as they moved along; however, it could not have been more than half an hour or so before it was obvious that every puppy in that group was pulling forward. When the team was stopped, the pups shook themselves but now intently watched the team leaders. As soon as the leaders stood up to move again, the pups immediately began heaving away at their small harnesses, hauling with all of their strength in the same direction that the lead dogs were moving. The fact that they were taking their cues from the lead dogs was obvious, and within an hour or so, this batch of puppies had taken its first instruction in what would become their lifetime work as sled dogs. Their lesson had simply been learned by watching the dogs who knew the job and the dogs around them.

Group-coordinated Learning

This form of learning is based upon what scientists call "allelomimetic behaviors"—group-coordinated behaviors that depend upon an inborn inclination to want to be with other dogs and to follow their lead and do the same thing. Puppies show tendencies to imitate the behaviors of others from an early age and continue to do so throughout their lives. Many significant behaviors are learned as a result of participating in such organized social behaviors. Many knowledgeable dog trainers know that the easiest way to train puppies is to take advantage of these tendencies. Thus you can train a pup to come when called by having him chase after the trainer who is running away, but who then stops and rewards the pup for coming (adding the word "come" as he does so). Heeling can easily be taught to the pup, since there is an allelomimetic tendency for pups to walk by a trainer's side, and this can rapidly be brought under control if the puppy is taken out on a number of walks and rewarded for being beside the trainer, who adds the word "heel" to cement the concept in the pup's mind.

Many dog owners have learned that bringing a puppy into a house that already has a trained adult dog greatly simplifies the newcomer's training. The puppy learns to come when called by tagging along with the other dog. Teaching a pup to hop into your car on command is simple when you have another dog that responds to the command. Housebreaking is simplified because the pup will follow along with the adult and will eliminate at the same times and in the same outdoor locations as his companion.

Dogs seem to learn more complex tasks by observation, too. Some tasks are of sufficient complexity that it would be difficult to design a program to train dogs effectively. An example of this is the work of Saint Bernard rescue dogs. The breed was named for the hospice founded by Saint Bernard, located in the Swiss Alps on one of the principal roads that connects Switzerland to Italy. The hospice provided winter travelers with a refuge from wind, cold, blizzards, and avalanches. The dogs assisted the monks in their searches for travelers who had strayed off the main road. Monks seldom left the hospice without dogs, because mountain fogs can come on suddenly and without warning, making it impossible to see even one step ahead. Without the dogs, the monks could not find their way back to the hospice. Together the monks and dogs have saved thousands of travelers. These rescue dogs work in three-dog teams. When a lost traveler is found, two of the dogs lie down beside him to keep him warm while the third returns to the hospice to sound the alarm and bring back help. These dogs are not given any special training, and no one is exactly sure how one could train a dog to do these things in any event. Young dogs are simply allowed to run with the older, experienced dogs when they go on patrol. In this way the dogs learn what is expected of them. Ultimately, each dog learns his job and also decides for himself whether his professional specialty will eventually be to lie with the victim or go for help.

Dogs Training Dogs

Although dogs can learn by watching and interacting with other dogs, they can also learn by passively observing the behavior of other dogs. This fact was simply and elegantly demonstrated by Lenore and Helmut Adler at the City University of New York's College of Staten Island. They worked with dachshund puppies that were tested in pairs. One puppy, who they called the "demonstrator," was given the end of a ribbon that was attached to a little food cart on a rail. He had to figure out for himself that he could use the ribbon to pull the cart into the cage to get the food. Meanwhile, the other puppy, who they called the "observer," watched the learning process from an adjacent compartment, separated from the demonstrator by a wire screen. After five sessions the observers finally were granted access to the ribbon. The sixty-day-old demonstrator pups took 595 seconds, on average, on their first attempt to solve the problem, but the observer dogs took on average only 40 seconds. Since the demonstrators had taken 15 times longer, clearly the observers had learned by observation.

A fascinating demonstration of observational learning, which shows how useful it can be in training service dogs, was conducted at the South Africa Police Dog School in Pretoria, where German shepherd dogs were being bred to be used as narcotics-detecting dogs. One group of dogs was given special experience. Between the ages of six and twelve weeks, a few times each week they were permitted to watch as their mothers searched for, found, and retrieved sachets filled with narcotics. When the pups were young, the sachets were hidden near their kennel; later on, they were hidden along the side of the path that was used for their daily exercise walk. Each time their mother succeeded in finding the narcotics, the pups also got to see her praised and rewarded for her work. At no time were the puppies allowed to try to get the narcotics themselves. In total, over the six-week period they saw their mother perform this learned behavior fourteen times.

At the age of twelve weeks, all of the pups were separated from their mothers and entered into a program of standard police dog obedience training with their permanent handlers. None of the pups had any contact with narcotics, and they did not receive retrieving training. At the age of six months, the dogs were assessed for their ability to find hidden narcotic sachets and retrieve them for their handlers using the same tests used for trained dogs. There were five tests worth up to 2 points each and a perfect score was 10 points. These tests looked at (1) the dog's attention and interest in retrieving a narcotic-filled sachet; (2) the way it approached the hidden sachet; (3) the way the dog searched for the sachet; (4) how the dog picked up and carried the sachet; and (5) whether the dog carried the sachet straight back to the handler. If a dog showed no interest or ability for the task, he scored 0, while a dog that located and retrieved the narcotics immediately could earn 10 points.

The results were truly amazing. In order to understand how well the pups did, you must understand that a narcotics dog is considered to be fully trained when it receives a score of 9 or 10. One would not be surprised to find that no pup received a score of 10; however, four out of the twenty untrained dogs who had seen their mothers working got a score of 9, which means that they were performing at a level equivalent to that of a conventionally trained narcotics dog without any further training! These are the highest scores recorded for any untrained puppies since the establishment of the South African dog school. A score of 5 and above is considered the cutoff point for an aptitude for narcotics work and 85 percent of the dogs that had observed their mothers finding and retrieving narcotics scored higher than 5 compared with only

19 percent of puppies reared in the usual way without an opportunity to learn this work by observation. This seems like powerful evidence that dogs can learn by simply observing the behavior of other dogs.

All of the examples of observational learning I have given thus far involved puppies below the age of six months. Most trainers believe that observational learning is less efficient in older dogs for tasks such as sled-pulling, herding, and rescue work. Although there is little systematic research on the effect of age on observational learning, it has lately become clear that dogs never stop watching and learning.

What Dogs Watch and Understand

All of the data discussed so far has been based on dogs observing other dogs but, since dogs live in close quarters with humans, people might also serve as models for canine social learning. For a dog to use a person as a model or a source of information would require that dogs have a reasonable degree of sensitivity to the kinds of signals that humans use. Recent evidence suggests that this is certainly the case. Most dog owners have had the experience of merely glancing in the direction of where the leash is hanging, only to find that Lassie or Fido is now headed for the door in anticipation of a walk. While this seems like an everyday event to dog owners, to scientists it has special significance because of what it says about how a dog thinks. First of all, it shows that dogs can read human body language. In addition, it shows that dogs feel that our movements and gestures are communicating something about the world and what might happen next in the environment. If this is the case, then dogs should be able to use information from human actions to solve problems in much the same way that they use information from other dogs.

Since the middle of the 1990s, scientists have been studying dogs' "social cognition," or how well dogs read social cues. As a human you read cues automatically. Thus you know that when the person you are talking to is frequently glancing at his watch, you had best get to your point before he leaves. Research shows that dogs are surprisingly good at reading social cues. For a long time we thought that the only information that a dog extracted from social cues had to do with social intentions. Thus we were quite willing to grant that a dog could tell when another dog or a human is annoyed and might be deciding upon aggressive actions. Dogs can also read human social signals when humans mimic typical dog signals. For example, a team of researchers, mostly from the Anthrozoology Institute at the University of Southampton, was able to demonstrate that when a human imitates the play bow of dogs by getting down on hands and knees, placing elbows and forearms flat on the floor, and stretching forward to lower the body, a dog will often respond by giving a play bow of his own and starting to play. Similarly, dogs also respond to a quick short lunge forward by a human as a play signal.

When a "demonstrator" is a dog, dogs can learn a job or task, but can they also extract information to guide their behaviors from just observing human actions? The scientific test typically used to look for such behavior in dogs is quite simple. You start with two small bucket-like containers. Next, place a bit of food under one of them while the dog is out of sight. (Both containers have been rubbed with the food so that there is no scent difference.) Place one container on your right and the other to the left. When the dog comes in, give one of several different social cues to show which bucket contains the food. The most obvious cue would be to tap the container with the food. Less obvious is to point an arm toward the baited one. An even more muted signal is turning your head or body to face the direction of the container with the food. The subtlest signal is to hold your head still and move only your eyes toward the correct container. If the dog chooses the right container, he is rewarded by getting the food.

Now deducing that there is a reward in a particular location and that that location is indicated by a person's gestures appears as if it is a simple ability, but this is not so. Surprisingly, Daniel J. Povinelli, a psychologist at the University of Southwestern Louisiana, found that our closest animal relatives, chimpanzees, were very bad at this task. Three-year-old human children weren't very good at this either, although they were better than the monkeys. Both the chimps and the kids could quickly learn the task, however. The real surprise came when Brian Hare, a psychologist at Harvard University, ran the same test on dogs and found that they could interpret the signals indicating the location of the food four times better than the monkeys. Dogs were also more than twice as accurate as young children, even though the experimenter was a stranger.

An important question is where did dogs get this talent? The first guess might be that since dogs descended from pack-hunting wolves, their ability to pick up social signals might have evolved to help coordinate the hunt. If this were the case, then wolves should be just as good at this task as dogs. However, when Hare tested wolves at the Wolf Hollow Wolf Sanctuary in Massachusetts, he found that wolves were actually worse than monkeys and a lot worse than dogs. So the next guess is that dogs learn to read human language by simply hanging out and watching their human families. This would suggest that young puppies, especially those that were still living with the littermates and had not yet been adopted by a human family, should not be very good at picking up social signals. Wrong again. Even nine-week-old puppies, still living with their mother and littermates, do a lot better than wolves and monkeys. The conclusion then from these studies is that this ability is not inherited from the last common dog-wolf ancestor, and it does not take tremendous exposure to humans to bring it out.

With the scientific evidence failing to support the two most obvious explanations, we are still left with the question of "Where did dogs get this innate ability to read human signals?" There are two more candidate explanations, both concerning evolutionary changes in dogs that occurred during their domestication. Certainly, dogs that could figure out their masters' intentions and desires would be more likely to thrive in a human society. This means that the ability to read social cues would allow them to survive and produce more young. Then the question becomes, were the specific dogs chosen to be domesticated selected *because* they had the ability to understand people or was this ability some sort of unintended by-product that simply came along during the process of domestication?

Either of these two theories might work. Obviously people would tend to prefer and would more easily form a bond with dogs that could understand human body language. However, the alternative theory could also work. Domestication usually involves selecting the tamest, most easily managed animals—for safety's sake, if nothing else. Think of it this way: If you select against aggression, a whole suite of changes accompanies that reduction in aggression. A lot of unintended changes also occur as by-products, such as neoteny, which causes domestic dogs to look and act more like wolf puppies than adults all their lives. It is certainly possible that the ability to read human signals and extract information from human behaviors may be just another by-product of domestication. The calmer, more attentive animals might also happen to be the ones that are able to pick up these subtle social cues better.

Observing and Learning from People

The kind and amount of information that dogs can extract and use from a human's actions is quite varied and significant. Péter Pongrácz and a team of researchers from Hungary's Eötvös Loránd University and the Hungarian Academy of Sciences have been testing whether dogs can learn to solve a problem that involves finding a particular path to a reward just by watching humans successfully complete it. The general experimental arrangement that they use is a large V-shaped wire fence with the point of the V facing toward the dog and a special treat in the point behind the fence. Psychologists call this kind of situation a "detour problem." It is an interesting problem to test animals with because the solution involves moving some distance away from the goal before going back to it. In this case a dog must move down the side of the V-shaped fence for a good distance (which seems to take him farther away from the treat he wants) and then, eventually, he will reach the end of the fence and be able to curve around and enter the V from the open side and reach the goal. Although initially dogs experience difficulties in solving problems involving detours, they usually can learn to solve such tasks by trial-and-error. This trial-and-error learning, however, is slow, and the dogs usually need to blunder their way around until they successfully find their way around the fence and find the food at least five or six times before they catch on and have that "Aha!" experience. From then on they show significantly improved ability to get their reward quickly. If a small door is open near the point of the V that allows the dogs to get to the food faster, they seem to learn this solution more quickly than the more distant detour around the back of the fence.

Suppose that instead of just letting the dog poke around to find a solution, he is kept in one place and watches a human being taking the correct path. The dog clearly learns from the human's behavior and solves the problem quickly, in one single attempt, instead of the usual five or six. Furthermore, if now the door in the fence is opened to allow the shortcut solution to the problem, dogs that have observed people go all the way around the fence will ignore that better way to their goal and follow the path that they observed bringing the human demonstrator to the reward. In this instance the dogs walk right by the open gate that will take them more quickly to the reward, since they are modeling their behavior on the successful actions of the human that they observed rather than actively exploring for alternative solutions that might be better.

Another team of researchers from Hungary's Eötvös Loránd University and the Hungarian Academy of Sciences, this time headed by Enikö Kubinyi, showed that dogs can also learn to manipulate objects by simply watching their owners do so. In this case the object consisted of a box with a handle that stuck out horizontally from it. If the handle was pushed to the left or right, a ball rolled out of the side of the box; however, there were other ways that the ball could be removed from the box, including banging hard against it, flipping it on its side, and so forth. During the demonstration period the dog's owner held the collar of the dog to keep him looking at box. Next the owner directed the dog's attention to the handle by saying "Look at my hand!" When the dog was looking, the owner pushed the handle and the dog saw the ball roll out. The ball served as a reward, since his owner then played with the dog and the ball for a few seconds. This demonstration was repeated ten times. Now it is important to understand that we are interested in whether the dog will imitate the behavior he observed his owner use to get the ball. However, we have to be careful, since there is a phenomenon known as "local enhancement," in which the demonstrator's actions merely focus the observer's attention on a feature or place and thus attracts them to that location. Obviously, if the dog's attention is attracted to the lever, then the chance that he will push it by simply nosing around that region becomes higher. To avoid contamination by this phenomenon, there was also a group where the owner directed the dog's attention to the handle by saying "Look at my hand" and touched it with his or her forefinger but did not actually push the handle. Obviously no ball was released by this action, and therefore no play followed this demonstration.

After the demonstrations the dogs were given three test trials. They had sixty seconds to get the ball (and earn some play time) for each test. The results indicate that the dogs were learning about how to manipulate the box by watching their owners. Remarkably, in the handle-push-for-ball-reward group, the majority of the dogs (77 percent) went over to the box and touched the handle in all three trials, and every other dog in this group touched it at least some of the time. We can compare this to the group of dogs that did not see their handlers touch the handle. Here only 16 percent of the dogs touched the handle during all three test trials, and 53 percent did not touch it at all. Of the group that saw their owner push the handle to free the ball, 65 percent of them also pushed the handle to set the ball loose. Contrast this to the group whose handlers called their attention to the handle and watched him touch it—only 6 percent of those dogs managed to release the ball by pushing the handle on all three test trials. Thus the dogs that watched a person manipulate an object to get a ball were more than ten times more likely to manipulate that object in the same way and successfully get their reward!

In another study, this team of researchers discovered a major difference between dogs and wolves. When faced with a manipulation task that they can't solve, dogs will stop, look at the face of the person with them, and try to discover clues as to what to do from the person's actions. In comparison, wolves, even though those that had been tamed and were living with humans, do not look at the faces of people for clues as to what to do. Dogs can thus extract more information from human social sources around them simply because they are specifically looking for it.

The Social Brain

Recently, studies of animal cognition have put great emphasis on what might be called the "Social Brain Hypothesis," which says that one of the major reasons intelligence evolved and became more complex in the first place was that it was designed to solve social problems. The more complex the social organization in which an animal lives, the more intelligence he needs and the more his brain is oriented toward social issues. Humans, of course, are social animals and spend most of their time exchanging personal and social information. We are not usually having discussions about ancient Chinese philosophy, the theories of Einstein, or what happens to things when they are sucked into cosmic black holes. We seem to be much more involved in the everyday aspects of our social lives.

To study this behavior, two British psychologists sampled conversations. Robin Dunbar took samples from all over England, while Nicholas Emler sampled ordinary conversations in Scotland. Both found that more than two-thirds of our conversations are taken up with social and emotional matters. Typical topics dealt with who is doing what and with whom, and perhaps commentaries on whether that is a good or bad thing. Other topics include who is moving up in the world and who is moving down and why. Many of the most emotional conversations had to do with how to deal with difficult social situations and described complex interactions with lovers, children, fellow workers, neighbors, extended family, and so forth. Obviously there were some complex technical discussions, perhaps triggered by a problem at work or a recently read book. Yet in a study I conducted that monitored over a hundred discussions between my colleagues at the university, I never found a technical discussion that went on for more than seven minutes without lapsing, at least for while, back into social conversation. In fact, only about one-quarter of the time was spent on technical matters overall.

If both human thinking and communication are focused on social matters, it is not surprising to find that much of what we learn is obtained by listening to the spoken words of others and watching their communicative gestures. To the extent that the same is true for dogs, we might be able to use a dog's interest in social matters, plus our own spoken and visual communication signals, to teach the animal. Sue McKinley and Robert Young, of the Department of Animal Science at De Montfort University in Lincolnshire in the United Kingdom, tried to facilitate dogs' learning and performance of certain activities with "labels" that stood for objects and actions. Dogs learned labels by watching a person interact with someone who the dog knows as a trainer. That other person could be seen as a model for the desired behavior and also as a rival for the trainer's attention. Some of the more intense social interest on the dog's part is apt to be stimulated by a rival. The dog wants to know what that other person knows so that he can also get social and other rewards from the trainer.

The researchers began with a haphazard group of pet dogs and their owners. Each dog had to learn to identify a particular dog toy by name and retrieve it on command. Two sets of rubber toys were used. One set consisted of three red rubber dog toys (a boot, a fire extinguisher, and a strawberry), whereas the other set consisted of three yellow rubber dog toys (a saxophone, a toothbrush, and a hammer). All of the toys were about the same size, from 6 to 8 inches in length (around 15 to 20 cm). One toy was chosen randomly from each group. Each dog learned to retrieve these on command when asked to retrieve it by name. The names or labels assigned to the objects were quite arbitrary and had nothing to do with the actual items themselves, but to avoid confusing readers we'll use the real names to describe what was done.

Each dog was taught to retrieve a specific object using two different methods. In the standard operant-training procedure, suppose the dog was required to learn how to retrieve the yellow rubber hammer. This would involve shaping or rewarding successive approximations to the behavior that was wanted. This might begin with only a rubber hammer out on the floor, and if the dog nosed at it, he would get a food reward. Later the dog would have to pick the object up in his mouth to get the reward, and eventually he would be rewarded only for bringing the toy to the experimenter when he said "Get the hammer." When he responded to the command correctly three times in row, the dog was considered to be "trained" and was then tested. All three of the yellow rubber toys were put out and the dog was told to "Get the hammer."

The length of time that he took to learn the task measured how well the training worked.

The model-rival technique of training required the dog to watch a "conversation" between the trainer and a model about the toys. The dog was secured on a leash about half a meter (a foot and a half) away from the trainer and the model, who were sitting in front of the dog. There was only one toy and the two people "discussed" it using scripted sentences. Since research with humans shows that they remember the last part of a sentence best, the name of the object was at the end of each sentence. Suppose that the item that the dog was supposed to identify was the red boot. The conversation ran like this.

TRAINER: Can you see the boot? (At the same time, he hands the boot to the model.)

MODEL: Yes, I can, thank you for the boot. (He hands the toy back to the trainer.)

TRAINER: Can you pass me the boot? (He hands the toy to the model.)

MODEL: Thank you for the wonderful boot. (He hands it back to the trainer.)

This kind of dialogue was performed in a highly animated and enthusiastic style to keep the dog's attention focused on the object being passed back and forth, with both looking at the object but keeping their body orientation and voice direction toward the dog. While the conversation was going on, the dog was not allowed to touch the item. After watching the conversation go on for about two minutes, the dog was asked to retrieve the object from a distance of 3 meters (10 feet) with the command "Get the boot." If the dog failed to get the object, the training was repeated and the extra time was added to the total training time score. If the dog succeeded, he was tested by being asked to "Get the boot" when all of the red toys were put out at the same time.

It turns out that dogs are able to learn from simply observing this social interaction while they listen and watch two humans speaking to each other. Furthermore, the total training time and the speed and accuracy with which they perform this task is much the same whether the dog was trained by standard operant-conditioning methods or by simple observation.

The kind of data that we have been discussing is particularly important because of its implications for dog and human interactions. It says that your dog is always watching what you are doing. If you pull open a floor-level cupboard to get your dog a treat, you may have not only taught your dog where the treats are stored, but also that he can get at them by pulling on the cupboard door handle. Right now, your dog is probably watching, listening, and learning from you.

CHAPTER 14

Artists or Scientists?

SOME PSYCHOLOGISTS have suggested that people have one of two thinking styles. The first is analytic, logical, and mathematical, presumably controlled by the left hemisphere of the brain; the second is more artistic, creative, musical, and emotional thinking, controlled by the right hemisphere of the brain. Regardless of the neurology, one or another of these thinking predispositions tends to dominate in each person. Thus psychologists often talk about "cognitive styles," which are predispositions to think in particular ways. There certainly are people who tend to approach every problem using logic and rational consideration, while others' first response is emotional and their major concerns are oriented toward art and beauty. With this in mind, it might be interesting to consider if there is an aesthetic side to dog's thinking or whether dogs are simply practical problem solvers trying to find the rational solutions to the questions posed by life.

Dancing with Dogs

The two blondes, Carolyn (dressed in a red vest) and Rookie (wearing leather with bright studs), danced across the floor. The music was classic rock and roll from the musical *Grease.* As the speakers blared the refrain "You're the one that I want . . ." Carolyn twirled in one direction and Rookie the other. They backed away from each other and then moved forward in a sensuous rhythm. Carolyn's hands flared outward in classic rock dance style and Rookie wove his way in, around, and through her legs. Yes, you read that last statement correctly. Carolyn is Carolyn Scott from Houston, Texas, and Rookie is a seven-year-old golden retriever. They were participating in an event called "Canine Musical Freestyle," but it is really dancing with dogs.

When you look at a musical freestyle performance, it is easy to convince yourself that the dog is actually dancing to the music. This is not the case, however. The performance is definitely a choreographed set of movements that are performed with musical accompaniment. But these performances are really closely tied to the standard traditions of dog obedience training, and in some respects they are basically a complex heeling routine or the canine equivalent of the equestrian sport of dressage. Freestyle began as an expression of the changing attitudes toward dog training in the 1970s. More positive training techniques began to arise, with emphases on motivating the dog and getting him to work with a happy attitude rather than just getting him to work. With these new teaching techniques, dogs worked better and with more precision than had been seen before. Dog-training classes were getting to be a pleasant pastime and a regular social event, since the removal of force and overt physical corrections lightened the tone of the sessions quite a bit. As part of this change in attitude, some instructors begin to introduce music into the classroom and to use obedience routines set to music as demonstrations of what dogs could do.

I got involved in the first musical freestyle competitions that were held in North America, at the Pacific Canine Showcase in 1992 and 1993 in Vancouver. Although the sport would soon come to emphasize performances involving one handler and one dog doing a dance routine, at that time the idea of teams of four or six handlers with their dogs was encouraged. Various dog obedience clubs had been contacted to see if teams could be solicited, and our club, the Vancouver Dog Obedience Training Club, put together a wonderfully spirited but mismatched team consisting of Barbara Baker's Staffordshire terrier, Nutmeg; Cindy Merkley's Shetland sheepdog, Martin; Peter Reid's English cocker spaniel, Beau; and my cairn terrier, Flint. We viewed this musical event as being the canine equivalent to the performances of the Spanish Riding School, with their famous Lipizzaner horses, or the Musical Ride of the Royal Canadian Mounted Police. For us, the music was to be a background for an interesting, innovative performance that demonstrated the dogs' abilities, but we weren't pretending that we were dancing. Our team did well, taking second place, and the following year an expanded team of six dogs took fourth place. By that time it had become clear that the dance aspect, and the entertainment values and costuming, were going to be most important. Since none of us felt musically proficient enough to be comfortable with that format, we decided to rest on our laurels.

Our early performances left no doubts that the rhythm of the music was not being reflected by our dogs. In fact, we selected bagpipe music for our first team performance so that there would be no pronounced beat or rhythm to get in the way. Today, however, the dogs seem to move with the music, and watching a fine performer like Rookie, you do get the feeling that these dogs are dancing. Does this mean that dogs have sufficient musicality that they can learn to dance to a rhythm? Apparently, even the freestyle associations don't pretend this is actually the case. In one publication put out by the Canine Freestyle Federation the answer is spelled out explicitly: "A Freestyle presentation is always accompanied by music selected to suit the rhythms of the dog." This recognizes the fact that every dog seems to have a natural rhythm for particular speeds of movement. Some dogs trot with a high-stepping bounce that suggests up-tempo dancing, while others move with a sinuous grace that seems to fit with classical ballet music. With training you can adjust the dog's natural movements to some degree, but dogs do not have the same range of movement rhythms that people do. So the dog appears to be dancing to the music because the music has been selected to fit the dog's natural pacing, not because dogs have an appreciation for the actual rhythmic structure of the piece. If you change to another musical tempo, it will become much clearer that the dog is responding to the movements of the handler and not to the rhythm of the music.

If dogs don't dance, then, do they have any other musical abilities? Can dogs sing? Do they appreciate listening to music?

Singing with Dogs

People think of a dog's howl as a canine attempt to make music, because during some events where people are playing music or singing, some dogs will join in by howling. Thus a basset hound named Bourbon would howl whenever his family of humans had gathered around the piano to sing Christmas carols. He would howl only when the family was singing in unison and would stop when the singing stopped. His owner, who was musically talented, claimed that Bourbon was just trying to join in the music making. He explained, "It started after the kids were old enough to sing with us. I think that Bourbon felt that he had to balance their squeaky soprano voices with a bit of a bigger bass section. He certainly has a 'basso profundo' voice."

Dogs howl primarily as a means of communication. Compared to wild canines, domestic dogs bark a lot more and howl only occasionally, but their howling is still a means of communication that other dogs respond to by howling in return. Although the howling of an isolated dog may indicate loneliness, some howling can be purely social. Wolves use howls to assemble the pack and also to reinforce the identity of the group. Upon hearing one animal howling, the other group members often gather together and join in a song with their pack. The most familiar howl starts without any fanfare and produces a continuous prolonged sound. It may occasionally begin with a slightly higher pitch before moving to the main tone, and sometimes the pitch may lower a bit toward the end of the howl. It has a sonorous sound to the human ear and is often described as "mournful." The animals participating in this kind of group howling seem to enjoy it, but whether they enjoy the sounds themselves or simply the social interaction which group howling represents is not clear. It is easy for humans to imagine that a group of howling dogs or wolves feels that they are simply engaging in the canine equivalent of a spontaneous jam session.

Scientific analyses have been done of canines howling during these instinctive concerts, and some researchers suggest that dogs have a sense of pitch. Recordings of wolves have shown that a howling wolf will change its tone when others join the chorus. No wolf seems to want to end up on the same note as any other in the choir. This is why a dog howling along with a group of singing humans is instantaneously noticeable. He is deliberately not in the same register as the other voices and seems to revel in the discordant sound he is making. The kind of human music that most often induces a dog to howl is produced on wind instruments, particularly reed instruments such as clarinets or saxophones. Sometimes dogs can be induced to howl by a long note on the violin or even by a human holding a long note while singing. Perhaps these sound like proper howls to the listening dog and he feels the need to answer and join the chorus.

The Critics Reply

Probably the most famous dog and person duet ever recorded involved the president of the United States in 1967. President Lyndon Baines Johnson had developed a strong bond with a white mixed-breed terrier with the unassuming name Yuki. I remember the film footage that was probably shown on every televised newscast. In it Johnson was sitting in the oval office of the White House with the presidential seal behind him. On his lap sat Yuki. Johnson first sang a Western folk song and then a piece of an operatic aria, both hideously off key, while Yuki accompanied him with gleeful and vigorous howls. The press was rather demeaning when they spoke about this duet. Music critics suggested that having the dog howl part of an opera was equivalent to having the president make disparaging comments about classical music. Others simply wondered whether the scene damaged the image of the president and the respect that people were supposed to have for the office. Johnson, however, enjoyed "singing" with the dog and he was not the least disturbed by the furor that it caused. He even proudly displayed an article that described one performance, noting, "Not all the comments are bad. This one says that I sing almost as good as the dog!"

Johnson was not the only president to enjoy canine music. In 1936, Franklin Delano Roosevelt invited the Golden Gloves boxing champion Arthur "Stubby" Stubbs and his bull terrier, Bud, to the White House. He later reported that while Stubby played the banjo, Bud sang a medley of Stephen Foster songs. Unfortunately, we do not have any recordings of this performance, but Roosevelt's wife Eleanor did comment on the performance, saying, "I don't know if it was music, but it was interesting."

There are reports that dogs can be just as critical of human attempts to sing as Eleanor Roosevelt was of Bud's vocalizations. I was told the story about a performance of the opera *Of Mice and Men,* written by Carlisle Floyd and based on the well-known story by John Steinbeck. This particular production was being put on by the opera company at San Jose, California. One critical scene in the story involves shooting a dog, so the company chose to have a live dog onstage. Her name was Jessie, and although she was well trained, it was never a sure thing that she would stay in her place during any given scene. She often got up and wandered around or even tried to leave the stage. At one of the rehearsals before the show opened, the director, Lillian Garrett-Groag, was getting rather frustrated with one of the performers whose timing was off and who was ruining the flow of this pivotal dramatic scene. As the scene was repeated for what felt like the hundredth time, and the errant performer was again demonstrating his musical incompetence in ringing tones, the dog Jessie rose from her place, walked over to the player, and urinated on his shoe. Garrett-Groag stopped the performance and while someone ran for a mop, she turned to the person beside her and muttered, "She may not be polite, but that dog is certainly a perceptive musical critic!"

Anecdotes like this raise a valid issue. While we cannot say that dogs produce music as humans do, there certainly have been many reports of dogs that had definite tastes in music and some sense of what constitutes good music. A bulldog named Dan was owned by Dr. George Robinson Sinclair, the organist at Hereford Cathedral in London, who was friends with Sir Edward William Elgar, the English composer best known for writing *Pomp and Circumstance* and *Land of Hope and Glory.* Sinclair had even set aside a room for Elgar that he used to compose his music while visiting. Elgar developed a fondness for Dan because he felt that the dog had a good sense of musical quality. Dan would frequently attend choir practices with his master, and it was said that he would growl at choristers who sang out of tune, which greatly endeared Dan to the composer.

Eventually Elgar ended up writing a musical tribute to the dog. It came about this way. Dan, like many bulldogs, seemed to have a particular dislike of being in water. One day, on a walk along the banks of the River Wye, Dan fell in. As quickly as he could he scrambled out and vigorously shook himself, soaking both Sinclair and Elgar. Greatly amused by this incident, Sinclair challenged Elgar to put this to music. Elgar took up the challenge and on returning to the house immediately began his musical interpretation, which later became one of the *Enigma Variations* (number 11). Thus Dan, a dog that had a sense of when people were singing in tune or not, became immortalized in music.

Canine Musical Preferences

Richard Wilhelm Wagner, best known as the composer of the series of four operas that make up *The Ring Cycle*, had a strong faith in the musical appreciation of dogs. His dog Peps, a Cavalier King Charles spaniel, was required to be present when Wagner was composing. A special stool was provided for Peps, and he was expected to stay awake and listen while Wagner would play on the piano or sing passages that he was working on. The composer kept his eyes on the dog and modified passages based upon how the dog reacted. Wagner noticed that Peps responded differently to melodies depending upon their musical keys. For instance, certain passages in E-flat major caused an occasional calm tail wag, while some passages in E major might cause him to stand up in an excited manner. This put a germ of an idea in Wagner's mind, which ultimately led him to a device called the "musical motif." The motif involves the association of specific musical keys with particular moods or emotions in the operatic drama. Thus in the opera *Tannhäuser* the key of E-flat major was linked with the concept of holy love and salvation, whereas E major was tied to the notion of sensual love and debauchery. In all of his subsequent operas Wagner came to use musical motifs to identify important characters and other aspects of the drama. When Peps died, Wagner was devastated and found it difficult to apply his mind to composing until he obtained another dog (of the same breed). This new dog, Fips, soon took his place on a specially upholstered stool that was placed next to Wagner's piano so that he could render his canine musical expertise and criticism as needed.

Dogs apparently have certain musical preferences and react differently to particular types of music. A team of researchers led by psychologist Deborah Wells at Queens University in Belfast, Northern Ireland, exposed fifty dogs housed in an animal shelter to a variety of different types of music. They observed the behavior of the dogs when they were played either a compilation of popular music (including Britney Spears, Robbie Williams, and Bob Marley), a collection of classical music (including Grieg's *Morning,* Vivaldi's *Four Seasons,* and Beethoven's *Ode to Joy*), or a set of recordings by heavy-metal rock bands such as Metallica. In order to see if it were really the musical aspects of the sounds that the dogs were responding to, they were also exposed to recordings of human conversation and a period of quiet.

The kind of music that the dogs listened to made a difference. When the researchers played music by Metallica and other heavy-metal bands, the dogs became quite agitated and began barking. Listening to popular music, or human conversation, did not produce behaviors that were noticeably different from having no sound at all. Classical music, on the other hand, seemed to have a calming effect on the dogs. While listening to it, their level of barking was significantly reduced and the dogs often lay down and settled in place. Wells summarized her findings saying, "It is well established that music can influence our moods. Classical music, for example, can help to reduce levels of stress, whilst grunge music can promote hostility, sadness, tension and fatigue. It is now believed that dogs may be as discerning as humans when it comes to musical preference."

Canines at the Artist's Easel

There is, of course, more to art than just music. While a dog's visual artistic sensibility might be limited by considerations of the dog's restricted ability to discriminate colors and his sometimes diminished visual acuity, there are some reports that dogs may have an appreciation of the visual arts, and perhaps even some desire to create art.

Vitaly Komar and Alex Melamid are two Moscow-born artists who are best known for their satirical performance art. In the early 1970s they were expelled from the Moscow Union of Artists for giving unsanctioned exhibitions of art that did not fit the socialist realist art style of the time. They eventually fled the U.S.S.R. and ended up in New York, where they claim to have demonstrated canine artistry using a stray dog they had found in Jerusalem. In 1978, Komar and Melamid used this dog in a performance piece entitled *Canine Art: Teaching a Dog to Draw*. The process that they used, however, did not really show any artistic ability on the part of the dog. Basically, they dipped the dog's paw in ink and pressed it repeatedly on a sheet of drawing paper. In the end they had a pattern that generally resembled the shape of a chicken bone that they had laid in front of the dog to serve as a model. Komar's and Melamid's canine collaborator had no active understanding of the point of this procedure and, rather than being a canine artist, he was being used as a canine paintbrush manipulated by human painters. Komar and Melamid, however, declared the outcome as "proof" not only that dogs could paint, but that the instinct to produce art is inherent in all animals. They have since gone on to work with a monkey artist and have recently established several elephant art academies in Thailand.

A possibly more convincing example of the dog as an artist involves Tillamook Cheddar, a Jack Russell terrier from New York, who has already had several "one-dog exhibitions." Her art looks very much like what one might imagine as a Jackson Pollock abstract work had it been done with crayons. Most pieces are a welter of streaks and crosshatchings, sometimes emanating from the center of the piece, sometimes confined to one region of the "canvas," sometimes varying in density across the piece. There are also often dots, which on close inspection appear to be indentations caused by canine teeth.

The demonstration of Tillie's artistic technique that I observed started with some advance preparation by her owner, Bowman Hastie, whose day job involves writing teen romance novels. He first took a mat board and covered it with a wax-acrylic transfer paper that looks much like the carbon paper used in typewriters, only it comes in a variety of bright colors, including red, blue, yellow, black, and white. Hastie tapes the transfer paper onto the board, so that, in effect, it becomes a touch-sensitive recording device that will leave marks whenever Tillie pushes hard enough against it. When Tillie was given this "canvas," she immediately went to work. I suppose that it would be most accurate to say that she attacked her work. She grabbed at its edges with her teeth, then vigorously started scratching away at the surface. Her nails and teeth tore and scratched at it until Hastie decided that it was finished and took it away from her, unwrapped the remaining transfer paper (there was not all that much left in some sections), and showed the sunburst of lines which made up the pattern that Tillie had scratched.

One reporter, who may have been a bit dubious of the whole process but who also admitted that the works had "a certain primitive charm," asked how much of the art was actually Tillie's as opposed to Hastie's creation. Hastie responded by saying, "If I were a studio assistant for a human artist, I would have just about the same duties. My job is to pick up the supplies, stretch the canvas, lay out the colors, run errands, and clean up. Sometimes I am also called upon to motivate her and to stop her from being too critical of her own work (which means that I sometimes take a piece away from her when she has decided that she can do better and is trying to destroy it). But you can be sure that Tillie makes all the marks and puts in the creativity."

In 2002, none other than the National Arts Club held a New York exhibition of Tillie's work. This was a special collaborative exhibition. Twenty-six artists had agreed to collaborate with Tillie by either "finishing" a piece that Tillie had started or incorporating it in a larger work. At the exhibition I ran into a professor of fine arts from New York University and took the opportunity to ask him if Tillie's work could really be considered art.

"I think so," he replied. "Look at the work of Jackson Pollock. He didn't consider his later work painting, but rather the record of his actions. He claimed that he simply choreographed his movements, and the trail of paint drippings, splatters, and smears that resulted was his art."

"But," I protested, "Pollock knew that he was trying to create something artistic. He knew that he was painting, and he understood that the result might be graphically interesting. I doubt that Tillie knows what she is creating or has any aesthetic sense guiding her."

"I know, but suppose that a primitive tribesman somewhere in the world creates a mask to be used as part of a religious ceremony. He has no idea that he is creating art, but rather feels that he is creating a religious object. Yet we consider that work to be an 'artistic' creation, and we make no distinction between that product and another mask in a similar style that is deliberately crafted by modern artist to be sold to a gallery. Thus the intent of artist has little to do with whether the production is deemed to be art by those who look at it. It is simply the eye of the beholder that determines the artistic value." All the while that the professor had been speaking, he had been looking at one of Tillie's works that had red and white lines on a dark background. He looked at the card, which noted its title, number, and price, and then paused to jot down that information on a scrap of paper that he placed in his pocket. The smile on his face as he looked at it gave me the distinct impression that, whether that creation of Tillie's was art or not, it would soon be hanging in the professor's collection.

Dogs as Graphic Artists and Sculptors

Perhaps the largest gathering of canine artistic creations was presented by Vicki Mathison from New Zealand as a series of photographs in her book *Dog Works*. Mathison holds a degree in psychology and describes herself as an artist, teacher, journalist, and dog obedience trainer. She claims that she was fascinated by some chance observations of a Rottweiler–Labrador retriever cross named Titch, who had been rescued from an overcrowded dog pound. Titch's new mistress, an animal shelter worker named Bella, showed Mathison how Titch liked to draw. The dog would grab a large stick and then "draw patterns" in the sand with it that her mistress insisted were attempts to produce some form of art. Soon after, Mathison noticed that her own standard poodle, Minka, had developed a fascination with feathers and would compose "floating sculptures" with them, apparently deriving pleasure from simply looking at the patterns that she had created.

Four years later, a walk on a beach introduced Mathison to Jemima, a corgi–Shetland sheepdog cross. Jemima dug holes, but they seemed to be arranged in a pattern with deliberate symmetry. This caused Mathison to wonder if she was again looking at some form of artistic attempts by a dog. To gather more data, she published some articles that requested information from anyone who knew of dogs that exhibited unusual artistic behaviors. Much to her surprise, she received 155 communications from owners and observers of such behaviors in dogs. She discarded those that involved dogs doing strange things with tennis balls and also those that were unverifiable or unbelievable. This left her with ninety-three cases that still seemed valid enough to investigate. In an interview she noted that she tried to make sure that each of the final forty cases that she photographically documented was valid, and tried to avoid any possible fraud. She did report that in at least one case she found a deliberate attempt to fake artistic behavior in a dog by sending instructions via a transmitter arrangement to a receiver in the dog's collar. In other instances the dog simply did not perform once she and her associates arrived with camera equipment.

If we can believe the validity of the final set of photos that Mathison presents us with, then dogs do show a variety of behaviors that might, under some interpretations, be seen as art. Drawing was represented by dragging a stick to make designs in the sand, or digging patterns such as spirals in the sand, or producing symmetrical arrangements of holes. Sculpture seemed to be more common, if we consider making piles of objects to be sculpture. We have pictures of tent-like structures made of sticks or bones and piles of leaves or brush set with what appears to be deliberate and regular spacing. Perhaps the most impressive "artistic creations" are those where the dog appears to go and collect items (sticks, bones, ropes, pine cones, rocks, and so forth) and then arranges them in patterns that are meaningful to the human eye, such as circles, X's, and triangles. An Alaskan malamute named Luke arranges stalks of pampas grass so that they radiate from a common center in a starburst pattern and finishes the creation by then lying down in that center himself. Mathison clearly thinks that all of this is art. "I suspect that the dogs have some kind of aesthetic awareness. Why else would Emily [a Staffordshire terrier] have put those old bones in a perfect circle? And Titch, her drawings were so elaborate—and never duplicated."

There are also other cases in the collection where labeling a particular behavior as artistic is more questionable, such as the dog who hangs socks on fence wires or those that carry rocks or bones to a high place and just leave them there with some space between each item. But then again, I may be being too harsh. Perhaps these are forms of canine "performance art," similar at some level to when the human artist Christo wrapped some islands in the Florida Keys in pink plastic ribbon.

Part of the problem of speaking about a canine artistic sense is that all of the data that we have is based on our casual observations, and we can't know why the dog is indulging in these behaviors. Is the dog doing this because of a sense of aesthetics and an appreciation of beauty? Perhaps making piles of things is left over from nesting or denning instincts. Do dogs think what they have created is pretty, or pleasing to others' eyes? Nicholas H. Dodman, a well-known dog behaviorist who is also part of the veterinary faculty of Tufts University, might disagree that these creations are art. He describes a situation that Vicki Mathison might call an artistic attempt, where a dog would always arrange exactly six pieces of kibble in buttonhole depressions in a couch and then carefully place a seventh piece of kibble by the leg of the couch, and then it would happily lie down. After all, there is no reason to think that dogs that do their "art" in kibble are any less serious about their work than dogs that do their art in bones, sticks, or pampas grass. However, Dodman does not describe this behavior as the result of aesthetic motives but rather an example of obsessive-compulsive disorder. Humans with such a disorder collect things, often useless things, and spend much of their time arranging objects in orderly patterns, such as an obsessive-compulsive mother who constantly checked her baby's crib and then carefully arranged the stuffed animals so that there was one in each corner and one next to the child. Any deviation from this pattern caused her stress and anxiety. Was the kibble-arranging dog's behavior to be interpreted as evidence of a canine artistic sense or evidence of canine neurosis? Without any ability to understand the dog's motivation, we cannot answer this question. For now at least, as that professor of fine arts said earlier, "It is simply the eye of the beholder that determines the artistic value."

The Mathematical Mind of Dogs

If dogs can't be classed as artistic thinkers, can we conclude that they have scientific minds? Many people believe that their dogs show complex reasoning, but just how much intelligence can we grant them? Human beings have come to believe that of the highest forms of reasoning is mathematics. The Greek philosopher Pythagoras went so far as to say that "Numbers rule the universe," and Roger Bacon rephrased this idea by saying "For the things of this world cannot be made known without a knowledge of mathematics." Surely no one would think that dogs are capable of such high-level reasoning.

Some people even dismiss the fact that dogs can do the most rudimentary type of quantitative reasoning, such as the estimation of size. Thus Samuel Johnson, the eighteenth-century English writer, critic, and creator of the first "Dictionary of the English language," once rejected dogs' abilities in this area of intelligence. "Did you never observe," Johnson asked "that dogs have not the power of comparing? A dog will take a small bit of meat as readily as a large, when both are before them." Johnson's dismissal of the dog's ability in this instance, however, is wrong. Dogs *can* estimate size and respond appropriately. It is true that if you present a dog with two bits of meat, one larger than the other, dogs will snatch the closest, regardless of size, but this seems to be an expression of simple opportunism, a sort of "A bird in the hand is worth two in the bush" mentality. The closer bit of meat is easier to get and a more sure thing.

Norton Milgram, a psychologist at the University of Toronto, and his team of researchers have shown experimentally that dogs can judge size well. Their studies involve a tray that has two objects on it that differ in size. If the dog pushes the correct object, then underneath it he will find a food treat. Dogs can be taught always to pick the larger (or smaller) of two objects, regardless of the shape or identity of the objects, and they learn this fairly easily. Dogs can also be taught what is called a "same-different" task, where they have to look at three objects on a tray, two of which are the same size and the other which is larger or smaller. They must pick the one that is different, and dogs do this quite easily, demonstrating that they understand the concept of size.

A common example of dogs judging size can be observed in any dog that has been trained to jump hurdles. A dog will readily jump hurdles even if they are different in height from the ones on which he has been trained. If the hurdles are lower than usual, the dog readily jumps them, and if they are moderately higher than usual, the dog will attempt them. However, as the hurdles are made higher and higher, at some point the dog will shy away and refuse to attempt the jump. Clearly he has made some sort of size judgment and also gone one step further and compared that size to his own estimation of how high he can jump.

Another aspect of mathematics is the judgment of numerosity. This simply refers to the ability to compare two groups of items and then, without needing to count them, decide which group has the larger number. A mathematician would say that we are asking the dog to verify that X is greater than Y. Thus a dog who runs to a pile containing five pieces of kibble, rather than to the pile next to it that contains only two pieces of kibble, may have made that decision based upon his judgment of the number of pieces in each pile.

There is some evidence that dogs can learn numerosity judgments. In one study, dogs were shown pairs of panels. Each panel could have a number of dots on it. Some dogs were then taught that if they always picked the panel with the largest number of dots, they would get a food reward, while others were taught to choose the panel with the fewest dots. The training was slow, and it took many repetitions, but the dogs did learn this task.

Dogs That Count

Numerosity judgments don't really require any counting. Can dogs actually count? I have seen several instances where this seemed to be the case. The first one was after a dog obedience competition in the town of Saanich on Vancouver Island. I had completed my time in the ring and had taken my dog out of the building to enjoy the spring day. One of the other competitors had also finished for the day and was out on a large nearby field with his small black Labrador retriever named Poco. He had a box of large plastic retrieving bumpers with him and told me that he would use these to demonstrate that his dog could count.

"She can count to four quite reliably, and to five with only an occasional miss," he said. "I'll show you how it works. First you pick a number from one to five."

I picked the number three. While the dog watched, he then tossed three lures out into the field. The bumpers were tossed in different directions and at different distances and disappeared from sight in the high grass. To be sure that they were not visible, I got down on my hands and knees at the dog's eye level and assured myself that the bumpers couldn't be seen from the starting position. Then, without pointing or giving any other signals, he simply told the dog "Poco, fetch." Obediently she went out to the last (most recently thrown) bumper, picked it up, and brought it back. He took the orange-colored object from the dog and repeated "Poco, fetch," causing the dog to start to cast about and search for the next one. After the second bumper was returned he again commanded "Poco, fetch" and the dog went out after the third and last lure. Removing this last bumper from the dog's mouth, he still continued as if he believed that there was yet another object out there to be retrieved and again gave the command "Poco, fetch." At this, the dog simply looked at him, barked once, and moved to his left side, to the usual heeling position, and sat down.

He gave Poco a pat and murmered "Clever girl," then turned to me and said, "She knows that she's retrieved all three, and that is all that there were. She keeps a running count. When there are no more bumpers to find, she lets me know with that 'They're all here, stupid' bark that you just heard, and then goes to heel to let me know that she's ready for the next thing that I want her to do."

I was impressed but not convinced, so we spent the better part of a half hour, varying the number of bumpers up to five, with me and another dog handler tossing the bumpers and sending the dog to fetch as sort of a check to see if it was the something in the way that the items were placed or the commands were given that made any difference. Once we even had someone toss out a set of lures but in such a way that the dog saw it and the person sending her out to retrieve could not. This meant that the handler didn't know how many bumpers the dog needed to return and couldn't give any kind of useful clues to the dog, such as knowing glances or inadvertently signaling that all of the objects had now been picked up. None of these changes seemed to matter, and even with five objects, the dog never missed the count once. If I had conducted a similar experiment with my young grandchildren, by tossing toys behind items of furniture, and they had performed as well as Poco, I certainly would have taken that as proof that they could count from one to five!

If we accept the fact that dogs can count, how about the possibility that dogs can do simple arithmetic? I am not suggesting that dogs can multiply 233 by 471 and then divide the result by 16 and present us with an answer, but how about something simple, like demonstrating that they understand that 1 + 1 = 2? Two researchers, Robert Young of the Pontifical Catholic University in Brazil and Rebecca West of the University of Lincoln in the United Kingdom, attempted to test this idea using a group of eleven mixed-breed dogs and a set of large tempting dog treats.

These researchers modified a test that has been used to prove that human infants at the age of five months have a rudimentary ability to count. The technique involves something called "preferential viewing," which simply measures the amount of time that infants spend looking at things. It has been shown that infants (just like adults) will stare at something unexpected or unusual for a longer time. The human test for counting is quite simple. First the child is a shown a small doll on a table and then a low screen is put in front of it to block the child's view. While he watches, the experimenter takes another doll, shows it to the child, and then puts it behind the screen. If the child can count, he should expect that when the screen is raised he should see two dolls, and sometimes he does. However, sometimes the experimenter secretly removes one of the dolls so that now when the screen is raised there is only one doll visible. When this occurs, the results reveal that the babies stare at what is on the table for much longer after the screen has been raised, suggesting that they have made the calculation and worked out that the number of dolls that they are seeing is different from what they expected it to be.

In the canine version of this test, Young and West first showed the dog a single large treat. Then a low screen was lowered and the dog watched as the experimenter obviously placed another treat down behind the screen and out of his view. In the normal situation, where

1 + 1 = 2, the dog should expect that when the screen was raised there should be two dog treats visible. However, just like in the case of the babies, sometimes the experimenters cheated and surreptitiously removed the second treat, so that when the screen was raised the dog saw only one treat. In effect, he was faced with an equation that said 1 + 1 = 1. Just as in the case of the babies, the dogs stared at this unexpected outcome for a longer time than they did when the arithmetic came out correctly, apparently "surprised" at finding only one object and spending a longer amount of time searching for the missing treat. Now before granting that dogs can count based on this finding, we must consider the possibility that they are simply making a numerosity judgment by reasoning that one object plus another object should equal more than one object, not specifically two objects. To check for this possibility, the experimenters also presented the dog with the result that 1 + 1 = 3 by secretly slipping another treat behind the screen so that when it was raised the dog saw three objects rather than expected two. The dogs appeared to be equally surprised by this outcome and spent just as long staring at this odd result as they did when the outcome was smaller than they might have predicted. This suggests that the dogs expected that 1 + 1 = 2, and no other answer is correct. If this is so, then dogs can not only count but can also do simple addition and subtraction.

Simple counting and arithmetic ability might seem to be a superfluous ability for dogs, but it is a useful skill that would have been vital to dog's wild ancestors. Wolves, for instance, have a very complex social structure and often form allegiances and coalitions to take and hold leadership of the pack. If the Alpha wolf had basic mathematical abilities, then he could determine how many allies or enemies he had within his pack, which is knowledge that might be essential to his ability to maintain his position of leadership. This is also a useful skill for trying to keep track of where all your pack members are. For a breeding female wolf, this same numerical skill would allow her to know if her entire litter of wolf cubs was present, or if one of them had somehow gone astray and required a search-and-rescue mission to be launched.

Canine Calculus

Addition and subtraction are simple arithmetical skills, but how about higher mathematics, such as calculus? Actually, Timothy Pennings, of the Mathematics Department at Hope College, believes that he has proven that dogs solve problems in calculus. He reports his discovery resulted from a walk along the shore of Lake Michigan with his Welsh corgi, Elvis. He was tossing a ball into the lake and watching Elvis retrieve it. It was just a coincidence that this walk with his dog was just after he had given a lecture in his class that analyzed a particular problem type found in calculus. In his class he had set up the problem as if it were part of a movie scenario involving Tarzan and Jane, but with a reversal of the usual heroic roles. It seems that this time Tarzan blunders into some quicksand and Jane has to get to him in time to save his life. Pennings explains the problem this way, "So Tarzan is in the quicksand, and Jane is across the river and down the bank a ways, and she's got to get to him as quickly as possible. Now, she can run at a certain speed, and she can swim at a certain speed, which is obviously slower than she runs, and the question is what's her best strategy for getting to Tarzan in the quickest amount of time?"

Although Pennings was dramatizing the situation to hold the interest of his class, he was actually presenting a fairly basic problem in calculus that concerns calculations used to find the maximum and minimum values of various things. The situation here is to find the quickest route (the minimum time traveling) between some point A and another point B in the world. The trick involved is that the quickest route is not always the one that involves the shortest distance. For example, if Jane jumped into the river immediately and then swam directly in a straight line toward Tarzan, this is the shortest distance, but since her swimming speed is considerably slower than her running speed, this is not the way for her to get to him fastest. The quickest time is achieved by running along the riverbank until she gets to a point that is closer to Tarzan, and only then should she jump into the river and swim across. But how far should she run? Calculus allows you to find the exact point at which Jane should stop running and start swimming.

Since Pennings had just explained the solution of the problem to his students, mainly by drawing appropriate lines on the blackboard to illustrate various combinations of running and swimming times, and demonstrating that where certain lines intersected represented the quickest route, all of this was fresh in his mind as he tossed a ball into the lake for Elvis to fetch. As he watched the dog, it suddenly dawned upon him that Elvis was doing exactly what he had been drawing on the board, running a certain distance along the shore before jumping into the lake to swim for the ball. His curiosity as a scientist was piqued, and he decided to see just how accurately Elvis was solving the problem. First he measured the dog's average running speed and then his average swimming speed. Next he got a long tape measure and a screwdriver, marked his starting place, and then threw the ball and ran along with the dog. As soon as Elvis turned to start swimming, Pennington marked the point by driving the screwdriver into the ground. Then, tape measure in hand, he had to wade quickly to get to the ball before the dog did, in order to get an accurate measurement of its location. After several hours of such measurements (much to the dog's disappointment), the mathematician stopped the game and went home to check on the dog's solutions to the problem. It took the adult human mathematician about three hours to compute the same solution that his three-year-old dog had achieved in a fraction of a second. Furthermore, it showed that the dog's calculations were correct within a foot or so of distance.

Should we believe that the dog is really doing the math and solving the calculus equations? At one level we have to believe that the dog is doing calculus in the sense that he is solving a problem that requires calculus and somehow he knows how to find the path that gets him to the ball in the minimum time. However, this is obviously not conscious mathematical processing but rather a form of mathematical solution that comes with the rest of the dog's genetic endowment. Humans are probably performing the same kind of calculation when baseball players instinctively track fly balls and choose the quickest route to intercept and catch them. Certainly, having this kind of calculation prewired into a hunting animal is important. It would have allowed the wild ancestors of dogs to compute the quickest path to intercept a running rabbit or other prey. Furthermore, in the competitive social environment of the pack, perhaps the issue is that if a duck inattentively floats close to shore, whichever dog picks the correct distances and gets to it first will end up with the largest share of that meal. Thus being wired to do certain types of mathematical computation might well provide a survival advantage for the swift-running hunters from which dogs were bred.

Despite proof of all of this mathematical ability that dogs appear to have, I still steadfastly refuse to relinquish my pocket calculator to my beagle puppy. The last time that he got hold of it, rather than coming up with great mathematical insights, like $E = mc^2$, he simply did the most natural doggy thing and used it as a chew toy.

CHAPTER 15

The Wrinkled Mind

THE FRENCH ESSAYIST Michel Eyquem de Montaigne noted in 1580 that "Age imprints more wrinkles in the mind than it does on the face." For human beings it is certainly the case that age changes the clarity and speed of thought and also alters certain patterns of thinking. The same is true of dogs—in fact, some psychologists have suggested that age-related changes in the brain and in thinking processes are so similar between dogs and humans that dogs can actually serve as a model for studies of age-related changes in the thought processes of people.

For the researcher, although certainly not for the person who loves his canine companion, it is actually a great benefit that dogs have a shorter life span and show the effects of age much faster. Thus a human being might not start showing gray in his hair until his thirties, while a six-year-old dog will often be showing gray around his muzzle. This rapid maturing process benefits the researcher, who can track and monitor the aging process in a much shorter period, and thus he or she will live long enough to study many lifetimes worth of aging.

How Old Is Your Dog?

Translating a dog's age into human years depends upon several considerations. You may have heard that one year in a dog's life is equal to seven years in a person's life. This is not actually true. In the first year of life a dog grows and changes very quickly. On his first birthday, your dog has all of the physical abilities that a human who is sixteen years old will have, and his thought processes have also entered the canine equivalent of the teenage years. When the dog is two years old he is at the same stage as a twenty-four-year-old human. After that, we can say that each year adds about five human years in terms of the way your dog's body (including his brain and nervous system) is changing.

Therefore if you want to calculate your dog's age, it works like this. Suppose that your dog is 12 years old. You would start with 24 years for his first two years, and then add 5 years each for his next 10 years. This would give him a total of 24 plus 50, which is 74 years in human life. Right now 74 years is the average length of life for humans, and 12 years is the average life span for dogs. As far as we can tell, the oldest dog who ever lived was an Australian cattle dog named Bluey. In 1939 when he died, his age in chronological years was 29 years and 5 months old. In human years that would mean that he was more than 160 years old!

This method to compute a dog's age is complicated by its breed. Generally speaking, bigger dogs have shorter lives than smaller dogs. For instance, the tallest purebred dog is the Irish wolfhound, which tends to have a life expectancy of only a bit more than seven years. The large, elegant Great Dane has an average life of eight years, and the powerful Rottweiler, which is smaller than the Great Dane, nine years. Standard poodles live about eleven years, miniature poodles thirteen years. The small, tough Jack Russell terrier and the tiny Chihuahua both live to about fourteen years.

Even within certain size ranges there are other complications. For example, the shape of your dog's face can help predict how long he will live. Dogs with sharp, pointed faces that look like wolves generally have longer lives. Dogs with very flat faces, like bulldogs and pugs, often have shorter lives. Of course, dogs that are well cared for can often live much longer than average.

The same kinds of considerations play a role in the mental age of dogs. For human beings some slowing of thought processes and limitations on memory begin to appear at around fifty-five years of age. The giant breeds, like the Saint Bernard, will start showing the kinds of thought patterns, problem-solving changes, and learning problems that we associate with humans of that age somewhere between five to seven years of age. Large breeds, like the Alaskan malamute, start thinking like seniors between six and eight years of age. Medium breeds, like the fox terrier, won't enter their senior stage until seven to nine years of age, while the small breeds, such as the Bichon Frise, won't act like a senior until nine to eleven years of age.

When we are talking about mental abilities and behaviors, however, it is important to recognize that there is a large degree of variability even within a single breed. Some individual dogs seem to age more rapidly, while others go many years past when we might expect a slowing of the thought processes with no dimming of ability or loss of learning capacity. This is also true in humans, where some people seem to show the mental effects of aging at a younger age. In some respects the process of mental aging seems to be related to the individual's behaviors. People who remain mentally active, who read more, take courses, do puzzles, and engage in games that require problem solving seem to slow the aging of their brains. They are less likely to develop Alzheimer's disease and other problems that cause memory losses and impair thinking. This also seems to be the case for dogs. For the mind and brain the key phrase is "Use it or lose it!"

The Aging Brain

No one knows exactly why dogs or humans decline in their abilities when they age. One theory suggests that as the genetic material (DNA) reproduces itself in each new cell, the successive transcriptions become less accurate, sort of like making copies of copies of copies on a photocopier, where each one gets progressively grainier and harder to read. Damage to the DNA can also come about due to natural radiation damage from cosmic rays and more terrestrial sources (such as breathing in air pollutants or fumes from certain solvents), which in turn might lead to faulty enzyme production. When this happens, it will often result in cell deaths in the nervous system and elsewhere. Other theories of aging blame simple wear and tear, suggesting that various physical and neural systems break down from frequent use and may break down even faster if they are put under stress. Other theories suggest that aging results from the accumulation of metabolic waste products in the cells or the increase in unstable chemicals (free radicals) that interact with molecules in the cells and interfere with their functioning.

Regardless of the source of aging effects, the brain and nervous systems of dogs (and humans) change markedly as they age. Old dogs have smaller, lighter brains than young dogs. The change is quite significant and the older brain might be up to 25 percent lighter. It is important to note that this change is not necessarily due to brain cells dying off. When I was first learning neuropsychology, many textbooks claimed that humans lose a hundred thousand cells a day once they are mature. Although we do lose many nerve cells as we age, this number has proven to be a gross exaggeration. Actually, we mostly lose parts of the nerve cells, the branches (dendrites and axon filaments) that connect with other nerve cells. These connections to other cells start to break down with age. If we could consider the brain as a complexly wired computer, it would be the same as if various circuits in the central processor simply stopped functioning because connections were broken. Neurologists refer to this as a "pruning" of branches that are no longer used or needed, much as one might prune a bush in the garden. For the most part, it is the loss of these connections that reduces the size and the weight of the brain.

Another neurological change is that the transmission of information from one place in the nervous system to another becomes noticeably slower, and the reflexes that they control are also slowed. Jacob Mosier of the veterinary school at Kansas State University has observed that the age-related changes in dog behaviors are similar to those in humans. In a healthy young dog, neural information travels at about 225 miles per hour (360 kilometers per hour) while in an older dog this will often slow down to 50 miles per hour (80 kilometers per hour).

Various measures also show that the efficiency of the nerve cells diminishes with age. Some brain-scanning techniques measure how vigorously various brain cells react by measuring the amount of blood sugar (glucose) that is metabolized at any one time. The metabolic rate is a good measure of activity level. One study compared the rate at which various brain tissues in beagles used glucose. In the frontal portion of the brain, where we believe that most judgment, evaluation, and problem solving takes place, there was a steady decline in glucose utilization starting after the age of three years. By the time the dogs were between fourteen and sixteen years, the glucose use had dropped to roughly half that of younger dogs. In addition to a slowed metabolic rate, there is also a reduction in the oxygen supply to the brain, which can directly affect a dog's long-term memory. Although there is a general age-related reduction in neural activity in the brain, researchers did find that certain parts of the brain show a faster decline and others seem to be more resistant.

Slowing Age Effects

Exercising the brain by providing enriched sensory experiences (through vision, hearing, smell, and touch) and increased opportunities for problem solving and making choices can offset some age-related changes. The best evidence for this comes from the laboratory of William Greenough of the Department of Psychology at the University of Illinois. He has been using rats in most of his studies, but the results apply to dogs (and humans) as well. He began by taking a group of elderly, out-of-shape, overweight rats that had lived their entire lives in standard laboratory cages. Dull and boring environments, with little to do and not much to look at or listen to, these cages are the rat equivalent of solitary confinement in prison. These animals were moved to a new, exciting environment that could be viewed as the rodent equivalent of an amusement park. Their new living quarters had ramps, ladders, running wheels, swings, slides, and various toys and objects hanging from the ceiling. In addition, there were other rats to socially interact with. Initially, as you might expect, these old rats were quite frightened by their new surroundings, but after a while they learned that there was nothing to fear. Once that happened, they began to explore. They began to climb the ramps and ladders and use the slides, swings, wheels, and rat toys. Furthermore, they began to socialize and interact with the other rats in their new and complex world. They became more fit, lost weight, and seemed to be very happy in their new living quarters.

The real surprises, however, came when the brains of these animals were examined. There were many more neural connections in these animals than in their counterparts who were still living in the boring isolation of the usual lab cage. In fact, in one study Greenough found that the number of neural connections increased in the range of 25 percent to 200 percent, depending upon which types of neural connections they considered. Several findings make this research important. First, it shows that individual nerve cells are capable of growing new connections even when an animal has reached old age. Second, it shows that this new growth is triggered by exercising and stimulating the brain with new experiences and problems to solve. The significance of findings like this for an aging dog is obvious. While we cannot stop the effects of time on the reproduction of cells, production of hormones, integrity of DNA, or general wear and tear on body systems, we can control aspects of our dog's environment to give him more physical and mental exercise and to stimulate his senses to a greater degree. This stimulation, in turn, will improve the functioning of his brain and, in effect, slow the aging process. We should not follow the old adage and "Let sleeping dogs lie," but rather should encourage older dogs to think and experience life to a greater extent.

With age, chemical changes occur in the brain that affect behavior, memory, and learning. In dogs and humans the mitochondria, little strandlike structures in the nucleus of cells, are responsible for converting nutrients into energy. As dogs and humans age, mitochondrial efficiency decreases. The mitochondria begin to act as if they have become leaky, since they now begin to release "free radicals," chemicals that oxidize compounds essential for normal cell function. The loss of these compounds places the cell at risk. As the tissues degenerate, protein deposits called "amyloids" accumulate in the brain. High levels of amyloids, especially when associated with clusters of dead and dying nerve cells, are taken as part of the evidence that the individual is suffering from Alzheimer's disease. Studies conducted at the University of Toronto by a team of researchers, including psychologist Norton Milgram, have shown that dogs with high levels of amyloids in their brains have poorer memories and difficulties learning new material, especially if it involves more complex thinking and problem solving.

If the release of these oxidants is causing poor brain functioning and reduced behavioral efficiency in the dogs, then at least theoretically it should be possible to slow or even reverse the neural damage by administering high doses of antioxidant chemicals. Consuming more antioxidants could help provide the body with tools to neutralize those harmful free radicals. Antioxidants are quite common, and it's estimated that there are more than 4,000 compounds in foods that can fulfill antioxidant functions. Probably the best-known antioxidant is vitamin C (also called ascorbic acid). It is a water-soluble vitamin found in all body fluids and can work its way through the nervous system. It actively protects vital compounds that can be dissolved in watery body fluids from oxidizing. The difficulty with vitamin C is that it can't be stored by the body, so the individual has to get some every day. Another well-known antioxidant is vitamin E, which is fat soluble and can be stored with fats in the liver and other tissues. It specifically acts to protect cell membranes from oxidation damage. The carotenoids include some six hundred different antioxidant chemicals of which the best known is probably beta-carotene. These seem to help the mitochondria function more efficiently (and perhaps slow the "leaks"). Certain minerals, such as selenium, and fatty acids (such as DHA and EPA, carnitine and alphalipoic acid) will also help fight cell damage from oxygen-derived compounds.

Milgram's team had a specially prepared diet rich in antioxidants produced for testing. Their first study used young beagles (less than two years of age) and old beagles (older than nine years of age). Half the young and half the old dogs were put on the antioxidant diet while the other half had a normal balanced dog food. After six months Milgram tested dogs' mental abilities using an oddity discrimination test in which the dogs had to choose objects that were different from others.

The first important result that came out of this study was a verification that older dogs take longer to learn this task. The differences between old and young dogs were smallest when the task was easy but became larger as the task became progressively more difficult. The second important finding was that, as hoped, the antioxidant food seemed to reduce the effect of aging. The older dogs that were on the antioxidant diet performed much better on these tasks than the older dogs that were not on the special diet. The improvements were greatest for the most difficult problems. For these harder tasks the old dogs with antioxidant enrichment made roughly half the number of errors that the old dogs on the normal diet did. For the young dogs, however, the special diet made no difference.

In a follow-up study, the University of Toronto team combined the findings of their study on the benefits of antioxidant diets for aging dogs with Greenough's findings that mental exercise and stimulation helped offset the effects of aging. Using forty-eight old beagles, they put twenty-four of them on an antioxidant-rich diet and twenty-four on a regular-balanced diet. Within each of these groups, half the animals also received "cognitive enrichment" to exercise the brain. Specifically this meant that, five to six days a week, these dogs were challenged with learning tasks and puzzles, such as finding hidden food rewards. At the end of a year all four groups were retested, and the results showed that the diet-enriched, cognitively enriched group scored the highest. Milgram summarized his results this way: "We say that we can teach an old dog new tricks because it's possible to slow down, or partially reverse brain decline. Some dogs in our tests definitely became smarter."

The special food that Milgram used in his studies is now available as a prescription diet for dogs and is available through Hills Pet Nutrition, Inc. No equivalent diet is available for humans, unfortunately, at least at the time of this writing, but we can improve our diets and take vitamins and supplements to increase our intake of antioxidants. If you have an older dog and want to increase the amount of antioxidants available without a prescription or the need to rely on a commercial product, you can add certain fruits and vegetables to his diet. Important sources of vitamin C include citrus fruits (which many dogs don't like); however, green peppers, broccoli, strawberries, raw cabbage, and potatoes are foods that contain large amounts of the vitamin and many dogs do like them. You can also lightly steam or parboil green leafy vegetables and save the cooking water to add to the dog's food, since some of the vitamin will be dissolved in it. High concentrations of vitamin E can be found in wheat germ, nuts, seeds, whole grains, green leafy vegetables (steam or parboil them), vegetable oil, and fish-liver oil. Beta-carotene and other carotenoids are found in carrots, squash, broccoli, sweet potatoes, tomatoes, kale, collard greens, cantaloupe, peaches, and apricots. If you also want to add selenium to the diet, some good food sources are fish, shellfish, red meat, grains, eggs, and chicken.

Canine Cognitive Dysfunction

What we are trying to fight off by dietary manipulations and mental exercises is an age-related decrease in mental ability that is called "canine cognitive dysfunction." This was not a common problem fifty years ago simply because dogs did not live as long as they do today. Because of advances in veterinary science there are now estimated to be 7.3 million dogs ten years or older in the United States.

I became personally aware of canine cognitive dysfunction (usually abbreviated CCD) a few years ago when my much-loved Cavalier King Charles spaniel, Wizard, was in the middle of his twelfth year of life. It started with a change in his greeting behavior. He always met me at the door, but if he missed hearing it open the thump of my briefcase on the floor would bring him running. But he began to take a minute or two before coming to greet me, even though both of the other dogs were already milling around me causing the usual happy commotion that I love when I enter the house. This was not due to aches and pains that slowed him, since his arthritis was under control, nor was it due to hearing loss, since his hearing had been bad ever since he was ten years of age but he still could hear loud sounds (like the door slamming closed), sense vibrations, and see and feel when his canine housemates left their resting places to dash to the door.

There were other signs that his mental abilities were slipping. At my dog-training club I had long since stopped working him in any athletic tasks involving jumping, but there were other exercises that he had always liked. One of his favorites was scent discrimination, where he had to go out to a pile of dumbbell-shaped articles on the floor and retrieve the one that had my scent on it. He had always dashed to the pile and sniffed around with his tail batting from side to side until he found it and proudly returned to me with it in his mouth. Now he would move out to the pile of articles but then stand there as if confused, looking as though he had forgotten what he was supposed to do. If I repeated the command for him to "Find it!" it would appear as though the lightbulb had come back on in his mind and he would search around and bring back the article to me.

These lapses in memory and mental processing were becoming more frequent. For instance, each day I'd let him out through the back door first thing in the morning so that he could eliminate. Normally he would dash down the steps with the other dogs and return to sit by the door when he was finished with his business. Now, however, he would walk out of the door and simply sit on the porch and watch the other dogs in the yard. When they returned to be let back in, he would come along with them. A few minutes later he would slowly wander to the door and look back at me with that "I have to go to the toilet" look. It became clear that once outside he simply forgot why he was there. Ultimately I had to snap his lead on, lead him down the steps, and then give him the "Be quick!" command that I had first taught him when I began housetraining him simply to remind him why he was out there.

Wizard was also more anxious than usual. He had always been a very placid, easygoing dog. Now he seemed worried, especially at night, when he would lie in bed panting heavily. Once or twice each week he would waken me with a bark growl, but when I checked there was nothing out of the ordinary and the other dogs were quite unconcerned and unaroused.

Wizard's problem was that age had finally caught up with him and he was showing symptoms of canine cognitive dysfunction. Currently, it is estimated that about 62 percent of dogs over the age of ten years will experience at least some symptoms of this problem. The major one is confusion or disorientation. This was obviously what Wizard was suffering from. I have been told of dogs that wandered out into their own fenced backyards, apparently become lost, and seemed unable to find their way back to the door of the house. I have also heard of dogs that got trapped in corners or behind furniture because they couldn't remember that they could escape by backing up. Other symptoms are decreased activity level and apparent loss of attentiveness. In Wizard's case this would show up as periods of several minutes where he would stare into space or at a blank wall. Changes in sleeping patterns are also symptoms, especially when accompanied by increased anxiety, pacing behaviors, or remaining awake for large segments of the night. Loss of well-established habits is another symptom. The habit that is most apt to be noticed by the owner is housetraining, where a previously house-clean dog will forget his training and make a mess where and when he normally wouldn't. Probably one of the most distressing symptoms is when the dog fails to recognize well-known friends, or even worse, familiar family members.

If you can rule out other factors (decreased activity might be due to an advancing arthritic condition, for instance, or apparent inattentiveness might be due to vision or hearing loss), then it is time to see your vet. Your first line of action may simply be to increase the number of antioxidants and exercise your dog's mind a bit more, but for some cases of canine cognitive dysfunction a new drug may help. Originally designed for human patients with Alzheimer's disease and Parkinson's disease, it is called Selegiline or L-Deprenyl, and is a prescription drug sold in various forms under various brand names. When it works, it improves activity level and mental functioning in your dog, and it also seems to protect brain cells from DNA damage and further oxidation-related damage. If the dog responds, he will need to receive the medication daily for the rest of his life, but since you are dealing with an older dog, you may simply be improving the quality of his last few months or his last year or so of life. This means the burden may be short but the benefit can be great.

Can Old Dogs Learn New Tricks?

Even for the healthy older dog without canine cognitive dysfunction, the mind becomes less efficient with age. University of Toronto studies showed that with age the learning process slows, and this is most noticeable in more difficult learning and problem-solving situations. A simple memory task that psychologists call "matching to sample" involves first showing the dog an item and then removing it and presenting two items, one of which is the same as the one he saw. The dog's task is simply to pick out the item that he saw before. Older dogs do fine on this task, although they do a bit more poorly than younger dogs if you introduce a delay between showing them the first item and then giving them the test. Apparently the memory fades a little faster for the older dog in this situation. Now let's complicate the task. Suppose that instead of asking the dog to pick out the target that he saw before, we ask that the dog pick out the item that is new or different from the one that we showed him. This is called a "non-matching to sample" task, and older dogs do more poorly at this. Now if we also introduce a time delay between showing them the item and testing them in the non-matching-to-sample task, the older dogs have a really difficult time learning the rule.

Psychologist Dwight Tapp, now at the University of California at Irvine, tested dogs on a different task. He first taught them the difference between big and small objects. For instance, a dog might always be rewarded when he selected the larger of two objects. The shape of the objects is irrelevant; only the size counts. So during one trial, the dog might have to decide which of two balls is bigger and during the next, which of two cans is larger, and so forth. Older dogs are a bit slower than young dogs at this task, but they make steady progress and do learn it. Once they've learned to reliably choose the large item, the situation is reversed so that now the smaller object is always correct and rewarded. Obviously the dog will make some errors at first, but young dogs quickly learn to switch over to the new rule to earn their rewards. Here, however, the older dog has serious problems.

When a variety of such memory tasks is analyzed, a general principle seems to emerge. It is not so much that older dogs have difficulty learning new material but rather that older dogs seem to have trouble inhibiting or suppressing material they have learned. They stick with the old solution that they have learned for a much longer time. Psychologists would describe this as "perseveration," by which they mean that there is a tendency for a memory or idea to persist and for behaviors to be continued or repeated—even though it should be clear that the rules have changed or that the old idea is no longer correct. In old dogs, earlier learning seems to compete with newer learning and prevents them from acquiring new concepts and new solutions to tasks.

A real world example of this occurred when my cairn terrier, Flint, was about twelve years of age. One day on our morning walk, a cat skittered out from under a parked white van. Flint, being a terrier, gave chase, at least as far as the long leash would let him go. For the next two weeks he persisted in checking under every light-colored vehicle parked along the street. He had learned that there might be a cat under a white vehicle, and this idea perseverated in his mind for a long time despite dozens of disconfirmations on each of his daily walks. My younger dog (at that time it was Wizard, who was five years of age) joined the hunt the first few times, but later he patiently stood aside and observed Flint's continued excited searches under parked cars with some apparent puzzlement and perhaps some disdain. He had quickly learned that the old idea that there might be a cat under any white vehicle was wrong.

Early memories are preserved better than later ones, however, and an old dog can still recall material that he learned when young. The old dog will even maintain the same likes and dislikes of people and places over the years. Stories of an old dog's memories are common and often touching. One was told to me by Stephen Birch of Norfolk Virginia, who left his black and tan coon hound, Flannel, when he joined the army at the beginning of World War II. Flannel was three years old when Stephen left and he was nearly ten years old when he returned. Stephen was sitting on his front porch stroking Flannel's great grandson and looking off into the distance as he recalled:

> Flannel was a neat dog. He got his name because his ears felt just like Flannel. He was my first coon hound and we spent a lot of time together. Whenever he thought that we would be going out for a walk, or to play, or just down to the garage where I worked, he would do this little dance where he would spin around, bouncing on his front feet, and then make this "Woo-woo" sound. If I had been away from home for a while he would do the same dance when I walked into the door. It wasn't just being excited, 'cause he would only do that for me. I used to

think of it as his way of saying he liked me and expected me to do something nice for him.

Anyway, it was around 1941 when I last saw him—before they sent me for training and then shipped me out to North Africa and later to Italy. When the war ended they started to send people back home, but I was assigned to take charge of a prisoner of war camp there, and that really delayed my release from the service. It was 1948 when I finally got to come back home.

Mom and Dad knew that I was traveling, but not when I would arrive, so when I got to shore and was offered a ride home I thought that I would surprise them. When I walked up to the door and opened it there was Flannel. He was obviously a lot older then, with gray on his muzzle—although his ears still felt soft like flannel. He saw me, and it was just like no time had passed. He did his little dance and sounded off with that "Woo-woo" song of his.

Mom was in the kitchen and didn't know I had walked in. When Flannel sang that little song she called out "What's gotten into you Flannel. Steve's not here yet but you act like you know that he's coming." She later told me that Flannel had not done his dance or "Woo-woo" in the whole time that I was gone. But he clearly remembered me, because he started doing it immediately after I came home, and he continued to do it every day for me until he died. That little "Woo-woo" told me that I was home again and that someone remembered me—had missed me—and still loved me.

Aging Minds and Bodies

While I have been focusing on the changes in behavior that occur because of changes in the nervous system, it is important to recognize that changes that occur in the dog's body and the efficiency of his senses can also affect his behavior, his thinking, and even his personality. One must remember that changes in muscles, bones, and joints have consequences that can have vast effects on his responses and attitudes toward things in his life.

As dogs age, their muscles, like their brains, tend to decrease in size and mass. Many older dogs also develop arthritis in their joints, which can be painful. The symptoms that you are most apt to see are slowed movements, limping, holding a leg up, or showing evidence that it hurts when you touch certain joints. If the problem is in the back and spine (where it is called spondylitis), the dog will be unwilling (perhaps unable) to go up or down stairs. A dog that formerly jumped up on a bed or sofa to be with its owner may not be able to do so any longer and may even find sitting or running to be uncomfortable. Certain surfaces that are smooth or slippery, such as wood, tile, or linoleum floors, now become barriers to movement as the dog walks unsteadily. Although you might think that these are simply changes in mobility, they have important consequences. Dogs are social animals, so it is important for them to be with their pack or family. The older dog may now find it difficult to follow his owner from room to room, which can cause depression. Simply as a consequence of reduced mobility, the dog may start to show signs of social isolation. A dog that had always seemed to be secure might now start showing separation anxiety even if his owner has simply moved to another room.

When my dog Wizard first showed signs of slowed and restricted movement because of aging, he also began to show some signs of insecurity. Therefore I resorted to several tactics to ease the situation. First (somewhat to my wife's consternation), I built a step so that he could still make it up to my bed, where he had slept since he was six months old. Second, I made sure that he had a floor pillow in a central place where he could observe us in the living room or as we passed back and forth to the kitchen without needing to move. This gave him the sense of being included rather than isolated.

Older dogs sometimes seem to lose their calm, easygoing demeanor and become more hostile and aggressive. Changes in the muscles and joints are often accompanied by pain. As you may recall from an earlier chapter, dogs often show little evidence that they are hurting, but when pain is present it can make the dog quite irritable. This irritability can change the dog's personality. The existence of pain due to age-related processes can lead to unexpected, atypical aggressive encounters with visitors, family members, and other pets in the house, since the dog may ascribe the pain to the person who has just touched him.

The fact that older dogs are likely to be more cantankerous is partly due to their reduced mobility. The natural response of most dogs when confronted with stressful situations is to move away from the people, animals, or environmental circumstances that are bothering him. Running away is a good self-protective strategy. Unfortunately for the older dog, in his present condition running away might not be an option. Pain and lack of mobility may force the dog to stay where he is. If the dog interprets the situation as dangerous or threatening, this can lead to warning snaps or even actual aggression as the dog tries to defend the tiny territory around his body. This is most frequently a problem when there is a new puppy or a very mobile baby in the house. Intrusions in the form of attempts to play or interact with the old dog may ultimately start to threaten or stress him. If he can't easily move himself to get out of the situation, his only other option is to try to get the puppy or child to leave him alone. This can result in hostility and aggression. Strangely, this means that you may have to monitor an older dog's interactions with pups and babies more carefully than you have to monitor those interactions with younger adult dogs. Sometimes the simplest solution is to give the older dog a protective "den" in the form of its familiar kennel crate. Once inside, with the door closed, the dog will feel more secure, and unless little fingers inappropriately poke at it, both puppies and babies will be considerably safer.

Aging Eyes

When we first started talking about the dog's mind and thought processes in the beginning of this book, I pointed out that the building blocks of thought and problem-solving are sensations. The quality of the information that we have about our world depends on the quality of the sensory information that we have available. Unfortunately, some of the largest changes that the aging dog undergoes affect their senses. Eyes and ears are the most vulnerable systems, which can cause many problems.

As the dog ages changes in the proteins that make up the lens of his eye cause it to become less flexible. The dog, who at the best of times has poor vision for objects that are near him, now becomes even more farsighted. In addition, the focusing of the eye seems to be somewhat slower, and it takes more time for the dog to recognize objects and people (although some of this slowing may have to do with slower mental processing as well). This problem is compounded by the fact that the pupil of the eye (the hole in the colored iris through which the light passes) loses its ability to open and close efficiently. Changing the size of the pupil is important in adjusting to the amount of light in the environment, and if too much or too little light is present, the quality of the visual image degrades even further.

The most visible change in the dog's eye is a haziness that appears on the lens of an older dog's eyes. This condition is called "nuclear sclerosis." Fortunately, unless this cloudiness gets to be very dense (when it appears to be almost white), it does not appear to have very much of an effect on the dog's vision. Some people observing this condition may mistake it for cataracts, which are a major concern and the leading single cause of blindness in older dogs. Basically a cataract in a dog comes about when cells within the lens become dark and opaque over time. Some breeds have a hereditary predisposition toward cataracts, particularly cocker spaniels, poodles, and Lhasa apsos. Cataracts can also come about as a result of diabetes, injuries, nutritional deficiencies, and certain toxins. In addition, exposure to ultraviolet light, as from too much bright sunshine, can cause these opaque regions in the lens. Fortunately, veterinary science now has effective surgical treatments and often the same kind of prosthetics that are used with humans can be used with dogs to restore much of his vision.

The second major condition that causes blindness in dogs is glaucoma. The major problem in glaucoma is an increase in the fluid pressure in the eye, which then rises to the point that it damages the retina and optic nerve. In a normal eye the fluid is drained away at the same rate new fluid is introduced, but in glaucoma the outlet for the fluid is narrowed or closed. Again heredity is a factor, with some breeds (including cocker spaniels, Siberian huskies, basset hounds, and beagles) being especially susceptible to these problems. Aging dogs with high blood pressure are also more susceptible. If detected early, drugs and surgery can often stave off the loss of vision for quite a while, although the long-term success is disappointingly low.

Many people with blind dogs believe that their dogs lost their vision fairly suddenly, but most dogs suffer a gradual loss of sight. The truth is that only when visual capacity finally drops to the point that it is virtually useless does a dog's owner usually notice. Often subtle signs, such as behavioral or personality changes, indicate a visual loss. Thus, a dog that is losing its vision may become more fearful, show greater dependence on its owner, be more lethargic, and sometimes more aggressive. Sometimes the most obvious symptoms are seen in a reduced ability to retrieve or a disinterest in chasing balls. The dog may seem to be more cautious when climbing steps or jumping onto or off of furniture. Going up or down curbs might be accompanied by a cautious or high-stepping gait.

Some simple tests can help you tell if your dog is losing its vision. The simplest one involves the "pupillary light reflex." Use a concentrated bright light (a flashlight is good for this) and shine it in one of your dog's eyes. When the light hits the dog's eye, you should see the pupil grow smaller. In addition you should also see the pupil of the other eye grow smaller. A failure to find the pupillary light reflex is a sure sign that there is a visual problem and perhaps blindness. It is possible, however, for the dog to have the pupillary light reflex but still not have enough vision to make out objects, patterns, and movements, since this reflex is based on brightness alone.

If the dog passes the pupillary response test but you still feel that his vision is poor, you can use a couple of other tests. The first is the "looming response," which is simply based on the fact that when an object threatens to hit you in the eye or the face, you tend to blink, and so do dogs. The easiest way to test this reflex is to move your hand quickly toward your dog's eye. However there is a problem with this, namely that small air currents stirred up by this movement can affect the vibrissae, which would also cause the eye to blink. Placing a piece of clear glass or plastic in front of the dog's face and then moving your hand quickly toward his eye is the solution. A blink indicates that he is seeing your hand and its motion.

A more sensitive measure of vision is called the "visual placing reflex." This works best for small to medium dogs, since it actually involves lifting the dog. Lift the dog in such a way that the front paws are freely hanging down. Now move him toward a surface such as the edge of a table or a counter. If the dog's vision is working, he will automatically reach forward with his front legs and try to place them on the edge of the approaching surface. This is a visually guided response, so if your dog does this, he still has some useful visual function.

One last test that may also be useful is a "tracking test." You are going to toss an object and see if the dog follows it, but you want to avoid giving him any sound clues, as he would get when the object hits the floor. Therefore, throw a wad of absorbent cotton. Wave it to one side of the dog's head and then, using the fingers to flip it out of your hand, shoot it across the room, making sure that it passes in front of the dog's head. He should follow it with his head and eyes.

Of course these home tests are not as sensitive as those a veterinarian would use, but if the dog fails them, it certainly suggests that you need to get a more formal checkup to see if his vision is functioning.

A blind dog can still have a good quality of life, but you can expect some permanent behavioral and personality changes. The vast majority of these involve greater timidity and caution and a much greater dependence on the owner. Dogs seem to be much more comfortable on a leash, since their sense of touch then tells them where you are and helps them sense your movements. Blind dogs will tend to walk rather than run. Many blind dogs will become much more vocal. Since they can't see you, they may increase the amount of barking to solicit their owner's attention. Blind dogs are most comfortable in environments that they know well, so it is best to avoid moving the furniture in the house.

Other senses can take over for the lost sense of sight. A bit of cheap perfume or scented oil applied to particularly important places, such as where the dog sleeps or eats, or specific rooms or areas that the dog might be encouraged to avoid (such as the top of a stairwell), will help. Different scents for different places work best. A bit of distinctive carpet near the dog's sleeping area will tell his sense of touch that he has arrived. A friend of mine also got a series of bells of different sizes (and hence different tones) and put them on her two normally sighted dogs and on a cord that she and her daughter wore around their necks. Their blind cocker spaniel rapidly learned the significance of the bells and then could monitor where his family members were. This reassured and calmed him quite a bit. It is also important always to speak to the dog before touching him, since a startled blind dog may react by snapping in the direction of the touch without checking to identify the source.

Aging Ears

Just as it does in elderly humans, an older dog's hearing can also begin to fail. There are a number of signs that your aging dog may have lost some hearing, some of which we discussed in Chapter 3. The main thing is to look for a change in responsiveness to sounds. Since the dog has been living with you for a long time, you should have an idea of how he normally behaves, so changes in behavior should be quite noticeable. One obvious change is when a dog that has always responded to commands now ignores your call, especially if he is looking away from you. Other signs are that the dog sleeps more soundly than he used to, instead of bolting awake at a loud noise. Outdoors he may appear to be oblivious to the sound of approaching cars. For my old cairn terrier Flint, the first sign of his failing hearing was that he failed to show up at the sound of the refrigerator opening or closing or at the sound of things being placed on the kitchen counter. Some of the same personality changes that are associated with failing vision may occur as well, such as the dog becoming more fearful, dependent, lethargic, and sometimes more aggressive. In addition, the dog may awaken with a growl or a snap if touched while sleeping. If you suspect that your dog has hearing problems, please refer to the simple tests to check his ears in Chapter 3.

Age-related hearing loss in dogs is really mostly a matter of physical wear and tear. The little bones in the inner ear (called ossicles) that transmit the sound from the eardrum to the inner ear begin to grind at their joints and lose their mobility because of something that looks like arthritis. In the inner ear (the cochlea), tiny hair cells flex to register the arrival of sounds, but repeated flexing over the years causes a weakness in the material and the hair cell can break, just like a wire coat hanger that has been bent in the same place many times. These hairs do not regenerate in the way hair on your head or body does, so for each hair cell that is damaged, you lose a bit of your hearing ability. This happens first for the cells that register the higher frequencies of sound in both aging humans and dogs because the higher frequencies cause the hairs to flex more often and thus they break earlier. Hair cell damage, which is often caused by exposure to loud sounds, is more common in dogs that have been exposed to gunshot noises in hunting or that have lived in cities and been exposed to high levels of urban noise. Finally, there is sensory-neural hearing loss due to the death or damage of cells in the auditory pathways and processing centers that happens as a result of simple aging but which may be accelerated by exposure to various common solvents, such as cleaning fluids, paint thinners, and plastic solvents. A lifetime of minor stresses due to loud sounds and environmental chemicals can add up to a major loss of hearing in an old dog. Most dogs in the twelve- to fifteen-year-old range show some evidence of hearing loss.

In many cases, however, what appear to be age-related hearing losses may be due to other preventable factors. The dog's ear canal is much longer than that of humans, and it takes a right angle turn as it reaches the eardrum. This means the ear has a shape that is ideal for collection of debris. Wax, dirt, and hair build up in the canal and create a plug that keeps the sound from reaching the eardrum. These substances can also attract ear mites and cause ear infections (called "otitis"). The resultant swelling and fluid accumulation can greatly reduce the intensity of the sound waves reaching the middle ear. Dogs that spend a lot of time in the water (especially pond or lake water, which might not be so clean) are more susceptible to these problems. Finally, although appealing to look at, the long floppy ears of dogs like hounds and spaniels tend to trap moisture and limit air circulation, which in turn cause the ear to become a good breeding ground for ear infections.

There are several signs that suggest a problem with a dog's ears. Commonly, the dog will shake its head or scratch its ears, or the ears may be sensitive to the touch. Lift the flap of the dog's ear and give a sniff. A bad smell is a common sign of ear problems. Healthy ears are pink, and a small amount of amber wax is normal (and actually helps to protect the ear canal). Any discharge, blood blisters, excess reddening, or crumbly material may indicate an infection or ear mites that may be reducing your dog's hearing ability. If these signs exist, it is likely that a trip to the veterinarian is needed.

Some routine ear-cleaning procedures can often prevent or cure such difficulties. First you have to take care of some visible problems. For some breeds of dogs, including most spaniels and terriers, poodles, schnauzers, Lhasa apsos, Bouviers des Flandres, Old English sheepdogs, and others, hair actually grows inside the ear canal. This tends to block air circulation and to hold moisture, which in turn makes these dogs prone to ear infections. The hair around the outside of the ear canal can be easily trinned with clippers. You can remove the hair down to about half an inch (1 cm) from the opening of the ear by plucking a few hairs at a time, but go no further into the ear than this.

To clean the ears and dissolve the wax, you will need either some commercial ear-cleaning drops, some olive oil, or light mineral oil. Depending on the size and energy of the dog, you may also need someone to help you hold him. First take a cotton ball or a soft piece of cloth and dip it in some hydrogen peroxide or oil. Wipe away any visible debris from around the opening of the ear. Never use a cotton swab to poke into the ear; not only can it cause damage, but it may actually push waxy material down further into the ear and may lead to a compact and dense plug that becomes a veterinary problem to remove. Put the bottle of oil in a bowl of hot water until the oil feels just barely warm. Now turn the dog's head so that one ear is upward and fill up the ear canal to the top with the warm oil. Then gently massage the base of the ear with your forefinger and thumb to loosen the debris. Wipe away the excess with a cotton ball. During the application or removal of the oil it is common for the dog to shake its head violently, so be sure that you are working someplace where oil splashes won't matter. After the dog has shaken the material out, wipe the visible portions of the ear. Both ears should be treated twice a week in this way if you suspect that the canals are blocked, although once a week as routine maintenance is fine. The effect of this treatment is to soften the wax in the ear, which should ultimately run out on its own accord. Removing the wax and making the ear canal a hostile environment for ear mites can often do wonders for a dog that appears to be losing its hearing.

When age-related deafness comes on slowly, personality changes will be less dramatic. The most important thing that you have to worry about is that the deaf dog, like the blind dog, will feel a sense of isolation leading to bouts of separation anxiety and perhaps even panic. These can be eased by adapting one of the tricks that we used for the blind dogs. One way to make the older deaf dog feel more secure is for his owner to consistently use a perfumed body lotion or scented after-shave. The dog's sense of smell is the most robust of the senses and suffers least from the aging process. The scent you wear makes you a little easier to track down. Furthermore, since scents tend to persist in the air and cling to surfaces, the dog will recognize that you have been near recently, which will comfort him even if he can't hear you. You can also use his ability to recognize scents to avoid startling him from sleep. Simply approach the sleeping dog and hold your hand near his nose for a few seconds. Your scent will make it through to his sleeping brain, and he will normally awaken in a few seconds or so with the recognition that you are near. When his eyes open, you can reach out and pet him.

Strangely enough, one common problem with deaf dogs is that they bark a lot. Even though they can't hear their own barks clearly, they recognize the feeling of barking, and because they can't hear themselves well, they bark even louder to try to hear themselves. Frequently they bark to attract your attention because they feel socially isolated and anxious. Some owners actually inadvertently end up rewarding this activity by giving the dog a treat or patting him in order to comfort him. This encourages the dog to bark even more. A much more effective strategy is isolating the dog in a small room or his kennel until the barking stops. Wait for a pause in the barking of thirty seconds or more and then let him out and reward the quiet behavior.

For the blind dog we use bells on people and pets around him to help the dog locate them. Since your deaf dog can't hear, that strategy is of little value here. However, putting a bell on your deaf old dog himself will help you. Obviously a deaf dog won't come running when you call, but the tinkle of his bell will give you a much better chance of locating him.

Age-proofing a Dog

The other major problem is communicating with your old deaf dog. In my house I use a technique that I call "age-proofing." Since it is likely that if my dog reaches old age he will either lose his sight or his hearing, all of my dogs are trained to respond to both voice commands and to hand signals. This guarantees that I can communicate with them if they lose either of their senses. I even have a signal that means "Good dog!" which I use to reward them at a distance. The "Good dog" signal is just a momentary flash of my open hand, fingers flared wide, accompanied by the words "Good dog" and quickly followed by a treat. As you may recall from our discussion of learning, such a signal will soon become classically conditioned to produce a good feeling in the dog and can be used to tell him when he is doing something correctly.

Even if you did not teach your dog hand signals originally, it is easy to go back and retrain him to "come," "sit," "down," and "stay" using hand signals. Just make sure that the signals are clear and distinctive. One wise dog trainer many years ago showed me a simple trick that helped her communicate with her deaf Shetland sheepdog. She had a small flashlight that she hooked onto a long lanyard that she wore around her neck like a necklace. When she wanted her dog Minnie to respond, she clicked on the flashlight and gave the hand signals with the light in her hand. "It makes the hand signals more distinctive, and I think that even if Minnie's vision starts to go soon, she will be able to see the bright light better than she sees my hand. In addition, if I want her attention and she is across the room, I just flash the light in front of her and she knows that I want her to do something, so she starts looking for me."

Other easy techniques can help us make contact with our old deaf dogs. Stamping on the floor, so that the dog can feel the vibration, can get their attention. Once the dog looks at you, you can give a hand signal. Flicking room lights on and off will serve the same function. To call a dog in from the yard at night, flicking the porch light on and off can quickly be learned as a signal to return.

As long as the aging dog can still get information about his world, his mind will have the material that it needs to allow him to behave appropriately, solve problems, learn new relationships, and feel comfortable. If his senses fail, then we can often supply alternate ways of communicating with him and telling him about the world. For the aging dog we can also provide continuous assistance in another form. For the blind human there are guide dogs, and for the deaf human there are hearing-assistance dogs. Why not an assistance dog for your old dog? A young dog in the house will respond to your commands. The social nature of dogs will cause your older dog to watch or listen to the other dog and follow along. Thus when you call the young dog to you there is a very high probability that the old dog will pick up on his actions and follow along.

Elaine Dowd from Hull, Canada, deliberately established such a "guide dog for a blind dog" relationship. When her Doberman pinscher, Emma, became blind, Elaine got her a guide dog. The doggy guide is Amy, another Doberman, who wears a bell attached to her collar. Emma has simply been trained to follow the sound of Amy's bell. With Amy in the lead, Emma is able to go anyplace that Elaine wants to take them. She comfortably finds her way around (and onto) furniture, avoids walls and doors, has been out on hikes where she had to scramble up rocky slopes, and even has gone swimming. Elaine has also taken them out shopping with her. "No one ever suspects a thing," she says. "Once we tell them, they don't believe it!"

CHAPTER 16

Canine Consciousness

When my playful black dog Odin died, Dancer, the surviving dog in the house, began to grieve for his loss, or so it seemed to me. When Dancer arrived at my home at the age of eight weeks Odin was there to teach him his house manners, how to respect my wife's cat Loki, when to bark, and other vital lessons. They played together and ran together for hours each day. Now Odin was gone and Dancer was carefully checking each of the four places where the big dog used take his naps. He had done this before, virtually each hour, to see if his friend and mentor was there. Now, in an uncharacteristic way, he stood in the middle of the room, looking alternately at me and at the empty space under the end table that normally held the black dog, and he whimpered plaintively to express his grief.

Yet if this is grief that the little red dog feels, then he must have an image of Odin in his mind, and he must have a mental image of his world with Odin in it that he compares with the current picture presented by his senses, which does not contain his friend. He must notice the difference. Perhaps he may even now recognize his own aloneness and wonder about a future without his constant companion. All of that involves an incredibly high level of mental processing, including consciousness and self-awareness.

As I look at Dancer I wonder if I am committing what one of my old professors used to refer to as the "scientific sin of anthropomorphism." The term "anthropomorphism" comes from the Greek *anthropos,* meaning "human," and *morph,* meaning "shape or form," and it refers the to tendency to attribute human characteristics (either physical, mental, or behavioral) to things that are not human. In this case I am mourning the loss of my dog and I am conscious of his absence; therefore, I must ask if I might not be anthropomorphizing by acting and believing as if Dancer is capable of, and is thinking, experiencing, and feeling the same things I am.

Conscious Like Me

Anthropomorphism appears to be rooted in the human capacity for something psychologists call "reflexive consciousness," which is the ability to use knowledge about our own behaviors and feelings to try to understand and anticipate the behavior of others. In its simplest form, you look at a situation and imagine what you would feel or do under those conditions in order to predict what other people will feel or do in those circumstances. An individual who is good at thinking "what would I do in his place" is at a real advantage, since he can often predict what his rivals will do and perhaps outsmart them. It is also a great advantage in that it will anticipate conflict in enough time to avoid the trouble. Without such thinking we could not work together in cooperative teams on complex projects, which is necessary if you want to build a home or engage in agriculture, manufacturing, hunting, or war.

Viewing the world and estimating the reactions of others based upon the assumption that they act and think like we do is not unique to people. I have often heard people say, "My dog thinks that he's a person." This is not true. The dog really thinks that we humans are dogs. We may be strange-looking dogs who walk upright instead of on four paws, and we might not be very bright dogs, since we don't respond or engage in the full spectrum of canine behaviors, but we certainly act enough like dogs so that they can get along with us by assuming that we will react and respond like dogs. Our dogs are therefore engaging in what technically might be called "cynomorphism," from the Greek root *cyno* meaning "dog." That is why dogs wag their tails to us like they do to other dogs, sniff us as if we were dogs, try to get us to play with them by bowing with their outstretched front paws, and so forth. Most important for our ability to control their behaviors, they respect our leadership position in their social hierarchy and respond and submit to our controls in the same way that they would to a canine pack leader.

Without anthropomorphism on our part and cynomorphism on the dog's part, it is unlikely that dogs could have been successfully domesticated and eventually come to live in our homes and serve as companions and workmates. Using our own reflexive consciousness to predict a dog's behaviors gives us a reasonable working approximation of how the dog will react to certain behaviors that we might engage in. We know that inflicting pain on the dog will cause him to avoid a situation or a person in the future, while providing sustenance, play, safety, gentle physical contact, and positive social interactions will cause a dog to be attracted to us and respond to our controls. Likewise, the dog seems to recognize and respond to our intentions, behaving in a way that brings him the most benefits—just as if he were also using a form of reflexive consciousness.

In reality I recognize that for this entire book I have been dodging around, apparently trying to avoid confronting the question that most dog owners really want answered. That question is, of course, "Do dogs really have a conscious and rational mind that works like our own?" Another way of stating this question is, "Is the anthropomorphic assumption correct?" The simple answer is that at some level it must be correct or we would have abandoned it long ago as being a useless habit of thought. In our usual interactions with dogs, we normally treat them as if they had at least some lower level of consciousness.

Psychologists have not fully agreed on the best definition of consciousness. In everyday language, the word is used to mean being awake and responsive to one's environment, and we could contrast this to being asleep or being in a coma. This is a good start toward a definition, but psychologists will usually agree that some other properties must also be present. For example, an individual must not only be aware of the environment but also able to form some kind of mental representation of the world that can be used to plan future behaviors. A conscious individual will also have memories of events and things that guide what he does. An important aspect of consciousness is self-awareness, the sense that you have of being an individual, living in a body that is yours and different from others. Finally, you must have intentions or plans and be aware that others have intentions and plans that may be different from your own. In most of our interactions with dogs, we act as if they have consciousness and deal with the world in a manner similar to humans, or at least human children. In some cases our predictions of dog behaviors, based upon what we would do in certain circumstances, are wrong, but we appear to be successful frequently enough to justify our anthropomorphic assumption.

Sometimes our predictions of behaviors fail because we anthropomorphize about individuals who clearly lack the abilities we attribute to them. For example, we might say that a newborn baby is crying to get our attention, yet at the age of a few days or weeks this is only an anthropomorphic statement, since the baby is still too young to have developed its intellectual capacity to a level where it can reason something like "If I cry, then they will come and give me attention." Even more blatant is when we anthropomorphize about machines, as when my wife complains, "My car doesn't want to start this morning," or my colleague growls, "My computer is trying to sabotage my life," while another complains that, "The stock market hates me!" The difference, however, is that if each of the individuals was questioned carefully, they would admit that a car, desktop computer, stock market, and perhaps even the young baby do not have the mental capacities that we attribute to them and we are simply using convenient forms of speech to attach some emotional content to events. With dogs, however, the situation is different. Most people believe that dogs think and have consciousness.

Conscious Machines

So let's face the issue. What would Dancer, or any dog, have to do to convince a skeptical scientist that he has consciousness and rational thought? To understand the full scope of the problem, let's give you the same problem facing Dancer, namely to prove that *you* have consciousness and rational thought. Imagine that one day you woke up and your spouse or lover suddenly accused you of being an imposter. He or she might claim that you are no longer even human but an android robot imposter put there by some alien race or government conspiracy. Strangely enough, there is such a condition called Capgras delusion, and it is the result of brain damage. Victims of this disorder become convinced that their spouse or some close acquaintances are imposters and may not even be human. To them, this person or thing looks like their husband or wife, acts like that person, and even insists that they are the real individual, but the victims of Capgras delusion are absolutely certain that they are lying. In a few tragic cases, the mental disorder has caused its sufferers to attack and even kill the people they believed to be usurping "imposters" or "android robots."

Now, here is your problem: How could you prove to this Capgras victim that you are not a robotic device but are really a conscious, thinking individual? What could you say to convince him? If you know the answer to personal questions that he asks, that just proves that you have been programmed with the personal information of the human you are impersonating. There is really nothing that you could say or do to prove that there is a conscious brain inside of you. Of course, you might offer to get a brain scan to show to him, but that would only show him that there is something in your head that looks like a brain and has electrical activity going on within it. Computers can be produced in any shape, with weird-looking circuitry, and they also have electrical activity going on within them, so your brain scan simply proves that something is going on inside your head, not that you are a conscious being.

Actually tying the issue of computer intelligence to that of dog thinking provides us with a lead on to how one might deal with the dilemma of determining whether consciousness is present in our canine friend. Early in the twentieth century one of the pioneers of digital computer development, Alan Turing, addressed this problem. At that time science-fiction writers and the general public had become obsessed with the idea that "thinking machines," in the form of giant computers, would soon be developed. The rationale for this was that brain is made up of neurons, which are complex structures but behave like machines. We have billions of them in our heads, which means that we can view the mind as a machine. It must be considered a very complicated machine, but it is still subject to the laws of nature. Since we are already capable of creating many complex machines, it would seem that, in theory at least, we should be able to create machines that use the same information-processing methods found in the brain. Many fictional works of the 1950s and 1960s featured computers that developed consciousness and thought processes (usually on their way toward taking over the world). Although early computer developers insisted that this would never happen, the question arose as to how we could determine if and when a machine actually had reached the stage where it was engaging in conscious thought.

Turing tried to provide a test to determine if machines could actually think. He reasoned that since consciousness is subjective and thus inscrutable, the only way we can determine if a computer is intelligent is to ask it questions. He suggested that we might place a computer in one room and a human being in an other and have a person or a panel of people ask each questions. The experts would study the answers that both the computer and person gave and try to judge which was which. He concluded that "If we can't tell the difference between 'intelligence' that is human and one that is machine, the machine might as well be considered human." Turing was basically presenting the old idea that "If it looks like a duck, acts like a duck, flies like a duck, swims like a duck, and quacks like a duck, then we might as well consider it a duck," only here we must replace "duck" with "conscious mind" (with an appropriate modification of the duck-like behaviors).

Turing's Test for Dogs

As you might imagine, not everyone would agree that Turing's test is a valid way of determining whether we are dealing with a thinking and conscious mind; however, no one has offered a workable alternative. One advantage of Turing's test is that we could certainly apply it to dog behaviors and compare them to human behaviors that seem to require conscious thought. If the behaviors are indistinguishable, then at least we must entertain the possibility that dogs do have conscious rational thought. Consider, for example, the following situation, where we can apply Turing's test to dog behavior.

This is just a simple domestic situation, rather than rooms with dogs and people and scientific judges, but it illustrates the issue. I was out at our little farm and my youngest daughter by marriage, Kari, had been visiting along with her own daughter, Centainne. Since it had turned out to be a drizzly gray day, outdoor activities were out of the question, so Kari and my wife Joan decided to go into town to do some shopping, leaving me behind to watch and entertain my granddaughter. After a while Centainne's toys and the television could not hold her interest and she was looking for something else to do. Fortunately, since she was just a bit older than two years, I knew a "game" that could amuse her.

The game that I hit upon that day involved my beagle, Darby, who was about nine or ten months old at the time but was already showing the typical beagle traits associated with a love for social interaction and a love of food (not necessarily in that order). Our game involved having Darby sit in front of us on the floor while I draped a bath towel over his head. Then in a singsong voice I asked Centainne, "Where's Darby?" She would then totter over to the dog and clumsily pull the towel off of him. She was rewarded with a singsong "That's right! There's Darby!" accompanied by hand clapping. Darby was rewarded for putting up with this indignity by getting a treat, either from me or my granddaughter, plus a little pat. He clearly was enjoying the game, since his tail was batting from side to side, and more important, he remained sitting there rather than seeking some safe refuge from all this noise.

As is typical with children of this age, we repeated the same little game about a dozen times, varying it only slightly by sometimes turning her around so that she actually didn't see me cover the dog and once or twice by having her do the actual covering. Darby sat quite happily through it all, accepting the treats and the attention. Eventually, Centainne called a halt to the proceedings by looking at me and smacking her lips, and then making a sound much like "mmm," which I interpreted as meaning that she was thirsty and wanted a drink of milk. I gave Darby a final pat and then tossed the towel onto a nearby chair as I headed for the refrigerator to get Centainne some milk.

Once the little girl had her spillproof cup of milk in her hand, the television (which was still on) again caught her attention, and she wandered over to sit in front of it. Meanwhile, I noticed that Darby had been quietly sitting in the same place where we had played the game. Now, as I let myself look away from my granddaughter for a bit, I noticed that he had stood up and was casting his gaze around the room. Next he walked over to the chair where I had tossed the towel, reared up on his hind legs, and caught it in his mouth. He next dragged his terrycloth prize to the middle of the floor and sat next to it. When I did nothing, he looked first at the towel, then at me, and then back to the towel. I was fascinated by what I thought was an attempt at communicating to me that he wanted the game (or at least the flow of treats associated with the game) to continue. When I still didn't move, the little dog reached down and grabbed the edge of the towel in his jaw. He then rolled onto his side, carrying the towel with him, and continued twisting his body until he had completely rolled over and his feet were again pointed toward the ground. Then, with some difficulty, he struggled back into a sitting position, with the towel now hanging mostly over his head and back. He looked for all the world like a character from some low-budget science-fiction movie, where a big-nosed priest from some alien religious cult tries to hide his identity by pulling the hood of his robe over his face.

As I gave a little laugh at this scene, he punctuated it with a little whining bark to make sure that I was paying attention. The sound caught Centainne's attention, and she dropped her cup and immediately, and with a squeak of her own, waddled over to the hooded dog and pulled the towel off and clapped her hands. Obviously the game was going to continue for a few rounds more, so I gave Darby another treat and watched his tail bat even more quickly in what appeared to be satisfaction.

While I smiled at what appeared to be Darby's childish attempt to communicate that he wanted the game to continue, I also knew that many very bright scientists would insist that this should not be happening. As a psychologist I know that many of my colleagues would not be easily persuaded that Darby's behavior indicated any form of conscious reasoning, logic, or directed intelligence. They would argue that dogs simply don't have such reasoning ability. They would go on to explain that self-awareness, planning, and anticipation of future events could not be involved here. They would probably conclude by suggesting that I was anthropomorphizing.

Now for the sake of argument, let's suppose that the roles played by Darby and Centainne had been switched. Now we would be playing "Where's Centainne?" while covering my granddaughter with a towel. This, by the way, is another popular game for children at that age, since they get to prove how clever they are by pulling the towel off their own heads in response to the dramatically asked question. Suppose that it was the child who had retrieved the towel and draped it over her head and made noises to bring me back when I had indicated that I was stopping the play. These same careful psychological scientists would have no problem using phrases like, "She wanted to continue the game and thought that she could entice you into it again by covering herself with the towel and using one of her limited speech sounds to get you to look at her." This would then suggest that the child had the planning ability, a sense of future outcome, logic, and self-awareness that my dog Darby did not have. Yet both were performing the same actions in response to the same situation!

Suppose that we change the situation slightly so that we apply Turing's test to the observable behaviors. We could remove the obvious visual information as to which was the child and the dog by having the actions described verbally by someone rather than observed directly by the panel of judges. Thus the critical action would be described as "the individual has now gone over the chair where the towel was thrown and has draped it over his or her head and is now looking at you, making sounds that have attracted your attention." Phrased in this way, it would be very difficult to distinguish between the two behaviors we have described. This means that either we would have to grant that my dog Darby was engaging in reasoned and likely consciously planned behaviors, or that my granddaughter was responding in an unconscious, unthinking, and automatic sequence of movements. Since we are most likely to accept that a child has reasoning ability and consciousness (even if we agree that their reasoning is not as acute as that of an adult human and their consciousness may be more limited in scope), according to the rules of Turing's test I believe that we must grant the same to the dog.

Some people might still quibble, arguing that this may be thinking and even reasoning, but does it prove consciousness? According to Turing, it should. I sometimes fall back upon the words of Sigmund Freud, who wrote in *The Interpretation of Dreams,* "It is essential to abandon the over-valuation of the property of being conscious before it becomes possible to form any correct view of the origin of what is mental." After all, as we noted earlier, it is impossible to prove to anyone else that we ourselves are conscious and not simply well-programmed machines.

Dreaming Dogs

Actually, since I have mentioned Freud's famous book on dreams, I might as well use these special experiences to further our understanding of whether dogs have consciousness. I believe that everyone would accept the fact that dreams are events that exist only in our consciousness. Although they can be tied to actions occurring in our brains, they have no outside reality. They are basically "movies in our minds" that spring into our awareness when we sleep. If dreams are just mental pictures, perhaps replayed or edited from the day's events or from the fantasies of a sleeping being that is normally capable of experiencing conscious images, the presence of dreams might be evidence of a mind capable of consciousness.

Most people have observed their dog sleeping and have been come away with a strong impression that their pet is dreaming. At various times during sleep, some dogs may quiver, make their legs twitch, or even growl or snap at some sleep-created phantom, giving the impression that they are dreaming about something. At the structural level the brains of dogs are similar to those of humans, and during sleep their brain wave patterns follow much the same time course and go through the same stages observed in people, all of which is consistent with the idea of dogs dreaming.

Actually, if dogs didn't dream, this would be a much greater surprise given that recent evidence suggests that animals that are simpler and less intelligent than dogs seem to dream. Matthew Wilson and Kenway Louie of the Massachusetts Institute of Technology offered compelling evidence that the brains of sleeping rats function in a way that irresistibly suggests dreaming. Much of the dreaming a human does at night is associated with the activities that person engaged in that day. The same seems to be the case in rats—namely, they might dream about the complex maze that they were learning to run earlier. Electrical recordings taken from the hippocampus, an area of the brain associated with memory formation and storage, found that some of these electrical patterns were quite specific and identifiable while the rat was awake and learning a maze. Later, when the rats were asleep and their brain waves indicated that they had entered the stage where humans normally dream, these same patterns of brain waves appeared. In fact, the patterns were so clear and specific that the researchers were able to tell where in the maze the rat would be if it were awake and whether it would be moving or standing still. Wilson cautiously described the results, saying, "The animal is certainly recalling memories of those events as they occurred during the awake state, and it is doing so during dream sleep, and that's just what people do when they dream."

Since a dog's brain is more complex than that of a rat and shows the same electrical sequences, it is reasonable to assume that dogs are dreaming as well. There is further evidence that not only do they dream, but that they dream about common dog activities. This kind of research takes advantage of the fact that there is a special structure in the brain that keeps all of us from acting out our dreams. As some people age, this place in the pons (which is part of the brain stem) becomes less able to inhibit our tendency to physically do what we are doing in our dreams, so the person might actually jump up, move around, or act out bizarre and sometimes dangerous activities when dreaming. When scientists removed the part of the brain that suppresses acting out of dreams in dogs, they observed that the dogs began to move around, despite the fact that electrical recordings of their brains indicated that the dogs were still fast asleep. The dogs started to move only when the brain entered that stage of sleep associated with dreaming. During the course of a dream episode these dogs actually began to execute the actions that they were performing in their dreams. Thus researchers found that a dreaming pointer may immediately start searching for game and may even go on point, a sleeping springer spaniel may flush an imaginary bird in his dreams, while a dreaming Doberman pinscher may pick a fight with a dream burglar.

It is really quite easy to determine when your dog is dreaming without resorting to brain surgery or electrical recordings. All that you have to do is to watch him from the time he starts to doze off. As the dog's sleep becomes deeper, his breathing will become more regular. After a period of about twenty minutes for an average-sized dog, his first dream should start. You will recognize the change because his breathing will become shallow and irregular. There may be odd muscle twitches, and you may even see the dog's eyes moving behind its closed lids if you look closely enough. The eyes are moving because the dog is actually looking at the dream images as if they were real images of the world. These eye movements are the most obvious characteristic of dreaming sleep. When human beings are awakened during this rapid eye movement, or REM, sleep, they virtually always report that they were dreaming.

Different types of dogs have different patterns of dreaming. It is an odd fact that small dogs dream more frequently than big dogs. A small dog, such as a toy poodle, may dream once every ten minutes, while a dog as large as a mastiff or an Irish wolfhound may spend an hour and a half between each dream.

There is one other way in which the dreams of dogs follow the same pattern as the dreams of people. Just as in humans, the amount of time that dogs spend dreaming depends upon their age. Younger dogs spend much more of the sleep time dreaming than older dogs. At any age, however, dreams seem to exist only as events occurring in a special state of consciousness that can be monitored by recording electrical activity. This means that the presence of dreams strongly suggests the presence of some level of conscious imagery in the dreaming animal, and dogs do dream.

Knowing Is More Than Sensing

At a technical level psychologists would want more evidence than the existence of dreams to credit dogs with any consciousness. Here we have to start getting very specific as to what we mean by consciousness. Obviously we mean more than the everyday distinction that an animal that is awake has conscious awareness as compared with when he is asleep or in a coma. Philosophers and psychologists argue continually among themselves about what we mean beyond being aware. For some, simply being able to perceive the world, process information about it, and lay down memories of what we have sensed is enough. Thus the Oxford philosopher Michael Lockwood says that "consciousness is the leading edge of perceptual memory." More stringent requirements as evidence for consciousness might include having a picture of the world that goes beyond our immediate sensations, such as knowing that the existence of objects is independent of whether we can still see them right at this moment. More recently, some theorists have suggested that we must be self-aware and have a concept of self, perhaps even an awareness of our own existence. The highest demands require that we be conscious of being conscious and understand that other individuals also have minds and consciousnesses that might be the same or different from ours.

Let's consider dogs in light of some of these more stringent demands of proof of consciousness. The first of the stringent requirements for consciousness is that we have a mental representation of the world that goes beyond what our senses are registering at the moment. In simple terms, I know that my wife still exists even though she has walked out of the room and I can't see her at the moment, and I also know that my Cavalier King Charles spaniel, Banshee, exists even though he has slipped under my desk for a nap and is no longer visible. To know that an object's existence does not depend on our ability to sense it at the moment was labeled "object permanence" by the Swiss psychologist Jean Piaget. He demonstrated that this is not an ability that we are born with. This is easily demonstrated by taking a young child, a year or so of age, and showing him a toy that he really wants. Naturally he will reach for it. Now while he is watching the toy we slip a sheet of typing paper in front of it so that the piece of paper now blocks his view of the toy. Under these circumstances the child will not try to reach past or around the paper, but rather acts like the toy no longer exists, perhaps looking around blankly or crying because it is gone. In very early childhood, even a child's parent is simply another object that passes in and out of existence as it appears and disappears from view. This would explain why babies seem to get so much pleasure from games of "peek-a-boo." Somewhere around a year and a half to two years of age the child will develop object permanence and know that the toy is still there, just out of sight. He will prove this by trying to look or reach behind the paper barrier, or trying to move it to get the toy. Piaget would say that the child has formed a "mental representation" or a "cognitive map" of the world. He then brings this picture of the world into his consciousness: It tells him that the object still exists and it gives its location. In his consciousness he becomes able to manipulate representations of objects first in a concrete way and later more abstractly. I do not think that Piaget is suggesting that before the development of object permanence children have no consciousness but rather that when they do develop this aspect of thinking their consciousness has risen to a higher level and now can be used for more complex forms of thinking and problem solving.

Even without going into the laboratory to verify this, it should be apparent that dogs have object permanence. Obviously, if the wild ancestors of dogs believed that a rabbit or any other quarry ceased to exist simply because it was no longer visible after it ran behind a rock or around a bend in a path, they would have long ago died of starvation. We have all seen a dog excitedly trying to recover a ball that has rolled behind a sofa or another piece of furniture and is now out of sight. Furthermore, every good retriever can see two birds shot from the sky which then fall out of sight in the high grass and still know that both exist, since he will confidently move in direct lines to fetch them back to its master.

Formal laboratory testing of object permanence in dogs has been done by psychologists Sylvain Gagnon and François Doré of Laval University in Quebec, Canada. They found that this psychological ability appears much more quickly in dogs than in humans. In puppies of only five weeks of age there is already a basic understanding of object permanence. By the age of eight weeks it is just as reliably present as the object permanence seen in an eighteen-month-old human child.

While this level of performance might be enough to convince some people that dogs have a conscious representation of the world, others have insisted on proof of a higher level of consciousness. When working with children, it's possible to make the object permanence test more difficult and thus make it depend more definitely upon a conscious representation of the world. This involves something called an "invisible displacement test." In this task an experimenter places an object in a container so that now the object is no longer visible and its existence requires some level of object permanence. Next the experimenter moves the container behind a screen and, while it is still out of the child's sight, the object is removed from the container and left there. After this invisible position change (remember, the child saw the container holding the object, not the object itself, moved), the experimenter brings the container back into view and shows the child that it is now empty. Obviously the sight of the now-empty container should allow him to conclude that the object must have moved, even though that movement took place out of sight. If the child has a conscious representation or map of the world, then he should be able to deduce that if the object moved, and it still exists, then the only place that it could be would be behind the screen. This then allows him to quickly find it. As you can see, this simple judgment really requires a high level of conscious processing, so it requires more mental maturity for children to be able to do this than was needed to solve the simple object permanence problem. Yet by about two years of age human children are doing well at this. Gagnon and Doré also tested dogs using the invisible displacement test and found that they could successfully solve this problem quite easily at the age of about one year. Additional research shows that if we increase the difficulty of object permanence tests even more, by introducing up to five different locations where the object could be, and also using a delay of up to four minutes between the disappearance of the object and the time that the dog has to go and find it, the dog still does reasonably well at the task (although not as well as he did with fewer screens and a shorter time). In this revised task the need for some kind of conscious memory map and some reasoning based upon it is difficult to deny.

Memory and Consciousness

Several years ago the philosopher Daniel Dennett, from Tufts University, told me quite unambiguously that he was convinced that dogs have no episodic memory and without this he could not accept the fact that dogs have consciousness anything like that which people have. I later learned that this is a view that is shared by a number of other philosophers and some behavioral scientists. To understand what he meant, you must first know that there are many types of memory. Psychologists often start by dividing memory into large groupings that they call "explicit" or "implicit" memory. The easiest way to distinguish these is to note that explicit memories are the ones that you can describe or call into your mind at will, whereas implicit memories are automatic and not really conscious. Learned skills are good examples of implicit memories. Thus, although you might remember how to ride a bicycle (since you can easily do it), trying to describe to someone else what you have to do to stay upright on a bicycle is virtually impossible. You know what to do, but you can't make these actions conscious in such a way as to communicate them to others.

When we consider explicit memory, we first have to note that there are two varieties, namely "episodic" and "semantic" memory. Episodic memory is memory for what you have personally experienced. When you answer a question about what you had for dinner last night or which clothes you wore yesterday, or you describe your first romantic kiss, you are recalling episodic memories. This is different from semantic memory, which involves memory for facts. To answer a question such as "Who was George Washington?" or "What is the climate like on the moon?" involves semantic memory. It is not episodic memory, since you never met George Washington, nor have you visited the moon. Some people say that episodic memory is a sort of mental time travel in which you revisit events that you experienced by bringing them into consciousness. Episodic memory is not based upon practice or repetition, since most life events occur only once and nonetheless are remembered. An important characteristic of episodic memories is that each contains specific data about "what," "when," and "where."

Dennett's statement puzzled me, even in light of only casual observation of dog behaviors. For example, many dog owners have a variety of "Find the object" phrases that they use and to which the dog responds appropriately. For example, my dogs respond to "Where's your ball?" by dashing around to find the ball and then bringing it to me. If it is inaccessible, they will usually stand near where they believe it to be and bark. My dogs also respond to "Where's Joannie?," which is a convenient phrase that helps me to locate my wife. On hearing it, the dog goes to the room where he last saw my wife. If she is upstairs or in the basement, the dog will move to the appropriate set of stairs and wait there. If she is out of the house, the dog will usually go to the door that she used when she left. If the dog doesn't know where she is, or if she has moved since he last saw her, he will usually start to search for Joan. Each of these is an instance of episodic memory, since the dog must remember where he last saw the item. This memory clearly has the required "when," "what," and "where" components, since we are asking for a location of a particular object when it was most recently seen.

I pointed out the "Where's Joannie?" situation to Dennett, who did not seem much impressed. He would only grant that this was "episodic memory-like behavior." He went on to note that he would have to think about it further and would get in touch with me when he found the flaw in my reasoning. He never did contact me again about the matter.

Actually, the episodic memory in dogs is so good that there is the possibility that, in addition to guide dogs for the blind and hearing assistance dogs, we may one day have memory assistance dogs. Although this may sound bizarre, there already is one such dog, owned and trained by John Dignard of Wetaskiwin, Alberta, Canada. Dignard was hit by a car at the age of five, and the accident caused brain damage. In the end he was left with learning difficulties and a very unreliable short-term memory. Before anything makes it into his long-term memory, it must be repeated and relearned many times. Early memories are still there, so that he can remember his phone number from when he was four, but new ones are a problem. For instance, it took him a year after his marriage to remember his wife's name. He told me, "When you ask someone's name six hundred times because you can't remember, it's very frustrating." Sadly, I also doubt that he will remember being interviewed for this book by the time it comes out.

At a very pragmatic level, in the absence of short-term memory, simple tasks became nightmares. If Dignard goes to a shopping mall, by the time he comes out he usually will have completely forgotten where his car was parked. This is where the episodic memory ability of a dog becomes important. Dignard can now go shopping with confidence because of a German shepherd dog named Goliath, who is his memory aide. Goliath is the third such service dog that he has had. Obviously Goliath can't help with names, phone numbers, or shopping lists, but the dog does serve the same purpose as the ball of string that Theseus let out as he wended his way through the labyrinth in order to find his way back out after he slew the Minotaur. Goliath's task is to lead his master back to the places that he can't remember, such as the way out of a building he's never been in before.

Dignard says, "I'd be lost all the time without him. Now I just tell him 'go to the exit door,' or I tell him 'back to the car,' and he takes me there." It is thus Goliath's episodic memory that substitutes for the episodic memories that his master has such difficulty producing. I wonder what Dr. Dennett would say about this.

The Self-aware Dog

For some theorists, consciousness must go further. It must include a self-consciousness, a recognition of the person's own individuality and identity. In effect, we must be able mentally to step outside of ourselves and consider ourselves as separate entities. Although it seems like it would be virtually impossible to investigate whether animals have self-awareness without using language, for primates, at least, all you need is a mirror and some red lipstick.

This series of experiments began, as is frequently the case, with Charles Darwin. While he was doing research on emotional expressions in animals and humans he visited a zoo and put a mirror in front of the enclosure containing orangutans. Then he simply watched and recorded what he saw. The orangutans looked in the mirror at first, then looked behind it as if looking for the ape they were seeing. Next they watched carefully as they made specific movements and then made a series of facial expressions while looking at the mirror. Darwin thought that the results were a bit ambiguous. After all, the facial expressions could be interpreted as expressions made toward what they thought was another orangutan. Darwin also suggested the possibility that these apes recognized that they were looking at a reflection of themselves and were simply making expressions in order see what they looked like. This "facial expression" game is often played by human children in front of mirrors as well.

Gordon Gallup, a psychologist from the State University of New York at Albany, picked up on Darwin's observations and went one step farther. First he introduced a mirror into the home cage of a chimpanzee. At first the chimp did exactly what the orangutans had done. However, Gallup knew that people who have been blind from birth but who have had their sight restored, and also young children who have never seen a mirror, initially react as if they were seeing another individual when they first see their own reflection in a mirror. Given time, however, they learn that this is their own reflection. Therefore, Gallup left the mirror in the cage for a period of time. Next Gallup anesthetized the chimpanzee and painted a red mark on its eyebrow and another over its ear. When the anesthesia wore off, the chimp failed to show any interest in the marks until it caught sight of itself in the mirror. On seeing its image with the red marks, the chimp began to selectively touch its own eyebrow and ear while carefully watching its image in the mirror. Gallup believes that this means that the chimp is self aware. The animal understands that he is an individual, that he is looking at a reflection of himself, and that that image has somehow changed—meaning that something about himself has changed. Orangutans, gorillas, and dolphins also respond with the same evidence of self-awareness when presented with mirror images of themselves.

Dogs and other species either treat the image as another animal or come to ignore it completely. From this, researchers concluded that dogs lack self-awareness and, thus, consciousness. Another conclusion that could be drawn, of course, is that dogs recognize their own reflection but are simply not as vain and concerned with their appearance as higher primates.

University of Colorado biologist Marc Bekoff interpreted these apparently negative results in another way. He recognized that dogs are considerably less affected by visual events than humans and most apes. Perhaps the difficulty resides with the sensory modality used to test self-awareness in dogs. The most important sense for dogs, as we have seen, is smell. Dogs certainly seem to recognize the scent of familiar dogs and people, and if they have a sense of self, then perhaps rather than asking them to recognize their own reflection, we should ask them to recognize their own scent. Instead of a "red dot test" for self-awareness, Bekoff used a "yellow snow test." His subject was his own dog, Jethro, a Rottweiler and German shepherd cross. He described the clever but rather inelegant experimental process this way.

> Over five winters I walked behind Jethro and scooped up his yellow snow and moved it to different, clean, locations some distance down the trail. I also gathered yellow snow from other dogs and moved it. There is a real advantage to doing this experiment on snow because it holds the urine and is easily portable. Since it took five winters to get all of the data you know that this was a labor of love.

All of this snow moving occurred while Jethro was elsewhere along the path and the dog did not see Bekoff transporting it. The testing was quite simple: Bekoff watched Jethro move down the trail, timed his arrival, measured how long the dog sniffed at the urine patch, and watched what else he did. As most dog owners could probably have predicted, the dog stopped at each yellow snow patch, sniffed at it, and then usually urinated on top of the yellow snow from other dogs. However, Jethro seemed to recognize his own scent, since when he encountered his own urine-stained snow he sniffed at it for a much shorter time than he did the patches of urine from other dogs and left it alone.

Based on this data, Bekoff concluded that dogs do have some of the same aspects of self-awareness that humans have. According to him, they have a sense of "body-ness," the feeling of possessing one's own body and owning the parts of his body, such as "my paw" or "my face." In addition, dogs have a sense of "mine-ness," which is the sense of what belongs to him and what belongs to others. This would include the sense of "my territory," "my sleeping place," and "my bone." What this data cannot establish is whether dogs have a sense of "I-ness," which, for lack of a more concise way of describing it, is what Tarzan was talking about when he said "Me Tarzan, you Jane." The experimental test for that quality of self-awareness in dogs does not yet seem to have been worked out.

Theory of Mind

Probably the most stringent test for consciousness involves what psychologist David Premack of the University of Pennsylvania called a "Theory of Mind." The first thing to understand about a theory of mind is that it is not a psychological theory proposed by scientists but rather the theory that each of us has about other people and their minds. Basically it says that we are self-aware and conscious, and know that other creatures are also self-aware and conscious. However, we must also recognize that these other creatures may have their own points of view and mental processes, and that these might be the same or different from our own. A theory of mind is needed for successful social interactions, since we need to be able to think about something like "If I do this, then he'll think that, and he'll do what?" This allows us to negotiate, avoid conflict, and lie and deceive as well. It is usually agreed that an animal that has a theory of mind has achieved the highest level of consciousness, in part because a theory of mind includes all of the other elements of consciousness—namely, active perception of the situation, a mental representation of the world, and self-awareness. Self-awareness, however, puts you in the position of using your own experience with your own mental processes to predict the mental processes and behaviors of others.

Young children below the age of four years do not have a well-developed theory of mind. They believe that what they see and experience must be the same thing that everyone else is experiencing. They can't imagine other viewpoints or other ways of thinking that are different from their own. This is clearly shown using a simple experiment in which an experimenter shows a child two hand puppets and then starts to act out a little scenario:

> This is Bert. Bert has a basket. This is Ernie. Ernie has a box. Bert has a box of crayons. He puts them into his basket. Bert is now going to leave the room and go for a walk. Ernie takes the crayons out of the basket and puts them into the box. Now here comes Bert after his walk. He wants to play with his crayons. Where will Bert look for his crayons?

The child has watched the entire scene in which the crayons were transferred from the basket to the box, so the child knows where the crayons are, but the puppet Bert, who did not see them moved, should not. Children aged three or less will almost always point to the box, since they are unable to separate what they themselves know from what another person (or puppet) knows. Their theory of mind, which says that other people can have a different view point and different mental processes, has not yet developed. By the age of four years, however, they will correctly understand that Bert can't know what they know because he did not see the crayons moved. They will point to the basket because they have developed a theory of mind and understand that Bert's viewpoint must be different than theirs.

This is one of the reasons why when you ask a young child to hide, they will often cover their own eyes. In the absence of a theory of mind, they reason that if they can't see you, then you can't see them.

An amusing (if slightly frustrating) conversation with one of my grandchildren, Ravi, also illustrates this. Ravi was around three years old and we had sent him three or four little picture books. Each was quite distinctive, one with animals, one with trucks and cars, and so forth. My daughter Rebecca had telephoned and said that Ravi really liked one of the books and he wanted to say thank you.

"So," I asked, "which one did you like best?"

"This one," he replied.

"Well, which one is that," I asked.

"This is the one. I don't like this one so much," he answered.

Obviously he had the books in front of him, and he might have been pointing to each in turn, which certainly conveyed no information to me across the phone line. However, he could not understand that another person could not necessarily see what he was currently seeing. He was not yet old enough to have a fully developed theory of mind.

Dogs, on the other hand, do seem to understand that other creatures have their own points of view and mental processes. If you consider why dogs should have developed the theory of mind, you must understand that it is extremely adaptive at an evolutionary level. Wild canines, such as wolves, may have evolved the ability to mentally "put themselves in the shoes" of others as a hunting skill. A theory of mind would tell the wolf that it must keep out of sight and hearing of prey, and this would encourage the wolf to stalk his quarry silently. Once the chase has actually begun, this ability would enable the hunting canines to predict, for example, which way the prey might run during a hunt. When engaged in pack hunts of large prey, wolves will often split the pack, sending one or more animals in a particular direction and then having them lie down, out of sight, setting an ambush. Once the ambushers are in place, the remainder of the pack then rushes at their quarry from particular angles designed to drive the animal in the direction of the waiting attackers. This requires quite a bit of foresight and planning, as well as the ability to predict how the victim will view the situation and then react. Thus for social hunters, like dogs, a theory of mind is very useful.

Dogs seem to be very aware of the fact that other individuals have a particular point of view that must be taken into account. Here is a simple proof of this that you can verify when you are out playing fetch with your dog. After throwing the ball a few times for him to retrieve, all you need to do is to intentionally turn your back on the dog. Inevitably the dog will run around and put the ball down in front of you. This means that the dog seems to understand that that the human has to see the ball before he'll throw it and that he can't see it unless he is facing toward it.

Stephen Budiansky, the author of several fine books on animal behavior and how animals and humans interact, gives another example of dogs using a theory of mind to their own advantage. He notes that his cats are fed in the tack room of his barn. He usually keeps the door closed so that the dogs can't get at the cat food, but sometimes when he went into that room to fetch something, his border collie would sneak in and start eating the food. Of course, when she was caught she was yelled at, so she soon stopped this behavior. However, there is also a telephone in that room. When Budiansky would go into the room to use the phone, as soon as his attention was focused on the conversation and his eyes drifted away, the collie would make a dash over to the cat food and eat some, and most of the time she would get away with it. While Budiansky is doubtful of a theory of mind in dogs, the collie's behavior is certainly consistent with the idea that the dog consciously calculated that he was distracted when he was on the phone and thus was not aware of the things that she was doing at that moment. This aspect of her theory of mind thus gave her an opportunity to make a quick grab at the forbidden food, with some confidence that her sneaky behavior would go undetected.

The fact that dogs take the viewpoint of other creatures into account has actually been demonstrated experimentally. For instance, Josep Call and a team of researchers from the Max Planck Institute for Evolutionary Anthropology were able to show that dogs understand what nearby humans are aware of and can determine what a human is paying attention to simply by monitoring where the people are looking. In their research a piece of food was placed on the floor and the dog was severely warned not to take it. If the person left the room, however, the dog immediately snatched up the food. If the person stayed in the room and looked directly at the dog, the animal was much less likely to take the food; or if the dog decided to snatch the food, he was more likely to attempt to sneak around, trying not to be seen, before making a grab at it. The most interesting situations were those in which the person stayed in the room but either turned her back, engaged in a distracting activity, or closed her eyes (obviously these situations are similar to Budiansky's turning away to answer the phone). Under these conditions, the dog seemed to recognize that the person's attention was not on them and it was more likely to make an opportunistic dash to retrieve the food. Clearly, these dogs were watching where the human was looking and using something analogous to a theory of mind to decide what the person was aware of and how they would react. The dogs then used those judgments to guide their own behavior.

Lying, Deceiving, and Knowing

The behaviors that we have been discussing not only suggest a theory of mind for dogs but also a willingness to use that information to achieve personal ends, sometimes by subterfuge. Putting it bluntly, despite the common belief that dogs are moral and honest, this kind of behavior suggests that our best friends are capable of lying and deceit. To get away with deception, however, requires that you believe that your victim has a mind and a viewpoint, and you can manipulate what he thinks and believes. This is a fairly high level of consciousness, but in living in a socially organized world, such deceits could obviously give a dog a competitive advantage.

One example of this kind of deceitful subterfuge involved Tessa and Bishop, two dogs owned by my daughter, Kari. We had taken the two dogs out to our farm for the weekend, where they would have a chance to play with my dogs. Tessa was getting old and was not as interested in romping with the other dogs as she used to be, but she did like the company and the chance to nose around in the foliage, which was a pastime denied to her in the city. Tessa's greatest love, however, was for smoked pig's ears. Out at the farm, each dog was given one of these every day. I had just distributed the pig's ears and Tessa, who liked to eat hers lying down, had settled down to munch on hers. Bishop had his in his mouth but had not yet begun to eat it. At that moment my wife returned from shopping and her van pulled up to the side of the house. Either Bishop recognized the sound of her vehicle, or he was simply reacting in his ever-vigilant "guardian of the family" mode. In any event, he dropped his ear and raced to the door, barking as he ran. Tessa glanced in his direction and the moment he disappeared down the hallway to the door, she dropped her own pig's ear and trotted over and picked up Bishop's ear. She then returned to her starting place and lay down on top of her own ear while she proceeded to munch on her companion's pig's ear. A few moments after my wife entered the door, Bishop greeted her and then dashed back to retrieve his treat. He checked the place where he had dropped it and then began to search around to see if he could find it. Tessa, who to Bishop's eyes would have appeared to have remained in her original place, continued to nonchalantly chew on Bishop's ear. She quickly finished it, but did not stand up. Instead she stretched her paws and head forward, and with eyes half closed surveyed the scene in front of her. After a few minutes Bishop gave up his search and then wandered out of the room (perhaps to check to see if his treat had been moved to the hallway). Once he was out of sight again, Tessa stood up and retrieved the ear that she had been lying on. She then resumed her original position and proceeded to consume the pig's ear that had been initially given to her. Bishop never appeared to catch on that she had not only robbed him but had cleverly concealed the evidence of her theft from his sight by lying down on top of it.

There are numerous anecdotal examples of dogs engaging in deception. Some of these involve a sequence of actions on the part of the deceptive dog. Brenda Edwards of Chicago told me one of these stories about her Doberman pinschers, Rolf and Fanny. Her account goes like this:

> There are two things that you have to know in order to understand why I think that Fanny is really a con artist. First, my dogs really love bones. I get them these hunks of beef shank bones and they get one every few days. When they get grotty or small, I pick them up and throw them out. Other times they just lose them. If there is only one bone around at the moment, though, Rolf and Fanny don't fight over it. They seem to have agreed that the bone belongs to whomever happens to have it in their possession at the moment.
>
> Second, the only thing that my dogs love more than their bones is my husband. I think that one reason for this is that whenever he enters the house, he doesn't only pet them, but he gives them a special treat from a jar that we keep next to the back door. Steve usually parks the car in the garage, which is behind the house, and enters using the back door, so that means that his arrivals are always an occasion for a treat.
>
> Anyway, what happened was that one afternoon Rolf was chewing on a bone and Fanny couldn't find hers. She stood and looked at Rolf, and then wandered around the room, stopping to stare at the bone. I walked into the kitchen to do something when all of a sudden Fanny rushes past me to the back door. She rears up and hits the back door with her front paws. Now it's an old door, and there's a bit of wobble in

> it, so that when you bang against it the door moves enough to sound like it's closing. Next she rushed back to the kitchen door and stood off to side, hugging close to the counter. This is a position where she was close to the door but not visible to someone coming through it. Within moments of the door banging, Rolf appeared. He clearly interpreted the noise as being my husband's arrival. As soon as Rolf entered the kitchen, however, Fanny made a dash out of the room and snatched up the bone as her own.
>
> I really believe that Fanny hit that door to make a slamming sound knowing that it would convince Rolf that Steve was home, and predicting that he would come for a treat—then she could steal the bone. What absolutely convinces me that this was planned was the way that after leaving the door, she hid out of sight next to door until Rolf passed her, and then she made her move. What a con artist!

The problem with stories like Tessa's and Fanny's deceptions is that they occur spontaneously and it is difficult to subject them to the kind of scientific verification that we might like. However, two psychologists, Robert Mitchell from Eastern Kentucky University and Nicholas Thompson of Clark University, recognized that there is a very common situation where dogs seem to show that they have a theory of mind by engaging in deception. This is when they are engaged in play. These researchers videotaped twenty-four different dogs playing with their owners or strangers and then did a second-by-second analysis of the interactions. Both people and dogs use lots of deception during play. We can call the two types of deceptions "keep-away" and "misdirection" When people are in control, their deceptions might go like this: They show the dog a retrieving object (such as a ball), entice him to come close by seeming to offer it to dog, but then quickly move it out of reach, hide it behind them, or throw it as the dog lunges for it. Alternatively, they might pretend to throw the object but not let it go.

The dogs played both of these games as well. In keep-away the dog holds an object in its mouth and moves toward the person, close enough to entice them to go after it but hopefully not close enough for the person to get it. Sometimes the dog deliberately stops and drops the object, standing over it or even backing up a step or two, as if offering it to the person. If the person is drawn in by this enticement and moves to grab it, the dog immediately grabs it or knocks it away and then grabs it, quickly making a dash to keep out of arm's reach. An alternate game involving more misdirection could be called "self keep-away," which involves the dog running toward the person but dodging their advances once the person is committed to moving.

Part of the fun of the game for both human and dogs seems to be not only the exercise of throwing and retrieving but also the testing of each other's theory of mind. Succeeding in deception seems to be part of the pleasure derived by both dog and person. This would explain why 78 percent of the people frequently tried to deceive the dogs and 92 percent of the dogs tried to deceive the people. This also suggests that dogs like deception a bit more than humans do.

Another interesting statistic that comes out of this study has to do with the success rates of these attempts at deception. When a human tries to deceive a dog during play, he succeeds around 47 percent of the time. When a dog tries to deceive a human during the game, he succeeds about 41 percent of the time. If a successful deception depends upon using your theory of mind to accurately determine what your counterpart will see, interpret, and do next, then this means that humans have a more accurate theory of mind than dogs, but the difference of only 6 percent is much smaller than most people would have predicted. Dogs deliberately try to deceive, and they seem to do it almost as well as people do!

It is interesting to speculate about an extension of this study. Suppose that we could use some special-effects technology to change the videos of play and deception obtained by Mitchell and Thompson so that the images of the dog and the person were replaced by equal-sized unrecognizable blobs. Suppose that we then asked people to judge the activities of the blobs and try to determine which was the person and which was the dog. My guess is that most of us would have great difficulty doing this. If their behaviors are indistinguishable, then this means that dogs are passing Turing's test. If so, then according to Dr. Turing we should accept as a reasonable working hypothesis that dogs and people could be using the same kind of reasoning, theory of mind, and consciousness, at least in this limited situation.

How far can we push this interpretation? I certainly am not going to suggest that dogs are merely a version of humans that happen to walk on four feet and wear fur coats. Dogs seem to have intelligence roughly equivalent to that of a two- to four-year-old child (depending upon the problems that you set for them), they seem to have some degree of self-awareness, and they also seem to have a theory of mind at least equivalent to that of a four-year-old human being. This does not mean that they have all of the aspects and qualities of consciousness that an adult human does, but, if we credit two- to four-year-old humans with consciousness and reasoning, then, in the absence of data to the contrary, it seems appropriate that we grant the same to dogs.

Nonetheless, it is always possible that dogs and humans arrive at the same behaviors, in the same situations, through the use of different mental processes. This fact was emphasized for me when a friend who happened also to be a psychologist offered to demonstrate to me that he had taught his golden retriever, Hojo, to read.

"Actually," Jim explained, "he can only read two words—the names of my daughters—but we use it as part of a game."

Jim then proceeded to print the names of his daughters, Stephanie and Pat, on separate file cards. He then called Hojo, held the two cards up to him, and said, "Okay, Hojo, deliver the mail."

The dog looked back and forth between the cards, selected the one marked "Stephanie," and carried it over to one of the two giggling girls on the other side of the room. He quickly returned and took the one marked "Pat" to the other girl, who hugged him and told him he was a smart dog.

"Let me try," I asked, since I knew that there is always the possibility that there might be unintended clues or signals that the dog could responding to.

I took two new cards, printed the girls' names on them, and held them up for the big blond dog to look at. He studied them carefully, then again selected the one marked "Stephanie" and carried it to the appropriate girl, returning a moment later to take and deliver the other. I was impressed, but as I gathered the cards, Jim appeared to be puzzled.

"That's strange," he said. "I always print the girls' names in block, capital letters, since I felt that those shapes would be easiest for a dog to learn. You printed everything, except the first letter of their names, in lower case. I never taught him to read lower-case letters."

I quickly grabbed two new cards and this time cursively wrote the names rather than printing them. Hojo did not appear the least bit perturbed by this. Again, the dog seemed to accurately read the words and delivered each appropriately. Jim was muttering in amazement, since his dog had never been taught how to read handwriting. As I stared at the cards, however, a faint glimmering of an idea occurred.

This time I took two cards and on one I wrote a row of nine Xs while on the other I wrote a row of three Xs. Hojo looked at the cards and confidently selected the one with nine Xs and carried it to Stephanie, and then took the one with three Xs to Pat. It was now clear what had happened. Jim thought that he was teaching the dog a simple word discrimination—how to read two different words—because that is the way that a human mind works. Hojo, however, had learned nothing about reading or letter shapes, rather he had learned that when presented with two cards with something drawn or written upon it, his task was simply to determine which had the longer line of marks and that one went to Stephanie, while the short line of marks went to Pat.

The caution is clear: Although dogs may have fine mental abilities and precise thought processes, just because a dog and a human reach the same conclusion does not mean that the dog arrived there by thinking in the same way that a human does.

AFTERWORD

As I WAS WORKING on the last section of this book I heard some excited whimpering. My beagle, Darby, was excitedly running back and forth between my office and the kitchen. Curious about what was wrong, I left my computer and went to investigate. Darby has a fascination with my wife's cat Loki, and seems puzzled about how the cat can get himself up onto tables and counters that are far too high for Darby to reach with his short beagle legs. Like all of my dogs, he also has a fondness for cat food if any can be stolen from the cat's bowl. For this reason, we have taken to putting Loki's food dish on the kitchen counter, where it cannot be emptied by dogs looking for an extra meal. In fact, I had fed Loki only twenty minutes or so earlier. Since the counter is high, we sometimes leave a little plastic stepstool near it so that a lazy cat doesn't have to exert himself so much in leaping to the counter. The stool is low, however, so it doesn't help greedy, short dogs reach the counter. As usual, Darby had been interested in the feeding process, watching carefully as I dished the cat's kibble into his bowl, and as usual he had made excited, hopeful sounds. Now as we entered the kitchen the cat had just jumped off of the counter. Darby glanced up, then at the cat, then at me, and next he did something very strange. He looked down and began to dig at the base of the counter. I looked down but saw nothing.

"What are you trying to say, Darby?" I asked him, as if I expected an answer.

Again he looked at me and then frantically began to dig at the base of the counter. I looked down more closely and still could see nothing. Darby paused and once more started to scratch at the base of the counter with even more determination. Finally, in order to examine what he was pawing at, I got down on my hands and knees to examine the area better. Suddenly I felt something on my back and when I looked up Darby was standing on the counter and scooping up some of the stray bits of kibble that the cat had left behind.

There are many ways that one can interpret this sequence of events. One of the most generous is to suggest that Darby had observed the cat using the stepstool but recognized that he needed a larger step to reach the counter. He also knew that I often came over to investigate what he was doing or places that he was paying attention to. Therefore, if he had engaged in conscious planning, his scheme was simple—namely to get me to bend down near the counter and to use me as a larger, more functional stepstool. That is a long chain of speculations on my part, and it credits the little dog with a high degree of consciousness and reasoning. As a scientist I know that I have no evidence that this is what went on his mind, but then again, I have no evidence that this was not what went on in his mind. Since it is clear that in this instance a dog apparently outsmarted someone who has a Ph.D. in psychology, it is more comforting for me to suggest that this is evidence of a dog's thinking and intelligence.

SELECTED BIBLIOGRAPHY

THE FOLLOWING CONTAINS a partial list of bibliographic references for the material in the book. It is arranged by chapters. If a source is used in more than one chapter, the full citation appears only for the first mention of the material. If a reprint or a later edition of a work was consulted, that source, rather than the original, was noted. I have tried to include review material whenever possible so that the reader can use these citations as a starting point for finding the more specific research that they may be interested in. A list of a few journal title abbreviations follows.

Journal Abbreviations Used Below

AABS	*Applied Animal Behavior Science*
AB	*Animal Behavior*
AC	*Animal Cognition*
AJVR	*American Journal of Veterinary Research*
BVJ	*British Veterinary Journal*
JABA	*Journal of Applied Behavior Analysis*
JAVMA	*Journal of the American Veterinary Medical Association*
JCP	*Journal of Comparative Psychology*
JCPP	*Journal of Comparative and Physiological Psychology*
VCNA	*Veterinary Clinics of North America—Small Animal Practice*

Chapter 1. The Mind of a Dog

Alanen, L. (2003). *Descartes' concept of mind.* Cambridge, Mass.: Harvard University Press.

Coren, S. (1994). *The intelligence of dogs: Canine consciousness and capabilities.* New York: Free Press.

Darwin, C. (1998). *The expression of the emotions in man and animals,* 3rd ed. With an introduction, afterword, and commentaries by Paul Ekman. London: HarperCollins.

Darwin, C. (1964). *On the origin of species.* Cambridge, Mass.: Harvard University Press.

Darwin, C. (1890). *The descent of man.* London: J. Murray.

Kirkness, E. F., V. Bafna, and A. Halpern et al. (2003). The dog genome: Survey sequencing and comparative analysis. *Science* 301:1898–1903.

Nagel, T. (1974). What is it like to be a bat? *Philosophical Review* 58:435–450.

Navia, L. E. (1998). *Diogenes of Sinope: The man in the tub.* Westport, Conn.: Greenwood Press.

Plato. (1997). *Complete works.* Edited, with introduction and notes, by John M. Cooper. Indianapolis, Ind.: Hackett.

Rosenthal, D. M. (2002). How many kinds of consciousness? *Consciousness & Cognition* 11:653–665.

Watson, J. B. (1930). *Behaviorism,* rev. ed. Chicago: University of Chicago Press.

Chapter 2. Getting Information into the Mind

Coren, S., L. M. Ward, and J. T. Enns. (2004). *Sensation and perception,* 6th ed. Hoboken, N.J.: John Wiley & Sons.

Gelatt, Kirk N. (2000). *Essentials of veterinary ophthalmology.* Philadelphia: Lippincott Williams & Wilkins.

Miller, P. E., and C. J. Murphy. (1995). Vision in dogs. *JAVMA* 207:1623–1634.

Murphy, C. J., K. Zadnik, and M. J. Mannis. (1992). Myopia and refractive error in dogs. *Invest Ophthalmology & Vision Science* 33: 2459–2463.

Neitz, J., T. Geist, and G. S. Jacobs. (1989). Color vision in the dog. *Visual Neuroscience* 3:119–125.

Peiffer, R. L., and S. M. Petersen-Jones. (1997). *Small animal ophthalmology: A problem-oriented approach,* 2nd ed. London: Saunders.

Rusinov, V. S. (1970). *Electrophysiology of the central nervous system.* New York: Plenum Press.

Smith, P. T., and R. A. Boakes. (1986). *Human and animal memory.* Hillsdale, N.J.: Erlbaum.

Squire, L. R., and N. Butters. (1992). *Neuropsychology of memory.* New York: Guilford Press.

Wheeler, C. A., et al. (1999). *Ocular disorders presumed to be inherited in purebred dogs,* 3rd ed. American College of Veterinary Ophthalmologists.

Chapter 3. Playing Life by Ear

Fay, R. R. (1988). *Hearing in vertebrates: A psychophysics databook.* Winnetka, Ill.: Hill-Fay Associates.

Harvey, R. G., J. Harari, and A. J. Delauche. (2001). *Ear diseases of the dog and cat.* Ames: Iowa State University Press.

Hedlund, C. S., and J, Taboada. (2002). *Clinical atlas of ear, nose and throat diseases in small animals: The case-based approach.* Hannover: Schlütersche.

Heffner, H. E. (1983). Hearing in large and small dogs: Absolute thresholds and size of the tympanic membrane. *Behavioral Neuroscience* 97: 310–318.

Heffner, R. S., and H. E. Heffner. (1992). Evolution of sound localization in mammals. In D. B. Webster, R. R. Fay, and A. N. Popper, eds., *The evolutionary biology of hearing.* New York: Springer-Verlag, pp. 691–715.

Kawabata, I. (2000). Two cases of acute acoustic trauma induced by dog bark. *Jibi Inkoka Tokeibu Geka* 72:115–118.

Lipman, E. A., and J. R. Grassi. (1942). Comparative auditory sensitivity of man and dog. *American Journal of Psychology* 55:84–89.

Mech, L. D. (1981). *The wolf: Ecology and behavior of an endangered species.* Minneapolis: University of Minnesota Press.

Poncelet, L. C., A. G. Coppens, S. I. Meuris, and P. F. Deltenre. (2000). Maturation of the auditory system in clinically normal puppies as reflected by the brain stem auditory-evoked potential wave V latency-intensity curve and rarefaction-condensation differential potentials. *AJVR* 61:1343–1348.

Strain, G. M. (2004). Deafness prevalence and pigmentation and gender associations in dog breeds at risk. *BVJ* 167:23–32.

Strain, George M. (1996). Aetiology, prevalence and diagnosis of deafness in dogs and cats. *BVJ* 152:17–30.

Chapter 4. I Sniff, Therefore I Am

Ackerl, K., M. Atzmueller, and K. Grammer. (2002). The scent of fear. *Neuroendocrinology Letters* 23:79–84.

Albone, E. S. (1984). *Mammalian semiochemistry investigation of chemical signals between mammals.* Chichester, U.K.: John Wiley & Sons.

Brooks, S. E., F. M. Oi, and P. G. Koehler. (2003). Ability of canine termite detectors to locate live termites and discriminate them from non-termite material. *Journal of Economic Entomology* 96:1259–1266.

Brown, R. E., and D. W. Macdonald. (1985). *Social odours in mammals.* New York: Clarendon Press.

Church, J., and H. William. (2001). Another sniffer dog for the clinic? *Lancet* 358:930.

Finger, T. E., and W. L. Silver. (2000). *The neurobiology of taste and smell.* New York: Wiley-Liss.

Halász, N. (1990). *The vertebrate olfactory system: Chemical neuroanatomy, function and development.* Budapest: Akadémiai Kiadó.

Kaldenbach, Jan (1998). *K9 scent detection.* Alberta, Canada: Detselig Enterprises.

King, J. E., R. F. Becker, and J. E. Markee. (1964). Studies on olfactory discrimination in dogs. 3: Ability to detect human odour trace. *AB* 7:311–315.

Rouby, C. (2002). *Olfaction, taste, and cognition.* New York: Cambridge University Press.

Schoon, G. A. A. (1996). Scent discrimination lineups by dogs (Canis familiaris): Experimental design and forensic application. *AABS* 49:257–267.

Scott, J. P., and J. L. Fuller. (1965). *Genetics and the social behavior of the dog.* Chicago: University of Chicago Press.

Settle, R. H., B. A. Sommerville, J. McCormack, and D. M. Broom. (1994). Human scent matching using specially trained dogs. *AB* 48:1443–1448.

Steen, J. B., and E. Wilsson. (1990). How do dogs determine the direction of tracks? *Acta Physiologica Scandinavia* 139:531–534.

Syrotuck, W. G. (2000). *Scent and the scenting dog.* Mechanicsburg, Pa.: Barkleigh Productions.

Thesen, A., J. B. Steen, and K. B. Doving. (1993). Behavior of dogs during olfactory tracking. *Journal of Experimental Biology* 180:247–251.

Watson, L. (2000). *Jacobson's organ and the remarkable nature of smell.* New York: Norton.

Wyatt, T. D. (2003). *Pheromones and animal behaviour: Communication by smell and taste.* New York: Cambridge University Press.

Chapter 5. A Matter of Taste

Beauchamp, G. K., and L. Bartoshuk. (1997). *Tasting and smelling.* San Diego: Academic Press.

Coren, S., L. M. Ward, and J. T. Enns. (2004). *Sensation and perception,* 6th ed. Hoboken, N.J.: John Wiley & Sons.

Ferrel, F. (1984). Preference for sugars and non-nutritive sweeteners in young beagles *Neuroscience Biobehavioral Review* 8:199–203.

Finger, T. E., and W. L. Silver. (2000). *The neurobiology of taste and smell.* New York: Wiley-Liss.

Fisher, C. (1997). *Food flavours: Biology and chemistry.* Cambridge: Royal Society of Chemistry, Information Services.

Forbes, J. M. (1995). *Voluntary food intake and diet selection in farm animals.* Tucson, Ariz.: CAB International.

Kincaid, D. (1983). *Taste and smell.* Windermere, Fla.: Rourke.

Kitchell, R. L. (1976). Taste perception and discrimination by the dog. *Advances in Veterinary Science and Comparative Medicine* 22:287–314.

Mugford, R. A. (1977). External influences on the feeding of carnivores. In M. K. Kare & O Maller (eds.), *The chemical senses and nutrition.* New York: Academic Press, pp. 25–50.

Rouby, C. (2002). *Olfaction, taste, and cognition.* New York: Cambridge University Press.

Chapter 6. In Touch with the World

Alanen, L. (2003). *Descartes' concept of mind.* Cambridge, Mass.: Harvard University Press.

Bateson, P. (1991). Assessment of pain in animals. *AB* 42:827–839.

Beck, A. M., and A. H. Katcher. (1984). A new look at pet-facilitated therapy. *JAVMA* 184:414–421.

Best, F., and M. Pearson. (2000). Docking is painful. *Australian Veterinary Journal* 78:238.

Carruthers, P. (1992). *The animals issue: Moral theory in practice.* New York: Cambridge University Press.

Field, H. L., and D. D. Price. (1994). Pain. In Samuel Guttenplan (ed.), *A companion to the philosophy of mind.* Oxford: Blackwell, pp. 452–459.

Fox, M. W. (1971). *Integrative development of brain and behavior in the dog.* Chicago: University of Chicago Press.

Friedmann, E., A. H. Katcher, J. J. Lynch, and S. A. Thomas. (1980). Animal companions and one-year survival of patients after discharge from a coronary care unit. *Public Health Reports* 95:307–312.

Friedmann, E., A. H. Katcher, S. A. Thomas, J. J. Lynch, and P. R. Messent. (1983). Social interaction and blood pressure: Influence of animal companions. *Journal of Nervous & Mental Disease* 171(8):461–465.

Gant, W. H., J. E. Newton, F. L. Royer, and J. H. Stephens. (1966). Effect of person. *Conditioned Reflex* 1:146–160.

Harlow, H. F., and R. S. Zimmerman. (1959). Affectional responses in the infant monkey. *Science* 130:421–432.

Hennessey, M. B., M. T. Williams, and D. D. Miller, et al. (1998). Influence of male and female petters on plasma cortisol and behavior: Can human interaction reduce the stress of dogs in a public shelter? *AABS* 61:63–77.

Igel, G. J., and A. D. Calvin. (1960). The development of affectional responses in infant dogs. *JCPP* 53:302–305.

Institute of Laboratory Animal Resources (U.S.). Committee on Pain and Distress in Laboratory Animals. (1992). *Recognition and alleviation of pain and distress in laboratory animals.* Washington, D.C.: National Academy Press.

Katcher, A. H. (1982). Are companion animals good for your health? *Aging* (331–332):2–8.

Katcher, A. H., and A. M. Beck. (1986). Dialogue with animals. *Transactions & Studies of the College of Physicians of Philadelphia* 8:105–12.

McGill, T. E. (1980). Amputation of vibrissae in show dogs. *Animal Problems* 1:359–361.

Melzack, R. (1982). *The challenge of pain.* Harmondsworth, U.K.: Penguin.

Morton, D. (1992). Docking of dogs: Practical and ethical aspects. *Veterinary Record* 131:301–306.

Noonan, G. J., J. S. Rand, J. K. Blackshaw, and J. Priest. (1996). Behavioural observations of puppies undergoing tail docking. *AABS* 49:335–342.

Park, G. R. (2000). *The management of acute pain.* New York: Oxford University Press.

Pettijohn, T. F., T. W. Wong, P. D. Ebert, and J. P. Scott. (1977). Alleviation of separation distress in 3 breeds of young dogs. *Developmental Psychobiology* 10:373–381.

Short, Charles, and Alan Van Poznak. (1992). *Animal pain.* New York: Elsevier.

Smith, H. S. (2003). *Drugs for pain.* Philadelphia: Hanley & Belfus.

Symons, L. A. (1988). *A behavioural examination of the intramodal and intermodal consequences of long-term tactile restriction by vibrissae removal in rats.* Vancouver: University of British Columbia.

Tellington-Jones, L., and S. Taylor. (1992). *The Tellington T-Touch.* New York: Viking Penguin.

Wall, P. D. (2000). *Pain: The science of suffering.* New York: Columbia University Press.

Zotterman, Y. (1967). *Sensory mechanisms.* New York: Elsevier.

Zotterman, Y. (1969–71). *Touch, tickle, and pain.* New York: Pergamon Press.

Chapter 7. A Canine Sixth Sense?

Bardens, D. (1987). *Psychic animals.* New York: Barnes & Noble.

Coren, S. (2001). Pooch predictions and Fido forecasts. *AnimalSense* 2 (1):14.

Schwarz, B. E. (1973). Possible human-animal paranormal events. *Journal of the American Society of Psychosomatic Dentistry & Medicine* 20:39–53.

Sheldrake, R. (1999). *Dogs that know when their owners are coming home.* New York: Crown.

Steiger, B., and S. H. Steiger. (1992). *Strange powers of pets.* New York: Donald I. Fine.

Wiseman, R., M. Smith, and J. Milton. (1998). Can animals detect when their owners are returning home? An experimental test of the 'psychic pet' phenomenon. *British Journal of Psychology* 89:453–462.

Chapter 8. The Preprogrammed Dog

Brenoe, U. T., A. G. Larsgard, K. P. Johannessen, and S. H. Uldal. (2002). Estimates of genetic parameters for hunting performance traits in three breeds of gun hunting dogs in Norway. *AABS* 77:209–215.

Coren, S. (1994). *The intelligence of dogs: Canine consciousness and capabilities.* New York: Free Press.

Coren, S. (2000). *How to speak dog: Mastering the art of dog-human communication.* New York: Free Press.

Feddersen-Petersen, D. U. (2001). Biology of aggression in domestic dogs. *Deutsche Tieraerztliche Wochenschrift* 108:94–101.

Goodwin, D., J. W. S. Bradshaw, and S. M. Wickens. (1997). Paedomorphosis affects agonistic visual signals of domestic dogs. *AB* 53:297–304.

Hepper, P. G., and J. Cleland. (1998–1999). Developmental aspects of kin recognition. *Genetica* 104:199–205.

Lorenz, Konrad. (1952). *King Solomon's ring: New light on animal ways.* New York: Crowell.

Lorenz, Konrad. (1965). *Evolution and modification of behavior.* Chicago: University of Chicago Press.

McConnell, P. B. (1990). Lessons from animal trainers: The effect of acoustic structure on an animal's response. In P. Bateson and P. Kloffer (eds.), *Perspectives in ethology.* New York: Plenum.

Neff, M. W., K. W. Broman, C. S. Mellersh, et al. (1999). A second-generation genetic linkage map of the domestic dog, Canis familiaris. *Genetics* 151:803–820.

Scott, J. P., and J. L. Fuller. (1965). *Genetics and the social behavior of the dog.* Chicago: University of Chicago Press.

Takeuchi, Y., and K. Houpt. (2003). Behavior genetics. *VCNA* 33:345–363.

Yin, S. (2002). A new perspective on barking in dogs (Canis familiaris). *JCP* 116:189–193.

Chapter 9. Early Learning

Cairns, R. B., and J. Weboff. (1967). Behavior development in the dog: An interspecific analysis. *Science* 1958:1070–1072.

Cartwright, J. (2002) *Determinants of animal behavior.* New York: Routledge.

Coppinger, R., and L. Coppinger. (2001). *Dogs: A startling new understanding of canine origin, behavior and evolution.* New York: Scribner.

Coren, S. (2000). *How to speak dog: Mastering the art of dog-human communication.* New York: Free Press.

Fox, M. W. (1971). *Integrative development of brain and behavior in the dog.* Chicago University of Chicago Press.

Hogan, J. A., J. J. Bolhuis, and J. P. Kruijt. (1994). *Causal mechanisms of behavioural development.* New York: Cambridge University Press.

Igel, G. J., and A. D. Calvin. (1960). The development of affectional responses in infant dogs. *JCPP* 53:302–305.

King, A. S. (1987). *Physiological and clinical anatomy of the domestic animals.* Oxford: Oxford University Press.

Lorenz, K. (1979). *The year of the greylag goose.* New York: Harcourt Brace Jovanovich.

Pfaffenberger, C. J. (1963). *The new knowledge of dog behavior.* New York: Howell Book House.

Scott, J. P., and J. L. Fuller. (1965). *Genetics and the social behavior of the dog.* Chicago: University of Chicago Press.

Serpell, J., and J. A. Jagoe. (1995). Early experience and the development of behaviour. In J. Serpell (ed.), *The domestic dog: Its evolution, behaviour and interactions with people.* New York: Cambridge University Press, pp. 79–102.

Wheeler, S. J. (1995). *BSAVA manual of small animal neurology.* Cheltenham, U.K.: British Small Animal Veterinary Association.

Wilkins, A. S. (1993). *Genetic analysis of animal development.* New York: Wiley-Liss.

Wilsson, E. (1984–1985). The social interaction between mother and offspring during weaning in German shepherd dogs: Individual differences between mothers and their effects on offspring. *AABS* 13:101–112.

Chapter 10. The Personality of Dogs

Bartlett, M. (1979). A novice looks at puppy aptitude testing. *American Kennel Club Gazette* (March):31–42.

Brody, N. (1998). *Personality psychology: The science of individuality.* Upper Saddle River, N.J.: Prentice-Hall.

Campbell, W. E. (1975). *Behavior problems in dogs.* Santa Barbara, Calif.: American Veterinary Publications.

Coren, S. (1998). *Why we love the dogs we do.* New York: Free Press

Goddard, M. E., and R. G. Beilharz. (1985). A multivariate analysis of the genetics of fearfulness in potential guide dogs. *Behavior Genetics* 15:69–89.

Hart, B. L., and L. A. Hart. (1985). Selecting pet dogs on the basis of cluster analysis of breed behavior profiles and gender. *JAVMA* 186:1181–1185.

Hart, B. L., and L. A. Hart. (1988). *The perfect puppy.* New York: Freeman.

Humphrey, E., and L. Warner. (1974). *Working dogs.* Palo Alto, Calif.: National Press.

Jagoe, A., and J. Serpell. (1996). Owner characteristics and interactions and the prevalence of canine behaviour problems. *AABS* 47:31–42.

Neff, M. W., K. W. Broman, C. S. Mellersh, et al. (1999). A second-generation genetic linkage map of the domestic dog, Canis familiaris. *Genetics.* 151:803–820.

Overall, K. L. (2000). Natural animal models of human psychiatric conditions: Assessment of mechanism and validity. *Progress in Neuro-Psychopharmacology & Biological Psychiatry* 24:727–76.

Podberscek, A. L., and J. Serpell. (1996). The English cocker spaniel: Preliminary findings on aggressive behaviour. *AABS* 47:75–89.

Reisner, I. R. (2003). Differential diagnosis and management of human-directed aggression in dogs. *VCNA* 33:303–320.

Serpell, J. (1996). Evidence for an association between pet behavior and owner attachment levels. *Applied Animal Behaviour Science* 47:49–60.

Serpell, J., and J. A. Jagoe. (1995). Early experience and the development of behaviour. In Serpell, J. (ed). *The domestic dog: Its evolution, behaviour and interactions with people.* New York: Cambridge University Press, pp. 79–102.

Svartberg, K. (2002). Shyness-boldness predicts performance in working dogs. *AABS* 79:157–174.

Svartberg, K., and B. Forkman. (2002). Personality traits in the domestic dog (Canis familiaris). *AABS* 79:133–155.

Thorne, F. C. (1944). The inheritance of shyness in dogs. *Journal of Genetic Psychology* 65:275–79.

Wilsson, E., and P. Sundgren. (1997a). The use of a behaviour test for the selection of dogs for service and breeding: I: Method of testing and evaluating test results in the adult dog, demands on different kinds of service dogs, sex and breed differences. *AABS* 53:279–295.

Wilsson, E., and P. Sundgren. (1997b). The use of a behaviour test for selection of dogs for service and breeding: II. Heritability for tested parameters and effect of selection based on service dog characteristics. *AABS* 54:235–241.

Wilsson, E., and P. Sundgren. (1998a). Effects of weight, litter size and parity of mother on the behaviour of the puppy and the adult dog. *AABS* 56:245–254.

Wilsson, E., and P. Sundgren. (1998b). Behaviour test for eight-week-old puppies—heritabilities of tested behaviour traits and its correspondence to later behaviour. *AABS* 58:151–162.

Chapter 11. Emotional Learning

Askew, H. R. (1996). Treatment of behavior problems in dogs and cats: A guide for the small animal veterinarian. Cambridge, Mass.: Blackwell Science.

Chance, P. (2003). *Learning and behavior.* Belmont, Calif.: Wadsworth.

Denny, M. R. (1991). *Fear, avoidance, and phobias: A fundamental analysis.* Hillsdale, N.J.: Erlbaum.

Frieman, J. (2002). *Learning and adaptive behavior.* Belmont, Calif.: Wadsworth.

Lavond, D. G. (2003). *Handbook of classical conditioning.* Boston: Kluwer.

Lindsay, S. R. (2000). *Handbook of applied dog behavior and training,* Vols. 1 and 2. Ames: Iowa State University Press.

Morillo, C. (1995). *Contingent creatures: A reward theory of motivation and value.* Lanham, Md.: Littlefield Adams Books.

Pavlov, I. P. (1960). *Conditioned reflexes: An investigation of the physiological activity of the cerebral cortex.* New York: Dover.

Pearce, J. M. (1997). *Animal learning and cognition: An introduction.* Hove, U.K.: Psychology Press.

Scott, J. P., and J. L. Fuller. (1965). *Genetics and the social behavior of the dog.* Chicago: University of Chicago Press.

Squire, L. R. (1992). *Encyclopedia of learning and memory.* New York: Macmillan.

Sudakov, K. V., D. Ganten, and N. A. Nikolov. (1991). *Reinforcement in functional systems.* New York: Gordon and Breach.

Chapter 12. Skill Learning

Chance, P. (2003). *Learning and behavior.* Belmont, Calif.: Wadsworth.

Clark, H., T. Rowbury, A. Baer, and D. Baer. (1973). Time-out as a punishing stimulus in continuous and intermittent schedules. *JABA* 6:443–455.

Denny, M. R. (1991). *Fear, avoidance, and phobias: A fundamental analysis.* Hillsdale, N.J.: Erlbaum.

Donaldson, J. (1996). *The culture clash.* Oakland, Calif.: James & Kenneth.

Dunbar, I. (1996). How to teach a new dog old tricks. Oakland, Calif.: James & Kenneth.

Frieman, J. (2002). *Learning and adaptive behavior.* Belmont, Calif.: Wadsworth.

Hammond, T. S. (1894). *Practical dog training: Training vs. breaking.* New York: Forest and Stream.

Iwata, B. (1987). Negative reinforcement in applied settings: An emerging technology. *JABA* 20:361–378.

Koehler, W. (1962). *The Koehler method of dog training.* New York: Howell Book House.

Lattal, K. A., and M. Perone. (1998). *Handbook of research methods in human operant behavior.* New York: Plenum Press.

Linsday, S. R. (2000). *Handbook of applied dog behavior and training* (Vols. 1 & 2). Ames: Iowa State University Press.

Morillo, C. (1995). *Contingent creatures: a reward theory of motivation and value.* Lanham, Md: Littlefield Adams Books.

Pearce, J. M. (1997). *Animal learning and cognition: an introduction.* Hove, U.K.: Psychology Press.

Reid, P. (1996). *Excel-erated learning.* Oakland, Calif.: James & Kenneth.

Scott, J. P. (1967). *The development of social motivation.* Nebraska symposium on motivation. Lincoln: University of Nebraska Press, pp. 111–132.

Skinner, B. F. (1951). How to teach animals. *Scientific American* 185:26–29.

Squire, L. R. (1992). *Encyclopedia of learning and memory.* New York: Macmillan.

Chapter 13. The Social Secret of Learning

Adler, L. L., and H. E. Adler. (1977). Ontogeny of observational learning in the dog (Canis familiaris). *Developmental Psychobiology* 10:267–280.

Caldwell, C. A., and A. Whiten. (2002). Evolutionary perspectives on imitation: Is a comparative psychology of social learning possible? *AC* 5:193–208.

Cooper, J. J., C. Ashton, S. Bishop, R. West, D. S. Mills, and R. J. Young. (2003). Clever hounds: Social cognition in the domestic dog (Canis familiaris). *AABS* 81:229–244.

Coppinger, R., and L. Coppinger. (2001). *Dogs: A startling new understanding of canine origin, behavior and evolution.* New York: Scribner.

Coren, S. (1994). *The intelligence of dogs: Canine consciousness and capabilities.* New York: Free Press.

Coren, S. (2000). *How to speak dog: Mastering the art of dog-human communication.* New York: Free Press.

Hare, B., and R. Wrangham. (2002). Integrating two evolutionary models for the study of social cognition. In M. Bekoff and Colin Allen (eds.), *The cognitive animal: Empirical and theoretical perspectives on animal cognition.* Cambridge, Mass.: MIT Press, pp. 363–369.

Hare, B., M. Brown, C. Williamson, and M. Tomasello. (2002). The domestication of social cognition in dogs. *Science* 298:1634–1636.

Kubinyi, E., J. Topal, and A. Miklosi. (2003). Dogs (Canis familiaris) learn their owners via observation in a manipulation task. *JCP* 117:156–165.

McKinley, S., and R. J. Young. (2003). The efficacy of the model-rival method when compared with operant conditioning for training domestic dogs to perform a retrieval-selection task. *AABS* 81:357–365.

Miklosi, A., E. Kubinyi, and J. Topal. (2003). A simple reason for a big difference: Wolves do not look back at humans, but dogs do. *Current Biology* 13:763–766.

Pongrácz, P., A. Miklósi, E. Kubinyi, J. Topául, and V. Csányi. (2003). Interaction between individual experience and social learning in dogs. *AB* 65:595–603.

Pongrácz, P., A. Miklósi, E. Kubinyi, K. Gurobi, J. Topául, and V. Csányi. (2001). Social learning in dogs: The effect of a human demonstrator on the performance of dogs in a detour task. *AB* 62:1109–1117.

Reid, P. (1996). *Excel-erated learning.* Oakland, Calif.: James and Kenneth.

Slabbert, J. M., and O. A. E. Rasa. (1997). Observational learning of an acquired maternal behaviour pattern by working dog pups: An alternative training method? *AABS* 53:309–316.

Soproni, K., A. Miklósi, and J. Topául. (2002). Dogs' (Canis familiaris) responsiveness to human pointing gestures. *JCP* 116:27–34.

Wyrwicka, W. (1996). *Imitation in human and animal behavior.* New Brunswick, N.J.: Transaction Publishers.

Chapter 14. Artists or Scientists?

Callahan, H., C. Ikeda-Douglas, E. Head, C. W. Cotman, and N. W. Milgram. (2000). Development of a protocol for studying object recognition memory in the dog. *Progress in Neuro-Psychopharmacology & Biological Psychiatry* 24:693–707.

Coren, S. (1994). *The intelligence of dogs: Canine consciousness and capabilities.* New York: Free Press.

Coren, S. (1998). *Why we love the dogs we do.* New York: Free Press.

Coren, S. (2000). *How to speak dog: Mastering the art of dog-human communication.* New York: Free Press.

Coren, S. (2002). *The pawprints of history: Dogs and the course of human events.* New York: Free Press.

Dodman, N. H. (2002). *If only they could speak.* New York: W. W. Norton.

Mathison, V. (2000). *Dog works: The meaning and magic of canine constructions.* Berkeley, Calif.: Ten Speed Press.

Mech, L. D. (1981). *The wolf: Ecology and behavior of an endangered species.* Minneapolis: University of Minnesota Press.

Pennings, T. J. (2003). Do dogs know calculus? *College Mathematics Journal* 34:178–182.

Wells, D. L., L. Graham, and P. G. Hepper. (2002). The influence of auditory stimulation on the behaviour of dogs housed in a rescue shelter. *Animal Welfare* 11:385–393.

West, R., and R. J. Young. (2002). Do domestic dogs show any evidence of being able to count? *AC* 5:183–186.

Chapter 15. The Wrinkled Mind

Adams, B., A. Chan, H. Callahan, and N. W. Milgram. (2000). The canine as a model of human cognitive aging: Recent developments. *Progress in Neuro-Psychopharmacology & Biological Psychiatry* 24:675–92.

Callahan, H., C. Ikeda-Douglas, E. Head, C. W. Cotman, and N. W. Milgram. (2000). Development of a protocol for studying object recognition memory in the dog. *Progress in Neuro-Psychopharmacology & Biological Psychiatry* 24: 693–707.

Chan, A. D., P. M. Nippak, H. Murphey, C. J. Ikeda-Douglas, B. Muggenburg, E. Head, C. W. Cotman, and N. W. Milgram. (2002). Visuospatial impairments in aged canines (Canis familiaris): The role of cognitive-behavioral flexibility. *Behavioral Neuroscience* 116:443–454.

Cunningham, J. G. (2002). *Textbook of veterinary physiology,* 3rd ed. Philadelphia: W. B. Saunders.

Gelatt, Kirk N. (2000). *Essentials of veterinary ophthalmology.* Philadelphia: Lippincott Williams & Wilkins.

Harvey, R. G., J. Harari, and A. J. Delauche. (2001). *Ear diseases of the dog and cat* Ames: Iowa State University Press.

Head, E., H. Callahan, B. A. Muggenburg, C. W. Cotman, and N. W. Milgram. (1998). Visual-discrimination learning ability and beta-amyloid accumulation in the dog. *Neurobiology of Aging* 19:415–425.

Klintsova, A., and W. T. Greenough. (1999). Synaptic plasticity in cortical systems. *Current Opinion in Neurobiology* 9:203–208.

Milgram, N. W., E. Head, B. Muggenburg, D. Holowachuk, H. Murphey, J. Estrada, C. J. Ikeda-Douglas, S. C. Zicker, and C. W. Cotman. (2002). Landmark discrimination learning in the dog: Effects of age, an antioxidant fortified food, and cognitive strategy. *Neuroscience & Biobehavioral Reviews* 26:679–695.

Mosier, J. E. (1989). Effect of aging on body systems of the dog. *VCNA* 19:1–12.

Oliver, J. E. (1997). *Handbook of veterinary neurology,* 3rd ed. Philadelphia: W. B. Saunders.

Overall, K. L. (2000). Natural animal models of human psychiatric conditions: Assessment of mechanism and validity. *Progress in Neuro-Psychopharmacology & Biological Psychiatry.* 24:727–776.

Ruehl, W. W., J. Neilson, B. Hart, et al. (1997). Therapeutic actions of L-deprenyl in dogs: A model of human brain aging. In D. S. Goldstein, G. Eisenhofer, and R. McCarty (eds.), Advances in pharmacology: Catecholamines. *Bridging basic science with clinical medicine* 42:316–319.

Swenson, M. J. (1993). *Dukes' physiology of domestic animals,* 11th ed. Ithaca, N.Y.: Cornell University Press.

Tapp, P. D., C. T. Siwak, J. Estrada, E. Head, B. A. Muggenburg, C. W. Cotman, and N. W. Milgram. (2003). Size and reversal learning in the beagle dog as a measure of executive function and inhibitory control in aging. *Learning & Memory.* 10:64–73.

Chapter 16. Canine Consciousness

Bavidge, M. (1994). *Can we understand animal minds?* London: Bristol Classical Press.

Bekoff, M. (2001). Observations of scent-marking and discriminating self from others by a domestic dog (Canis familiaris): Tales of displaced yellow snow. *Behavioural Processes* 55:75–79.

Bekoff, M., C. Allen, and G. M. Gurghardt. (2002). *The cognitive animal: Empirical and theoretical perspectives on animal cognition.* Cambridge, Mass.: MIT Press.

Budiansky, S. (2000). *The truth about dogs: An inquiry into the ancestry, social conventions, mental habits, and moral fiber of Canis familiaris.* New York: Viking.

Call, J., J. Braeuer, J. Kaminski, and M. Tomasello. (2003). Domestic dogs (Canis familiaris) are sensitive to the attentional state of humans. *JCP* 117:257–263.

Coren, S. (1996). *Sleep thieves.* New York: Free Press.

Crist, E. (1999). *Images of animals: Anthropomorphism and animal mind.* Philadelphia: Temple University Press.

Darwin, C. (1998). *The expression of the emotions in man and animals,* 3rd ed. With an introduction, afterword, and commentaries by Paul Ekman. London: HarperCollins.

Dennett, D. C. (1998). *Brainchildren: Essays on designing minds.* Cambridge, Mass.: MIT Press.

de Veer, M. W., G. G. Gallup, and L. A. Theall. (2003). An 8-year longitudinal study of mirror self-recognition in chimpanzees (Pan troglodytes). *Neuropsychologia* 41:229–234.

Domhoff, G. W. (2003). *The scientific study of dreams: Neural networks, cognitive development, and content analysis.* Washington, D. C.: American Psychological Association.

Doré, F. Y., and C. Dumas. (1987). Psychology of animal cognition: Piagetian studies. *Psychological Bulletin* 102:219–233.

Fiset, S., C. Beaulieu, and F. Landry. (2003). Duration of dogs' (Canis familiaris) working memory in search for disappearing objects. *AC* 6:1–10.

Fiset, S., S. Gagnon, and C. Beaulieu. (2000). Spatial encoding of hidden objects in dogs (Canis familiaris). *Journal of Comparative Psychology* 114(4):315–324.

Freud, S. (1978). *The interpretation of dreams.* New York: Modern Library.

Furth, H. G. (1981). *Piaget and knowledge: Theoretical foundations.* Chicago: University of Chicago Press.

Gagnon, S., and F. Y. Doré. (1994). Cross-sectional study of object permanence in domestic puppies (Canis familiaris). *JCP* 108:220–232.

Keenan, J. P., G. C. Gallup, and D. Faulk. (2003). *The face in the mirror: The search for the origins of consciousness.* New York: HarperCollins.

Mitchell, R. W., and N. S. Thompson. (1993). Familiarity and the rarity of deception: Two theories and their relevance to play between dogs (Canis familiaris) and humans (Homo sapiens). *JCP* 107:291–300.

Mitchell, R. W., N. S. Thompson, and H. L. Miles. (1997). *Anthropomorphism, anecdotes, and animals* Albany: State University of New York Press.

Povinelli, D. J., G. G. Gallup, and T. J. Eddy. (1997) Chimpanzees recognize themselves in mirrors. *AB* 53:1083–1088.

Povinelli, D. J., J. E. Reaux, and D. T. Bierschwale. (1997). Exploitation of pointing as a referential gesture in young children, but not adolescent chimpanzees. *Cognitive Development* 12:327–365.

Premack, D. (2003). *Original intelligence: Unlocking the mystery of who we are.* New York: McGraw-Hill.

Teuscher, C. (2002). *Turing's connectionism: An investigation of neural network architectures.* London: Springer.

INDEX

B

C

T

W

Y

Z

ABOUT THE AUTHOR

Stanley Coren, Ph.D., F.R.S.C., is a professor of psychology at the University of British Columbia and a recognized expert on dog-human interaction. He has appeared on *Dateline,* the *Oprah Winfrey Show, Good Morning America,* and National Public Radio, and hosts a weekly television show, *Good Dog!,* currently showing nationally in Canada, Australia, and New Zealand. He lives in Vancouver, British Columbia, with his wife and her cat, in addition to a beagle, a Cavalier King Charles spaniel, and a Nova Scotia duck-tolling retriever.